Big Data Systems

Big Data Systems

A 360-degree Approach

Jawwad Ahmed Shamsi
Muhammad Ali Khojaye

CRC Press
Taylor & Francis Group
Boca Raton London New York

CRC Press is an imprint of the
Taylor & Francis Group, an **informa** business

First edition published 2021
by CRC Press
6000 Broken Sound Parkway NW, Suite 300, Boca Raton, FL 33487-2742

and by CRC Press
2 Park Square, Milton Park, Abingdon, Oxon, OX14 4RN

CRC Press is an imprint of Taylor & Francis Group, LLC

Library of Congress Cataloging-in-Publication Data

ISBN: 978-1-4987-5270-1 (hbk)
ISBN: 978-0-3677-5523-2 (pbk)
ISBN: 978-0-429-15544-4 (ebk)

Typeset in Computer Modern font
by KnowledgeWorks Global Ltd.

Jawwad A. Shamsi would like to dedicate this book to his parents, his wife, and his children, all of whom have offered unconditional love and support.

Muhammad Ali Khojaye would like to dedicate this book to his parents, to his wife, and to his son Rayan. He also like to thank them for their enormous amount of support during this long process of writing this book.

Contents

Preface

In a simplistic term, a system which handles big data is considered as a big data system. This handling could include different services such as computation, storage, and networking. The term big data refers to enormous size of data, which could challenge the conventional systems for storing and computation. While there is no standard range, which can classify big data, normally systems which can handle a few terabytes of data can be considered as big data systems.

Large amount of data is useful in many ways. Organizations can get deep insights about many aspects and operations. End users can get enhanced services. For instance, a large search engine can offer customized search results to its users. Similarly, a government can enhance its security system through smart surveillance systems based on big data. Both these examples reflect the emerging potential of big data. While the benefits of big data are still emerging, it is necessary to understand and study different systems and platforms which can facilitate big data.

Objectives

The purpose of this book is to study different concepts related to big data. It has following major objectives:

- To elucidate different platforms for processing of big data systems.

- To highlight the role of cloud computing in computing and storing big data systems.

- To explain security and privacy issues in big data.

- To provide an overview of different networking technologies in big data systems.

- To describe pros and cons of different computational platforms for big data.

- To elaborate on different case studies of big data.

- To enlighten programming and algorithmic techniques available for big data processing.

Organization

The book is organized into five parts and 14 chapters:

Section 1: The first part covers introductory concepts. It consists of three chapters. The first chapter covers concepts related to fundamental concepts of big data including difference between analytical and transactional systems and requirements and challenges of big data. The second chapter elaborates on architectural and organizational concepts related to big data. The chapter explains the difference between lambda and kappa architectures. It also highlights cluster computing and different organization schemes for clusters. The last chapter in this section, chapter 3, is focused on cloud computing and virtualization. Cloud provides an important platform for big data and the chapter is focused on elaborating this requirement.

Section II: The second section is focused on elaborating efficient platforms for storing and processing big data. Chapter 4 explains various topics related to Hadoop and MapReduce. This chapter also covers programming examples using MapReduce. In addition, two important components of Hadoop, i.e., HDFS and HBase are explained. Chapter 5 explains a few important limitations of Hadoop v1, and describes how Hadoop v2 addresses these limitations. This chapter also covers YARN, Pig, Hive, Dremel, Impala, Drill, Sqoop, and Ambari. Chapter 6 explains Spark and its different components. It elaborates on how Spark is useful in solving a few major big data problems. The chapter also includes programming examples. Chapter 7 describes NoSQL systems. These include, column-base, key-value base, document oriented, and graph databases. The chapter covers illustrative examples for enhanced explanation. Chapter 8 is focused on introducing the topic of NewSQL systems. The chapter has introductory coverage of four different NewSQL systems. These include VoltDB, NuoDB, Spanner, and HRDBMS.

Section III: Section III elaborates on networking, security, and privacy for big data systems. There are several illustrative examples in this part. Chapter 9 explains various topics related to networking for big data. This chapter highlights different requirements for efficient networks for big data systems and provides an overview of existing networking solutions. Chapter 10 explains security requirements and solutions for big data. It includes various topics such as requirements, attack types and mechanisms, attack detection, and prevention. The last chapter in this section, chapter 11, provides an overview of privacy concerns in big data and explains existing solutions in ensuring privacy.

Section IV: The fourth part of this book includes computation for big data. It contains chapter 12 and chapter 13. Chapter 12 explains HPC solutions, which are being utilized by big data systems. This chapter describes the functionality of GPUs, TPUs, and supercomputing. Chapter 13 introduces the topic of deep learning. It covers explanations of various deep learning solutions. These include Feed Forward Network, RNN, and CNN. The chapter explains various examples of big data which can get leverage from deep learning solutions.

Section V: Section V contains chapter 14. This chapter covers various case studies on big data. These include organizational solutions on a Facebook, Uber, LinkedIn, Microsoft, and Google. The chapter also highlights a few open issues on big data systems.

Target Audience

The book adopts an example-centric approach, where various concepts have been explained using illustrative examples and codes. The book can be used either as a text book or as a reference book. It can be adopted for various courses such as cloud computing and big data systems. Moreover, individual chapters of the book can be used as reference for different courses related to networking, security, privacy, high-performance computing, and deep learning.

Contact Us

If you have any question or comment about this book, please send email to bigdataquestions@gmail.com

We have a web site for the book, where we list examples, errata, and any additional information. For access, please visit our web page at `https://sites.google.com/view/bigdatasystems`.

Jawwad Ahmed Shamsi and Muhammad Ali Khojaye

Author Bios

Jawwad A. Shamsi completed B.E. (Electrical Engineering) form NED University of Engineering and Technology, Karachi in 1998. He completed his MS in Computer and Information Sciences from University of Michigan-Dearborn, MI, USA in 2002. In 2009, he completed his PhD. from Wayne State University, MI, USA. He has also worked as a Programmer Analyst in USA from 2000 to 2002. In 2009, he joined FAST- National University of Computer and Emerging Sciences (NUCES), Karachi. He has served as the head of computer science department from 2012 to 2017. Currently, he is serving as a Professor of Computer Science and Director of the Karachi Campus. He also leads a research group – syslab (http://syslab.khi.nu.edu.pk). His research is focused on developing systems which can meet the growing needs of scalability, security, high performance, robustness, and agility. His research has been funded by different International and National agencies including NVIDIA and Higher Education Commission, Pakistan.

Muhammad Ali Khojaye has more than a decade of industrial experience ranging from architecting cloud-native applications to distributed systems design, continuous integration/delivery, and infrastructure. His current technical interests revolve around big data, cloud, containers, and systems architecture for distributed platforms. He holds a master's degree in Computer Science from the University of Leicester. Born in the mountain village of Chitral Pakistan, Ali currently lives in Glasgow with his wife and son. When he is not at work, Ali enjoys cycling, traveling, and spending time with family and friends.

Acknowledgments

The authors would like to acknowledge the contributions from Muhammad Nouman Durrani, Ali Akber, and Bara Raza Mangnani from National University of Computer and Emerging Sciences. The authors are also thankful to Abid Hasnain from Visionet Systems and Narmeen Bawany from Jinnah University for Women.

List of Examples

List of Figures

List of Tables

I

Introduction

Introduction to Big Data Systems

CONTENTS

B IG DATA has been increasingly used in our daily lives. From social networks to mobile applications, and internet search, a huge amount of data is being generated, collected, and processed. The purpose of this chapter is to explain the fundamental concepts related to big data that are useful in understanding the functionality and execution of big data systems.

1.1 INTRODUCTION: REVIEW OF BIG DATA SYSTEMS

In the year 2006, LinkedIn – the social networking giant, started analyzing profiles of its users by suggesting people they may know. The rationale behind this feature was to encourage users to expand their social network based on their interest and give them relevant suggestions. Through this feature, LinkedIn observed that most of its suggestions in inviting people were successful [352]. Similarly, in the year 2012, for the US presidential elections, President Obama's campaign experienced massive boost and success through predictive analysis using a big dataset consisting of voter's profiles, their likes, and their patterns [207].

The two examples cited above highlights the enormous potential of analyzing, linking, and extracting useful information from large data. The science of prediction requires a massive amount of data and methodological linkage of different attributes on big data.

While big data carries huge potential for information extraction; it requires thorough understanding and comprehension of underlying systems (software and hardware) that are used for storing, processing, linking, and analyzing.

1.1.1   Purpose of the Book

The purpose of this book is to explain different systems that are used for storing, processing, and analyzing big data. The book adopts an example-oriented approach in which each chapter contains examples and illustrations for better explanation.

1.2   UNDERSTANDING BIG DATA

The term big data has gained popularity [298]. It refers to the huge amount of data such that managing, analyzing, and understanding data at volumes and rates that push the frontiers of current technologies [225].

1.2.1   Important Characteristics of Big Data

Researchers have highlighted a few important characteristics of big data [369]. These are often referred to as five V's of big data.

1. **Volume**: Big data refers to the massive volume of data such that the amount of data challenges the storage and processing requirements. While there is no specific distinction about the volume of data, normally the volume could vary from Terabytes (10^{12}) to exabytes (10^{18}) and beyond.

2. **Velocity**: Data is being generated at a very fast pace. The high rate of data generation signifies the importance of data. The high velocity of data can be assessed by the fact that a large proportion of data being used belong to the recent past.

3. **Variety**: Data under consideration could be obtained from numerous sources such as web logs, Internet of Things (IoT) devices, URLs, user tweets, and search patterns etc. Similarly, data could have different formats such as Comma Separated Values (CSV), tables, text documents, and graphs. Further, it could either be structured, semi-structured, or unstructured.

4. **Veracity**: Data may vary in terms of veracity; i.e., data under consideration may be inconsistent or it may be highly consistent across all replicas; it may be useless or it may be of high value. Veracity refers to the trustworthiness, accuracy, or authenticity of data.

5. **Value**: Data must be of high value; i.e., stale data has limited value.

1.2.2   Big Data: How Big Is Enough?

One of the fundamental questions in big data is that for a given big data problem in consideration, how much data is enough? That is, how much data is needed to be analyzed in order to compute the result? The answer to this question is not trivial.

Often in data analysis, data is sampled to process results. For instance, opinion polls are based on data samples. In a similar context, gender-wise assessment and population are based on data sampling. Sampling induces likelihood of error – a scenario, where the data sample collected may not reflect true results.

An example of data sampling error could be derived from Google Flu Trends (GFT) [236]. In 2009, Google tracked the spread of Flu in the United States. The prediction was based on GFT, the search trends available on Google. The prediction was so successful that it outnumbered the prediction from the Center for Disease Control (CDC). However, in Feb

2013, a similar prediction appeared as erroneous. It was observed that the GFT prediction was overstated by a factor of more than two. The problem was that Google's algorithm was simply considering the search terms on the Google Search Engine. It was assumed that all the related searches made on Google are related to spread of flu. The Google team was unable to find the correlation between search terms and flu.

In a similar context, data sampling error could be induced during an election campaign. For instance, data for election tweets may favor a specific candidate. However, it may be the case that voters of the candidate are pro-active on social media as compared to the voters of other candidates. Similarly, sample size in any big data problem could have its own biases.

Determining the correct size of data for a given big data problem is not trivial. In addition, collecting or gathering the complete data is also an issue. Many experts believe that in the case of big data, N=ALL is a good reference point for data analysis [191]. That is, all the data needs to be analyzed. However, collecting such a large amount of data or determining what is included in N=ALL is not trivial. Therefore, in many cases, a big data problem is analyzed on **found data** – a term which is referred to donate the data which has found for analysis.

While collecting more data is often more useful for analysis; it is not necessary that more data would yield improved results. In this context, relevance of data being collected is also important [350].

1.3   TYPE OF DATA: TRANSACTIONAL OR ANALYTICAL

An important question is what type of data can be referred to as big data. In the literature, two types of systems have been mentioned:

1. **Transactional Systems**: These are the types of systems which support transaction processing. Subsequently, these systems adhere to ACID (Atomicity, Consistency, Isolation, and Durability) properties. They have proper schema and data for each transaction is uniquely identified.

2. **Analytical Systems**: Such systems do not necessarily hold ACID properties. Consequently, data does not necessarily adhere to a proper schema. It may have duplicates and missing values etc. Such systems are more appropriate for analyzing data.

Traditionally, the term big data has been associated for analytical systems – specifically due to the fact because such systems do not require strong consistency and have schema-less data with duplicates, multi-formatting, and missing values. However, as we will study in chapter 8 big data systems have evolved to include transactional systems bearing ACID properties.

1.3.1   CAP Theorem

The database community initially argued that lack of consistency and normalization in big data systems was a major limitation. However, later it was felt that big data systems do not need to maintain strong consistency and they can exploit CAP theorem to avail the benefit of relaxed consistency and improved performance.

CAP theorem was proposed by Eric Brewer [108]. It explains important characteristics for distributed systems. The fundamental idea of the CAP theorem is that in a distributed system, there are three important characteristics, i.e., Consistency, Availability, and Partition Tolerance (CAP). CAP theorem states that in case of a partition (or network failure) both consistency and availability cannot be offered together. That is, when network failure occurs and the network is partitioned, a distributed system can either offer consistency or availability but not both. Note that when there is no network failure, a distributed system can offer both availability and consistency together. Example 1.1 explains the concept of CAP theorem.

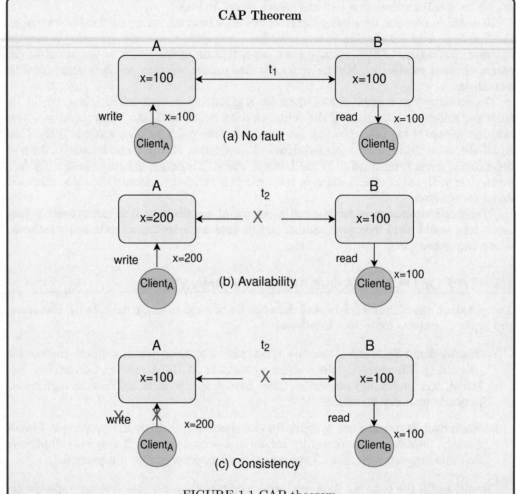

FIGURE 1.1 CAP theorem

Example 1.1 (CAP Theorem). *Figure 1.1 explains the CAP theorem. Two distributed servers A and B are shown. In part (a), at time t_1, $Client_A$ writes x=100 at $Server_A$. Assuming strict consistency, the value of x is immediately updated to $Server_B$. Consequently, $Client_B$ reads x=100.*

At time t_2, network fault occurs in the link connecting the two servers. Consequently, either availability or consistency can be met.

In part (b), availability is maintained, while consistency is relaxed. $Client_A$ writes x=200 at $Server_A$. However, since the network link is down, the value could not be immediately updated to $Server_B$. Therefore, $Client_B$ still reads x=100.

In part (c), in order to meet consistency, availability is compromised. $Client_A$ intends to write to $Server_A$. However, since the link between the two servers is broken, the value of x is not updated either to $Server_A$ or to $Server_B$.

Many big data systems exploit CAP theorem to provide availability at the cost of consistency. However, consistency is not necessarily compromised for availability. It can also be compromised for latency [74]. Systems which have relaxed consistency requirements are normally considered appropriate for data analytics as they do not necessarily maintain ACID properties. Maintaining ACID properties in the context of big data are challenging due to massive size and distributed nature of data. Therefore, by-n-large, big data systems have been normally associated with analytical systems. Figure 1.2 illustrates the difference between transactional systems and analytical systems.

1.3.2 ACID vs BASE

For distributed systems, meeting ACID guarantees is really challenging. Therefore, many big data systems employ BASE properties [87, 299]. BASE is an acronym for Basically Available Soft state Eventual consistency. BASE implies that in case of network failure, big data systems tend to compromise on consistency in order to provide availability. The main focus of such systems is to ensure availability, whereas eventual consistency model is followed.

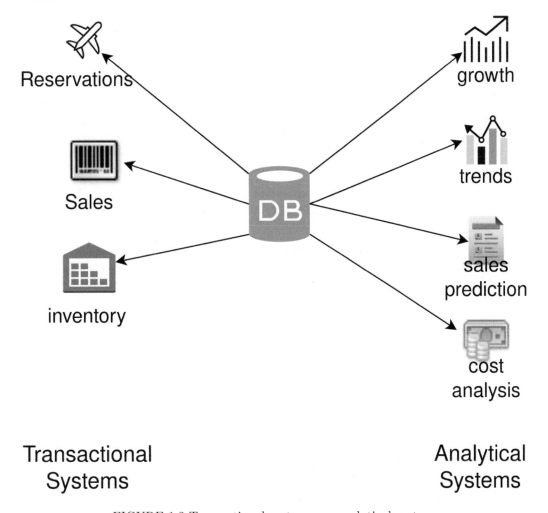

Reservations

growth

Sales

trends

inventory

sales prediction

cost analysis

DB

Transactional Systems

Analytical Systems

FIGURE 1.2 Transactional systems vs. analytical systems

1.4 REQUIREMENTS AND CHALLENGES OF BIG DATA

For big data systems, there are a few specific research challenges. These are needed to be catered:

1. **Scalability**: The foremost requirement for big data systems is to provide massive capability for processing and storage of huge amounts of data. Scalability should be achieved without any noticeable degradation in performance.

2. **Availability and Fault Tolerance**: An efficient big data system should be able to tolerate faults. Faults could either be transient such as network congestion, CPU availability, and packet loss, or they could be persistent such as disk failure, power faults, and network outages.

3. **Efficient Network Setup**: As big data system consists of a large number of machines and workstations, efficient networking setup is an important requirement. The network should be capable of providing access to big data, with low communication latency. Network setup should facilitate building big data systems through both Local Area Network (LAN) and Wide Area Network (WAN).

4. **Flexibility**: Big data systems may contain data from multiple sources such as textual data, images, videos, and graphs. Similarly, data can be assessed and analyzed through multiple means including visualizations, raw data, aggregated data, and queries. Big data systems should facilitate flexible mechanisms for accessing and storing big data systems.

5. **Privacy and Access Control**: As big data systems gather data from a large number of sources, privacy and access control are likely to be one of the major concerns. Questions such as which data should be made public, what information should be assessed, and who has the ownership of data are important and needed to be identified.

6. **Elasticity**: In a big data system, the number of users varies over time. An efficient system should be able to meet user's needs. Elasticity refers to the capability of the system in meeting these needs.

7. **Batch Processing and Interactive Processing** With the passage of time, big data systems have expanded from batch processing to interactive processing. For capable big data systems, possessing the ability to analyze and process big data in batch mode as well streaming mode is necessary.

8. **Efficient Storage**: As data is replicated in big data systems, efficient mechanisms for replication and storage are significant in reducing the overall cost.

9. **Multi-tenancy**: Big data systems are accessed by multiple users at a time. Multi-tenancy refers to the capability of the system in providing fair, persistent, and isolated services to the users of big data.

10. **Efficient Processing**: As data is massive, efficient algorithms, techniques, and hardware are needed for large-scale computation of big data. In this context, effective techniques for parallelization are also significant. Similarly, iterative computation for machine learning and data analytics are also important.

11. **Efficient Scheduling**: With multiple parallel tasks and concurrent users, methods and techniques for efficient scheduling are needed.

The above set of requirements are significant for big data systems. There are numerous solutions which have been developed to cater these needs. Over the course of this book, we will study various solutions pertaining to these challenges.

1.5 CONCLUDING REMARKS

Big data systems implement extensive analysis of the massive amount of data for prediction and analysis. These systems entail specific challenges and considerations related to system architecture, fault tolerance, computation and processing, replication, consistency, scalability, and storage. This book is aimed at explaining existing solutions which address these challenges.

The remainder of this book is organized as follows: Chapter 2 elaborates on architectural and organizational concepts related to big data. Chapter 3 describes cloud computing. These two concepts are well established for big data systems. Chapter 4 describes Hadoop – a popular platform for storing and processing big data. Chapter 5 explains a few important limitations of Hadoop v1, and describes how Hadoop v2 addresses these limitations whereas chapter 6 explains Spark. In chapters 7 and 8, we discuss NoSQL and NewSQL systems. Chapter 9 describes networking issues and solutions for big data systems. Chapter 10 explains security requirements and solutions for big data whereas chapter 11 discusses privacy issues in big data. Chapter 12 highlights high-performance computing systems and their impact for big data systems whereas chapter 13 introduces deep learning – an emerging concept for analytics in big data systems. Chapter 14 is the last chapter of the book. It describes different case studies of big data systems. It also highlights a few open issues on big data systems.

1.6 FURTHER READING

Examples of big data and its impact in analytics and predictions have been discussed in references [207, 236].

[191] provides further discussion on analytics and the size challenges for big data.

CAP Theorem and its impact on design of big data been discussed in many research papers. It was initially proposed in the year 2000 [111]. Later, in many research papers, different design principles of distributed systems have been explained [107–109, 178].

Difference between ACID and Base properties has been further elaborated in the literature. References [122, 294] explains these properties in detail.

Research Issues in big data systems have been discussed in detail in many research papers. These include architectural and hardware related issues, software, and platform related research, as well applications of big data [192, 238].

[208, 231] and [317] present a detailed discussion on all different challenges of big data.

1.7 EXERCISE QUESTIONS

1. Explain five V's of big data.

2. Explain CAP Theorem. How is it useful for big data?

3. Explain the difference between found data and all data.

4. What are the major challenges for big data systems?

5. What are ACID guarantees? Are they needed for big data systems?

6. Highlight major differences between transactional systems and analytical systems.

7. Explain major characteristics of BASE systems.

8. Explain how much data is sufficient to achieve high accuracy in big data systems?

9. Explain why Google flu trends were inaccurate in estimation?

10. Explain the difference between scalability and elasticity.

GLOSSARY

ACID: These are the set of properties which identify a database system. These stand for Atomicity, Consistency, Isolation, and Durability.

Analytical Systems: These types of systems are used to provide analytics on historically large volumes of data.

Atomicity: It is a database concept that a transaction either succeeds or fails in its entirety.

BASE: It stands for Basically Available Soft state Eventual consistency. These are the types of systems which provide relaxed consistency requirements than ACID.

CAP Theorem: It is a theorem which identifies a design model for distributed systems. It states that in case of a network partition (failure), a distributed system can either provide consistency or availability.

Cluster computing: It is a type of computing which allows multiple computers to work together to either solve common computing problems or provide large storage. It requires a cluster management layer to handle communication between the individual nodes and work coordination.

Data Visualization: It presents meaningful data graphically (from raw data) in order to understand complex big data.

Eventual Consistency: It is a type of consistency model, which support BASE model to the ACID model.

Fault Tolerant: It is a property of a system to make sure it recovers automatically even if certain parts of the system fail.

Processing: It refers to extracting valuable information from large datasets.

Reliability: The probability that a given system will perform its intended functions continuously and correctly in a specified environment for a specified duration.

Resiliency: A resilient system is one that can gracefully handle unexpected situations and bounce back from failures.

Transactional Systems: These are the types of systems which support transaction processing.

CHAPTER 2

Architecture and Organization of Big Data Systems

CONTENTS

A S WE DISCUSSED in the previous chapter, big data systems require massive amounts of resources in order to meet the challenge of computing, storing, and processing big data in a timely manner. The purpose of this chapter is to elaborate on suitable systems for big data systems, which can meet these challenges. We will begin the chapter with two possible architecture systems for big data. The chapter also elaborates into organization of big data systems.

2.1 ARCHITECTURE FOR BIG DATA SYSTEMS

In this section, we will study different architectures for big data processing. Our focus would be on analyzing strengths and limitations of these architecture systems. An efficient real-time data processing architecture needs to be scalable and fault-tolerant [169]. Further, it needs to support batch and incremental updates. We now discuss lambda and kappa architectures with their benefits and limitations.

2.1.1 Lambda Architecture

The lambda architecture was proposed by Nathan Marz in 2011 [260]. Nathan argues that it is possible to beat the CAP theorem. We should recall that the CAP theorem states that in a distributed system, in case of a network partition, both consistency and availability cannot be achieved at the same time. There are two important characteristics of data. First, data is a function of time, and the second, that data is immutable. Example 2.1 explains the two concepts of data.

Two important characteristics of data

Example 2.1 (Two important characteristics of data). *There are two inherent properties of data. First, data is time dependent. If Mike follows Cindy on a social network, even if he stops following her, that does not change the fact that he used to follow Cindy. Second, data is immutable. This is supported by the statement that the fact that Mike was following Cindy cannot be changed.*

Nathan argues that if availability is traded off then nothing can be done. However, it is possible to beat the CAP theorem if availability is chosen instead of consistency. This is because the system will be eventually consistent. That is, the updates will eventually be propagated. However, since data is immutable, i.e., data cannot be updated, it can only be added. This is true because data is a function of time.

The lambda architecture is illustrated in figure 2.1. The main idea of the architecture is based on the fact that a complex data system is composed of three components, a real-time layer, a batch layer, and a storage layer.

The batch layer manages and computes historical data. For instance, it can compute machine learning models over a large dataset. It can integrate the historical data and combines it with the arriving data. Results can be computed on the integrated dataset by going through iterations of computation. This allows higher accuracy at the cost of higher latency.

The speed layer provides results in real-time. It utilizes the model updated by the batch layer and the new data (not the complete dataset) to produce results in near-real time. Computation cost at the streaming layer is significantly low because in the model approximation algorithms are utilized. The purpose of the storage layer is to compute the results for fast retrieval.

The lambda architecture offers various benefits:

1. It facilitates near real-time data.

2. The master dataset can be used as an immutable dataset as it has a complete record of all the dataset.

3. Reprocessing of data is easier. Reprocessing implies to processing input data again to recompute the output. Reprocessing may be needed if the system is evolving or if the code is modified.

While the lambda architecture has several benefits, it also has a major limitation that it requires that the code is required to be maintained in two complex distributed systems. This requirement could create many issues.

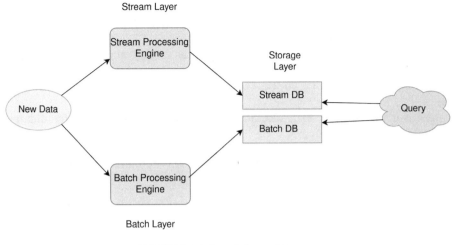

FIGURE 2.1 Lambda architecture

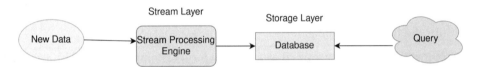

FIGURE 2.2 Kappa architecture

2.1.2 Kappa Architecture

The kappa architecture is introduced to cater the problems associated with the lambda architecture [228]. Jay Kreps argued that it is possible to bypass the need of maintaining two different data storage systems. This can be achieved using the following steps:

1. Use a stream processing engine such as Kafka (see section 5.8.2) to store logs of data from that point. For instance, if data of the past 10 days is to be processed then the system stores data from the past 10 days.

2. For reprocessing, another instance of stream processing could be started, which starts processing from the beginning.

3. Output of this processed data could be stored at a new location.

4. The old data location and the corresponding job can be deleted then.

Figure 2.2 illustrates the architecture of the kappa architecture.

The main benefit of the Kappa architecture is that it can bypass the need of maintaining the two different data storage systems. As compared to the lambda architecture, it requires fewer resources. However, it is not a one-size fit all model. That is, in some cases, absence of batch-layer may yield errors and two storage systems may be needed for efficiency [68].

2.2 ORGANIZATION OF BIG DATA SYSTEMS: CLUSTERS

In order to meet the scalability requirements of big data systems, a large number of processors are accumulated together to form a cluster. Cluster computing is a type of computing in which multiple computers, called cluster nodes, work together with the aim to either solve common computing problems or provide large storage. A cluster is a type of a parallel and distributed system in which a collection of interconnected processors are connected through hardware, networks, and software.

Clustering allows accumulation of resources such as storage and processing. This distribution facilitates parallelism and permits faster computation of data. Another advantage of accumulation is reliability, i.e., in case of a fault, replicated execution or storage can be utilized.

Clusters can be used for high availability, storage, load balancing, redundancy, and parallel computation:

1. **Storage**: A large dataset can be stored in a cluster to increase replication data availability and fault tolerance.

2. **Processing**: A large or computationally expensive task can be divided into smaller tasks for faster execution.

In the context of big data systems, clusters are used for processing as well as storage. A cluster can provide high availability and load balancing as well.

2.2.1 Introduction to Parallelism

Cluster computing is often generalized as a parallel form of computing in which a computationally expensive task is divided into smaller sub tasks. All of these smaller sub tasks can then be executed in parallel on the worker nodes of the cluster. A task can only be executed in parallel if there is no dependency among the sub tasks.

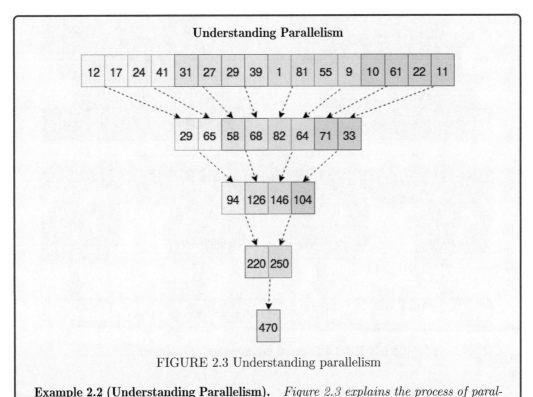

FIGURE 2.3 Understanding parallelism

Example 2.2 (Understanding Parallelism). *Figure 2.3 explains the process of parallelism through addition of 16 numbers. Suppose that the cost of adding two numbers is 1 unit. A serial program would require 15 time units for addition. Comparatively, a parallel version could reduce the cost to 4 time units.*

Example 2.2 illustrates parallelism through the process of addition. Parallelization decreases execution time. Consequently, large complex problems may be solved in a shorter time. A parallel program requires redundant resources.

Parallel computation can be implemented on a variety of architectures such as a desktop machine with few cores, a cluster, or a supercomputer. Parallel computing beyond desktop computing is often termed as High-Performance Computing (HPC).

2.2.2 Cluster Architecture

Figure 2.4 illustrates a typical architecture of a cluster [117]. It comprises of interconnected computers, interconnect hardware, communication software, middleware, and applications. Computers could include PCs, workstations, or symmetric multi-processors, working together as a single integrated resource. These computers could either have different operating systems, such as Solaris, Linux, and Windows or could have homogeneous OS. For big data systems, a high speed interconnect could be useful for faster transfer of data and reducing the overall time. We will revert to details of high speed networking solutions in chapter 9.

The figure also includes a parallel programming environment and a middleware. The main task of the cluster middleware is to manage computing nodes. It usually offers an illusion of a unified system image (single system image). The parallel programming environment consists of libraries, debuggers, profilers, schedulers, and deployment tools to facilitate computation of a big data system. Together, the middleware and the parallel programming environment offers high transparency, improved scalability, increased reliability,

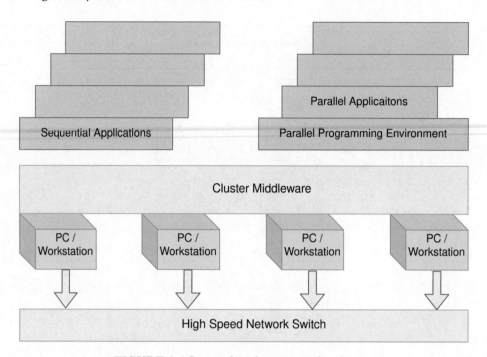

FIGURE 2.4 Layered architecture of a cluster

and effective task distribution and debugging. It is a common practice for big data systems to experience failures. In this context, redundancy and effective task distribution are utmost important.

Hadoop/MapReduce is an example of a parallel programming environment with redundancy, scalability, and task distribution. We will explain the architecture of Hadoop in chapter 4.

2.2.3   Services Offered by Clusters

Clusters can be classified on the basis of services they offer. In literature, four major types of clusters have been identified: (i) Storage clusters, (ii) High-availability clusters, (iii) Load-balancing clusters, and (iv) High-performance clusters which are discussed as under:

1. **Storage clusters**: Storage clusters offer a reliable file system image across the servers in the cluster. This allows servers to perform concurrent read and write operations to a single shared file system. Storage clusters limit the installation and patching of applications to a single shared file system, thereby simplifying the storage administration of such clusters. Further, these clusters eliminate the need for redundant copies of application data with a cluster-wide shared file system, and simplify backup and disaster recovery.

2. **High-availability clusters**: High-availability clusters are groups of computers that support and reliably utilize server applications. These clusters maintain redundant nodes that can act as backup systems. These clusters also offer continuous availability of services and eliminate single point failure through redundancy.

3. **Load-balancing clusters**: Load-balancing clusters balance the requested load by posting the network service requests to multiple cluster nodes. To provide better performance and optimize the overall response time, these clusters share computational

TABLE 2.1 Difference Between Cluster Computing and Grid Computing

Cluster Computing	Grid Computing
Homogeneous	Heterogeneous
Dedicated nodes	Non-dedicated nodes
Closed proximity or LAN	LAN, WAN, or MAN
Centralized management and single owner-ship	Individual management and multiple own-ership

load. For instance, a web server cluster may dispatch different service requests to different cluster nodes. These clusters offer cost-effective scalability, as the number of nodes required can be mapped according to the load requirements. Availability of load-balancing clusters is also important. If a node becomes inoperative; the load-balancing software detects the node failure and redirects the requests to other nodes.

4. **High-performance clusters**: High-performance clusters offer concurrent execution of applications to perform heavy computation, thereby enhancing the performance of the applications. Whenever required, nodes also communicate to execute their assigned tasks [117, 333].

2.2.4 Cluster Computing vs. Grid Computing

Cluster computing is often generalized as a parallel form of computing in which a parallel task is divided among worker nodes. However, this generalized notion is also applicable to grid computing. Therefore, it is pertinent to distinguish between cluster computing and grid computing. Rajkumar Buyya et al. [118] mentioned several differences between grids and clusters. A grid is generally spanned either over LAN or WAN. Nodes in a grid could be owned by different owners with decentralized management and heterogeneous computing environment. Comparatively, nodes in a cluster are located in a close proximity such as high speed LAN. They are dedicated for a specific task and are under the control of a single owner. Nodes in a cluster also have homogeneous environment such as a similar operating system.

Table 2.1 summarizes the differences between the two types of computing. A specific type of grid computing in which computing resources are voluntarily donated by users is called **volunteer computing** [285].

2.2.5 Flynn's Taxonomy

In order to comprehend different types of parallel machines, it is important to consider Flynn's taxonomy [168]. This taxonomy categorizes systems with parallel processing capability based on the number of instructions that can be executed and amount of data which can be shared. The classification is briefly discussed as follows:

1. **SISD**: In the Single Instruction Single Data (SISD) stream, a single instruction is executed on a single processing unit at a time. Uniprocessor PC and traditional mainframe computers fall in this category.

2. **SIMD**: In the Single Instruction Multiple Data (SIMD) stream, a single instruction stream is executed over multiple processing elements (or nodes). The control unit generates control signals for all the processing units, and the same operation is executed

on different data streams. In SIMD, each processing element has its own associated data memory, so that different processors may execute each instruction on a different set of data. Just like vector and array processor, data-level parallelism is achieved in this category.

3. **MISD**: In the Multiple Instruction Single Data (MISD) stream, a set of processing units executes different instructions on the same dataset. In fault-tolerant systems, the same instructions redundantly executed to detect and mask the errors.

4. **MIMD**: In the Multiple Instruction Multiple Data (MIMD) stream, a set of processing units simultaneously executes different set of instructions sequences on different datasets. MIMD-based systems can use the shared memory across heterogeneous network computers in a distributed environment or shared memory across in a memory. MIMD is primarily used in computer-aided design/computer-aided manufacturing, simulation, modeling, communication switches etc. Multi-core systems are examples of MIMD.

Big data systems such as MapReduce generally follow SIMD model in which the same program is executed on different worker nodes.

2.3 CLASSIFICATION OF CLUSTERS: DISTRIBUTED MEMORY VS. SHARED MEMORY

HPC systems are intrinsic for big data systems as they provide necessary computational and storage resources for execution of big data systems. These systems can be configured using many models such as:

1. **Shared Memory**: In a shared memory system, all nodes in the cluster share the same memory. As such an explicit mechanism for message passing or communication between the cluster nodes is not needed. Due to this feature, shared memory systems are considered much faster than distributed memory systems. An explicit mechanism for locking (or mutual exclusion) may be needed to avoid dirty reads. Shared memory systems have limited scalability due to the shared memory requirement of all the cores. Further, performance is limited by the speed of the system bus.

   Multi-core PCs, Graphics Processing Systems (GPUs), and high-end computing nodes such as Xeon are examples of shared memory systems.

2. **Distributed Memory**: In a distributed memory system, nodes are connected via network such that each node has a distinct memory. Network connection can be made either over a Local Area Network (LAN) or through a Wide Area Network (WAN). Communication between nodes is established through a dedicated communication paradigm such as Message Passing Interface (MPI). Due to the adaptive nature of distributed memory systems, they can achieve higher scalability. A Beowulf cluster is an example of a distributed memory system.

3. **Hybrid Memory**: A hybrid memory system is a combination of a distributed memory and shared memory models. In such a system, many shared memory nodes are connected via a distributed memory model.

In multi-processor shared memory systems, where each processor has its own cache, maintaining coherence among the contents of the cache is significant. **Cache Coherence** is a phenomenon, which avoids such conflicts and ensures that data remains updated among all the nodes in the parallel system. Parallel computing clusters incorporate increased fault tolerance through redundancy. In that, the same job may be assigned to multiple nodes to tolerate node failures.

Both the shared memory and the distributed memory systems differ in the mechanism of communication employed for communication among the processors.

Example 2.3 explains the difference between shared memory and distributed memory.

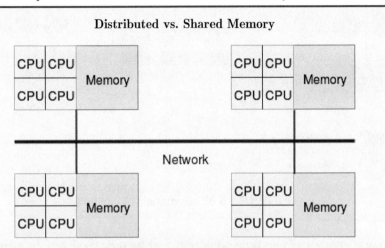

Distributed vs. Shared Memory

FIGURE 2.5 Hybrid memory

Example 2.3 (Distributed vs. Shared Memory). *We can better understand the difference between distributed memory, shared memory, and hybrid memory systems through figure 2.5. The figure shows four computers, which are connected over a network. Each of these four computers has four cores (also called CPUs) and a memory. This is equivalent to a hybrid model where message passing between the four computers is established over a network, whereas communication between the four cores of a PC is executed through the shared memory system.*

Shared memory systems are faster as they avoid network communication and utilize the shared memory medium for communication among the processors.

In comparison, distributed memory systems carry the potential of massive scalability as a large number of computers can be connected through the network.

A hybrid model integrates the advantages of both the systems, where low communication-latency is achieved through the shared memory model and scalability can be increased through the distributed memory system.

This arrangement in terms of distributed, shared, or hybrid is also referred to as loosely coupled, tightly coupled, or moderately coupled processors, respectively.

Figure 2.6 shows different models of clusters [302].

1. **Tightly Coupled**: In the tightly coupled architecture, a collection of multiple processors share a common memory using a shared bus system. In such an architecture, processors do not have their own private memory. An implementation of this architecture is also referred to as Shared memory systems. Shared memory systems are illustrated in figure 2.6 (a). Because of high connectivity, latency of communication between processors remains low.

2. **Loosely Coupled**: In a loosely coupled architecture, a group of machines are connected with each other using a minimum communication and cooperation among them. Each

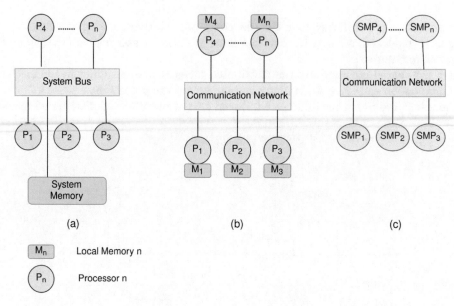

FIGURE 2.6 Three models of clusters

computer consists of one processing unit and its own local private memory. In such an architecture, a communication network and a data distribution and accumulation mechanism is required. This results in efficient usage of each individual computer, but limits the amount of coordination and sharing of workloads. Hadoop is an example of loosely coupled cluster. Figure 2.6(b) illsutrates the architecture of a loosely coupled system.

3. **Moderately Coupled**: Moderately or hybrid coupled clusters binds a loosely coupled system out of shared memory multiprocessor. In this configuration, from an operating system viewpoint, the programs and information needed during the boot process resides on the master node. The client node requires the master node for the boot process. Once the client node retrieves all the required file systems from the server, it acts like a stand-alone computer [302]. A hybrid of loosely and tightly coupled architecture is shown in figure 2.6(c).

2.3.1 Classification of Shared Memory Systems

In terms of organization, shared memory systems can be further divided into Symmetric Multi-Processors (SMPs) or Unified Memory Access (UMA) and Non-Uniform Memory Access (NUMA). Example 2.4 highlights the difference between the two types.

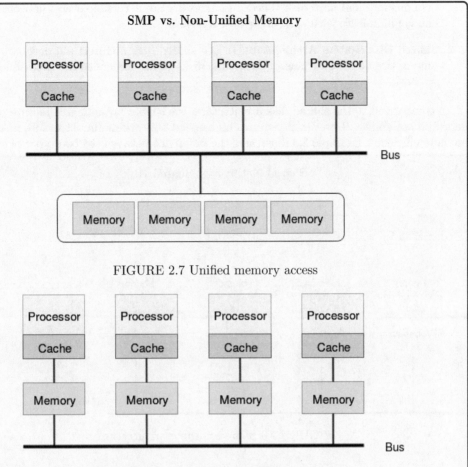

FIGURE 2.7 Unified memory access

FIGURE 2.8 Non-unified memory access

Example 2.4 (SMP vs. Non-Unified Memory). *Shared memory systems can either have Uniform Memory Access (UMA) or Non-Uniform Memory Access (NUMA). The former is also called a Symmetric Multi-Processor (SMP). Such systems are tightly coupled multi-processor systems in which there are numerous processors that are connected via a system bus. These processors are homogeneous, which share common resources of memory, I/O device, interrupt system, and so on. These resources are accessed via the common system bus. Each processor may execute different sets of data. A distinct feature is that access time to shared memory is the same for all the processors.*

On the other end, in Non-Uniform Memory Access (NUMA) systems, access to memory is asymmetric. This leads to variable memory access time for different processors and different memory units. Note that for both UMA and NUMA, each processor has a separate cache.

2.3.2 Classification of Distributed Memory Systems

Distributed memory systems can be organized into two categories [226]:

1. **Shared Nothing Architecture**: In the shared nothing architecture, each node has its

own memory and hard disk. These resources are not accessible over a network. Nodes can communicate with each other over a network.

2. **Shared Disk System Architecture**: In the shared disk architecture, disks are shared among the nodes of a cluster such that disks of all the nodes are accessible over a network.

In comparison to the shared disk architecture, the shared nothing architecture provides improved scalability. However, it requires high-speed networking infrastructure in order to promote efficiency. Example 2.5 illustrates the difference between the two types of systems.

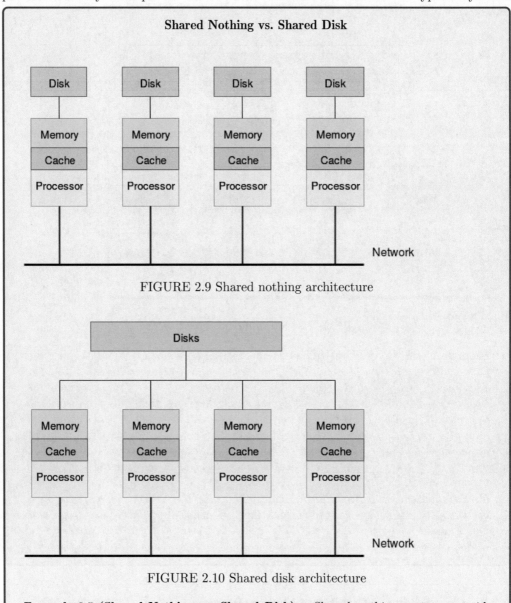

Shared Nothing vs. Shared Disk

FIGURE 2.9 Shared nothing architecture

FIGURE 2.10 Shared disk architecture

Example 2.5 (Shared Nothing vs. Shared Disk). *Shared nothing systems provide improved scalability; however they require faster network access.*

In terms of organization, **Beowulf cluster** is an example of loosely coupled systems. It is a collection of commodity computers networked into a local area network, which allows execution of workloads to be shared, and a high-performance parallel computing cluster can be formed, consequently. It usually consists of one server node (often called a head node), and one or more client nodes connected through Ethernet or some other network. The server node handles scheduling and management of computational nodes. In Beowulf systems, the server has two interfaces: one interface communicates with the clients, i.e., private client network, and the other deals with the organization of the network. The clients have their local memory, disk storage, and a version of the operating system. The private client network has a shared file server used for storing persistent data. The clients access the stored data when it is required. Large Beowulf systems may have multiple server nodes, in which some server nodes are dedicated to particular tasks, for example monitoring stations or consoles [341].

2.3.3 Cluster Example: Distributed File System

Distributed file system (DFS) is a file system, which is designed to efficiently store and retrieve massive amount of data. In DFS, data is distributed among a large number of nodes to provide increased availability. Data is also replicated to increase fault tolerance. A head node (master) is used to control the authorization and access of users. A DFS also provides transparency. For instance, the files are accessed, stored, and managed from a user's local node, while the process itself is being executed from servers. NFS from Sun Microsystems, DFS from Microsoft, and HDFS are examples of distributed file systems. Example 2.6 explains the architecture of a distributed file system.

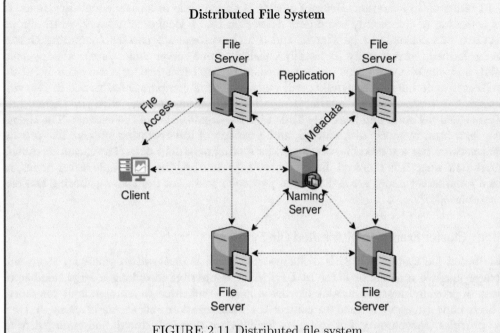

FIGURE 2.11 Distributed file system

Example 2.6 (Distributed File System). *Figure 2.11 illustrates a Distributed File System. A dedicated name server is used to store metadata and provide file lookup service to the clients. Files are replicated across the distributed system. Not all the files are available on all the servers. Clients access actual files through file servers. As files are replicated a client may select the nearest server in order to access files and reduce latency. In case of high load namespace may also be replicated.*

2.3.4 Cluster Example: Message-Passing Interface (MPI)

MPI utilizes message passing interface to provide a library of subroutines to be executed on parallel platforms. It is used for handling communication and synchronization or processes, which are running on parallel platforms. In MPI, data is moved from the address space of one process to the address space of another process. MPI is portable as it could be deployed over a network of computers connected via LAN (such as a Beowulf Cluster) or a distributed shared memory platform. MPI follows Single Program Multiple Data (SPMD) format. That is, each worker node executes the same program with different data. However, MPI is flexible to allocate diverse programs among worker nodes. We will study MPI programming in much detail in section 12.6. Example 2.7 explains the architecture of an MPI cluster.

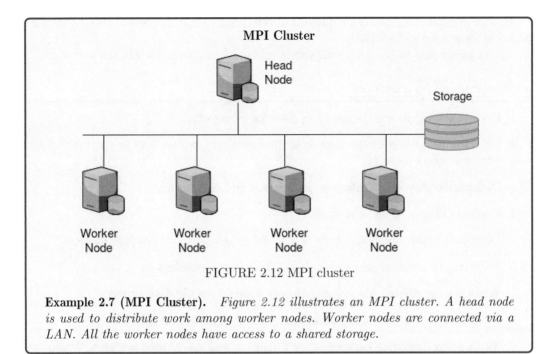

FIGURE 2.12 MPI cluster

Example 2.7 (MPI Cluster). *Figure 2.12 illustrates an MPI cluster. A head node is used to distribute work among worker nodes. Worker nodes are connected via a LAN. All the worker nodes have access to a shared storage.*

In the shared memory systems, another method of obtaining parallelism is through **OpenMP** paradigm. The paradigm utilizes shared memory architecture to exploit parallelism in high level languages such as C/C++ and Fortran. The choice exists between OpenMP and MPI paradigms for shared memory systems. However, for performance gain, MPI is specifically useful where communication between processes remains low and cluster is formed to achieve parallelism through distribution of tasks.

A hybrid architecture of OpenMP and MPI could also be deployed. This is specifically true for a cluster which employs multiple multi-core machines. MPI can handle distribution of tasks among different nodes, whereas OpenMP is useful for exploiting parallelism among multiple cores of a node.

2.4 CONCLUDING REMARKS

This chapter offers an insight on cluster computing. It forms the basis for many advanced applications. Internet search engines, social networking applications, distributed file systems, simulation, predictive analysis, and other big data applications [317], they all rely on cluster computing environment and parallel computing techniques for efficient operation. Cluster computing coupled with parallel processing techniques provides support for efficient operations in many big data applications.

In the next chapter, we explain cloud computing, which provides a basis for hosting scalable systems for big data.

2.5 FURTHER READING

The lambda architecture was initially proposed by Nathan Marz [260]. It has been further explained by Julien Forgeat [169].

The kappa architecture was initially proposed by Jay Kreps [228]. It has been further explained by Nicolas Seyvet and Ignacio Mulas Viela [315].

Cluster architecture has been explained in references [290, 312]. Details about grid computing is mentioned in Ref. [170].

Use of parallelism in big data analytics is explained in references [216, 387].

2.6 EXERCISE QUESTIONS

1. Explain the kappa architecture and describe its benefits.

2. Describe limitations of the lambda architecture and explain how kappa architecture addresses these issues?

3. Differentiate between cluster computing and grid computing.

4. Explain different types of clusters.

5. Describe Flynn's taxonomy. How is it useful in the design of big data systems?

6. Differentiate between grid computing and cluster computing.

7. What is a distributed file system? How is it useful for big data systems?

8. Differentiate between shared nothing and shared disk architecture.

9. Explain the difference between shared memory and distributed systems. Which one of them is useful for promoting scalability? and why?

10. Explain the functionality of a distributed file system.

GLOSSARY

Lambda: It is an architecture for big data systems, which require maintaining separate engines for stream processing and batch Processing.

Kappa: An architecture for big data systems in which stream and batch processing engines are merged together.

FLynn's Taxonomy: This taxonomy categorizes systems with parallel processing capability based on the number of instructions that can be executed and amount of data they can be handled at a time.

Clustering: it refers to the concept of organizing machines such that they are collectively organized to perform a coherent task. Machines in a cluster perform tasks in parallel.

Message Passing Interface (MPI): It is a communication paradigm used for distributed memory model. It is built upon send and receive architecture.

NUMA: It stands for Non Uniform Memory Access. In such systems, access to memory is asymmetric. That is, each processor may take variable time and delay to access the memory.

Shared Memory Systems: These refers to the types of systems in which all processing nodes share the same logical address space and has direct access to the memory.

Distributed Memory Systems: In such type of systems processing nodes have access to their local memory only.

OpenMP: It is an API for obtaining parallelism in shared memory systems. It provides abstraction of shared memory programming using threads.

Shared Disk Architecture: It is a type of distributed system architecture in which each processor has its own memory but all the processors share a common disk storage (clusters).

Shared Nothing Architecture: It is a type of distributed system in which each processor has its own memory and disk storage. That is, processors do not share anything.

Cloud Computing for Big Data

CONTENTS

C LOUD COMPUTING provides foundations for deploying big data systems. The purpose of this chapter is to elucidate the concept, the architecture, the service model, and the functionality of cloud computing in the context of big data systems.

3.1 CLOUD COMPUTING

The scale at which customers demand and consume technology-driven products is increasing exponentially. This results with new challenges requiring enterprises to rethink their technology approaches to cope with this demand. Cloud computing is one ecosystem which is continuing to evolve and innovating to create modern platforms for hosting and running applications.

In sections 2.2 and 2.3, we have explained clusters and their architecture. In the context of big data, there are a few fundamental questions, which are needed to be answered:

1. **Deployment**: Architecturally, how will these clusters be deployed? Should each big data application use a separate cluster? Or could there be sharing of clusters among different applications and users?

2. **Service Level**: Big data applications require long and extended operational hours. An important question is how to ensure a service level which meets a user's needs of fault tolerance and availability.

3. **Workload Management**: Workload for big data applications is expected to vary. A significant question is how to ensure higher efficiency and effective utilization of resources.

Cloud computing provides answers to these questions. A cloud is an abstraction of service in distributed computing. Fundamentally, it is a type of a utility computing model, which has a massive amount of resources and an enormous abstraction of availability, a colossal model of fault tolerance, and gargantuan functionalities of scalability. A cloud has several distinct features [170]:

1. **Elasticity**: Cloud is based on an elastic model of computing in which resources (e.g., storage space, CPUs) can either be added or removed as per the needs. The elastic model is supported through virtualization.

2. **Utility Computing**: The business model of the cloud is based on a utility computing model in which a user is charged as per usage.

3. **Multi-Tenancy**: The service model of a cloud allows multitenancy, i.e., a service could be shared by multiple users at a time. This increases hardware utilization and driving down costs.

4. **Deployment Model**: A cloud is physically hosted on a data center, a facility which consists of physical machines, networking setup, storage, cooling infrastructure, and power equipment.

5. **Layers of Service**: A cloud has a capable service model in which service to users can be provided at different layers.

6. **Resilient**: A cloud has highly distributed services which increase availability and reliability. This also limits impact if and when failure occurs.

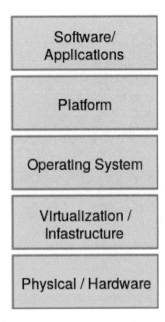

FIGURE 3.1 Layered architecture of cloud

7. **Agile**: Cloud provides capabilities for developers to build systems much faster. For instance, it can provision new IT resources or deploy application code in minutes rather than days or weeks with a simple click or API call. This results in a substantial increase in agility for the organizations.

3.1.1 Cloud Service Layers

A layered model of cloud is shown in figure 3.1. The lowest layer has physical infrastructure which is comprised of CPUs, storage, networking, and cooling. The second layer consists of virtualization, through which a cloud system can provide elasticity, multitenancy, and isolation. We should note that the virtualization could be of different types such as server/OS virtualization, storage virtualization, network virtualization, and application virtualization. Of these server/OS, virtualization is the fundamental requirement of a cloud. It enables a cloud to deploy and manage multiple VMs or containers over a multicore physical machine. We will revert to the topic of virtualization in section 3.2. On top of the virtualization layer is the operating system. Each virtual machine can have its own OS executing independently from other VMs hosted on that physical machine. Just like a normal physical machine, platforms and software are executed on top of the OS in a cloud.

The architecture provided above presents a simplified view for cloud computing. We will have a better understanding of the simplified architecture as we move along the chapter.

3.1.2 Data Center Architecture

In a data center, there are thousands of physical machines. These are organized into racks of PCs. These physical machines are connected to each other via a physical network. There could be virtualized network resources set up on top of the physical network. The networking setup and design vary in the data center.

Figure 3.2 illustrates a generalized architecture of a data center [145,183,307]. At the top of servers, there are Top of Rack (ToR) switches. These are connected to Layer-2 switches.

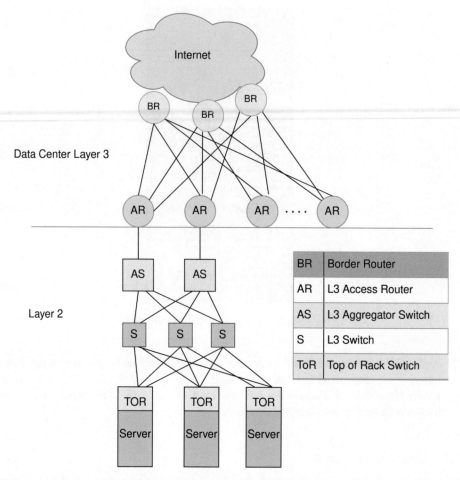

FIGURE 3.2 Data center architecture [145]

On top of layer-2 switches are aggregated switches, which are used to aggregate network packets and send them to access routers. At the topmost layer of the data center, there are border routers which provide data center's connection to the outside world.

3.1.3   Common Cloud Deployment Models

A cloud could be deployed in three different ways [263]. These include Public Cloud, Private Cloud, and Hybrid Cloud. Figure 3.3 illustrates the concept. We now explain the three models in detail:

1. **Public Cloud**: In the public cloud deployment model, a service provider provides resources, such as infrastructure, application, and storage. These resources are made available to the general public over the Internet. The service provider owns, operates, and manages the cloud. These services are typically offered on a pay-per-usage model.

    Infrastructure for public clouds is hosted on provider's premises. In addition, the environment is shared by multiple users. Therefore, deployment on public cloud may raise privacy concerns.

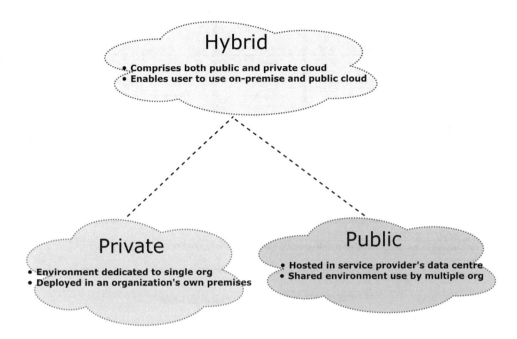

FIGURE 3.3 Cloud deployment models

Amazon EC2 [81], Microsoft Windows Azure [303], Google App Engine [384], and RackSpace [301] are popular examples of public cloud.

2. **Private Cloud**: In a private cloud, the infrastructure is provisioned exclusively for a single organization. It may be owned, managed, and operated by the organization itself or by a third party. The private cloud deployed inside customer-owned facility and the environment is dedicated to a single customer.

   Internal hosting on private cloud solves privacy concerns at the expense of the cost of hosting and management. OpenStack [149], Xen Cloud Platform [71], Eucalyptus [286], and VMware [70] are popular platforms for building a private cloud.

3. **Hybrid Cloud**: This cloud infrastructure comprises both private and public clouds. Public and private cloud remain distinct components. However, they are integrated together to offer the benefits of multiple deployment models.

   The deployed applications can utilize the benefits of both public and private cloud seamlessly. For instance, an organization may store and process sensitive data in a private cloud for security and privacy reasons and outsource the rest of the processing to public cloud.

   VMware [69] and Amazon VPC [2] are popular platforms for building hybrid clouds.

3.1.4 Cloud Platform Service Models

According to NIST (National Institute of Standards and Technology), there are three service models of Cloud [263]. However, additional service models have been emerged to cope with growing consumers and business needs for hosting applications. These models can be well-understood through figures 3.1 and 3.4.

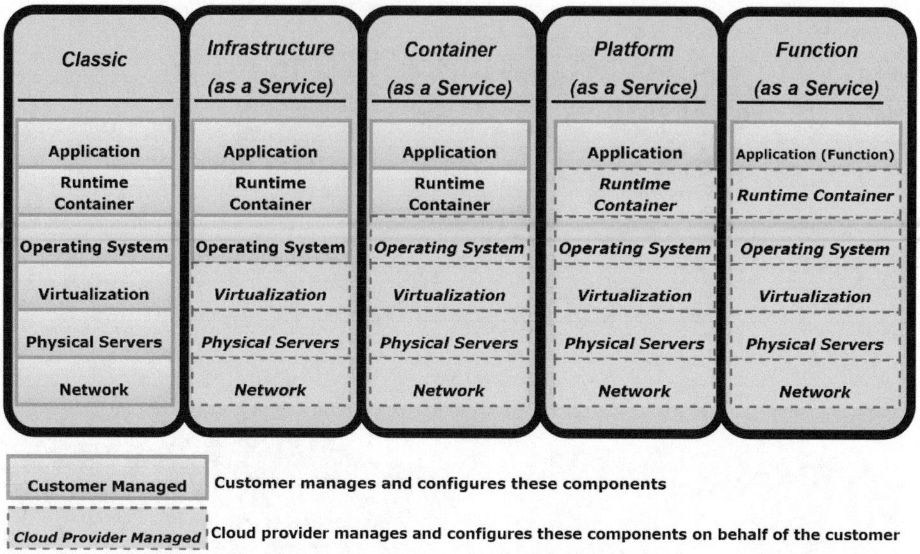

Classic	Infrastructure (as a Service)	Container (as a Service)	Platform (as a Service)	Function (as a Service)
Application	Application	Application	Application	Application (Function)
Runtime Container	Runtime Container	Runtime Container	Runtime Container	Runtime Container
Operating System	Operating System	Operating System	Operating System	Operating System
Virtualization	Virtualization	Virtualization	Virtualization	Virtualization
Physical Servers	Physical Servers	Physical Servers	Physical Servers	Physical Servers
Network	Network	Network	Network	Network

Customer Managed — Customer manages and configures these components

Cloud Provider Managed — Cloud provider manages and configures these components on behalf of the customer

FIGURE 3.4 Cloud service models

Each of these models provides an abstraction for masking complexities of these underlying components and therefore, allow users to focus on building applications while providing automation, scaling and ease of management. Also, these cloud service models can be used across each cloud deployment model we discussed in section 3.1.3.

When leveraging these cloud platforms, the users have a shared responsibility with the cloud service provider for securing the cloud services. As shown in figure 3.4, the further right the users go, the more responsibility the cloud service provider takes on.

1. **Infrastructure as a Service (IaaS)**

   This service model provides base-level infrastructure which includes servers, networking, compute, storage, and other infrastructure components. These are required to host user applications. IaaS provides flexibility to a user in providing computing, storage, networks, and other related resources on a self-service and pay as you go model. This service model allows a user to deploy and run arbitrary software, which can include operating systems and applications.

   (a) **Responsibilities**: In IaaS, a cloud provider manages the underlying cloud infrastructure on behalf of a user, while the user manages and configures operating system and applications. A user may also have limited control of networking components such as firewall.

   (b) **Examples**: IBM, Amazon, Microsoft, Google are some high-profile vendors in the IaaS market.

   (c) **Benefits, Concerns, and Considerations**: IaaS is the most mature and well-understood paradigm, which can be used to host several kinds of applications. These may include traditional or monolithic architecture applications and applications require specific hardware or infrastructure for the workloads, etc. It also provides complete control over infrastructure configurations and operating systems.

   IaaS delegates responsibility for patching, scaling, configuration, and management to the users. It supports limited portability and agility. The infrastructure cost for running applications (e.g., web apps) in IaaS compared to other models can vary significantly.

2. **Container as a Service (CaaS)**

An alternative to using an IaaS model, cloud platforms now also offer Container as a Service (CaaS) to deploy, run, and manage/orchestrate container instances. This cloud service model relies on containers – a lightweight virtual instance, which is capable of providing isolation and multitenancy.

The CaaS model allows users to build and deploy their containerized applications as portable virtual containers (e.g., Docker [23]) to a cloud provider. It therefore minimizes cloud vendor platform lock-in ensuring user applications can be migrated between different service providers. CaaS provides flexibility in packaging application components in an efficient manner while ensuring portability across multiple clouds. CaaS provides base infrastructure in addition to deployment, scaling, and orchestration of containers.

(a) **Responsibilities**: Unlike an IaaS model, where users have to manage the virtual machine the application is deployed to, with CaaS, the cloud provider manages or controls the underlying cloud infrastructure including network, physical servers, operating systems, or storage, and virtualization. The user has control over the deployed applications and container.

(b) **Examples**: Amazon's Elastic Container Service (ECS), Kubernetes [64], and Mesos [213] are some examples for container orchestration.

(c) **Benefits, Concerns, and Considerations**: CaaS provides increased server density and greater user flexibility. It also allows greater portability and efficiency across the environments than the IaaS service model. However, as it provides different layer of service, a user may have less control and higher service of abstraction.

Traditional monolithic or legacy architecture applications that have been modernized or containerized, and applications that developed using Microservice architecture are good fit for deploy into a CaaS-based platform.

3. **Platform as a Service (PaaS)** This service model enables users to run applications without the need to manage underlying infrastructure (e.g., operating systems, hardware). It layers on top of IaaS, provides users a platform, such as a set of tools, programming and development environment (e.g., Java), marketplace services, and database to develop, build, and deploy their custom applications.

(a) **Responsibilities**: In PaaS, a cloud provider provides support for the tools and development environment. They manage or control the underlying cloud infrastructure including network, physical servers, operating systems, patch updates, or storage, container, and virtualization, whereas the user has control over the deployed applications responsible for their configuration management and may also configure the application hosting environment.

(b) **Examples**: Google App Engine, AWS Elastic Beanstalk are some examples of PaaS products offered by cloud providers while Pivotal App Platform and Heroku are popular platforms for PaaS. Salesforce Apprenda and Jelastic are also some other proprietary offerings of PaaS.

(c) **Benefits, Concerns, and Considerations**: PaaS provides a platform that leverages and manages the complexity of underlying infrastructure and minimizes the overall operational overhead. Similar to CaaS, PaaS platform also provides portability across environments. PaaS also greatly simplifies the deployment process and experience.

PaaS platforms require a transformation of legacy applications in order to leverage their services. It also allows less developer control by providing prebuilt software services (e.g., database types), and therefore can lock our code into a cloud vendor platform if our application relies on many of the vendor-specific tools and technologies.

4. **Function as a Service (FaaS)**

Function as a Service (FaaS) is a cloud service model which takes advantage of serverless computing, provides hosting and dynamic scaling of functions – a small unit of code that can be executed in response to events. A function is a small piece of code that runs in response or triggered by an event or direct invocations by either other functions or platform services. Examples of events include changes to database records and new code commits to a code repository.

Functions should be designed with a single and well-defined purpose (efficient/single purpose code) with concise logic. It should always be designed to be idempotent.

Unlike other models where applications deployed on servers or containers run continuously, the FaaS-based platform only allocates resources when required and users only pay for the computing cycles required to execute the function.

(a) **Responsibilities**: A user only manages and configures the input function while the complete underlying cloud infrastructure including network, physical servers, operating systems, storage, visualization and container components manages and configures by the cloud provider on behalf of the user.

(b) **Examples**: FaaS is an emerging platform with growing users in both private and public clouds. The public cloud providers that provide serverless service are:

AWS Lambda from AWS (https://aws.amazon.com/lambda/)

Azure Functions by Microsoft (https://azure.microsoft.com/en-gb/services/functions/)

Cloud Functions from Google (https://cloud.google.com/functions/)

IBM Cloud Functions (https://www.ibm.com/cloud/functions)

(c) **Benefits, Concerns, and Considerations**: FaaS leads to increased server utilization efficiencies, cost optimization, and high level of abstraction. The FaaS-based model allows users to focus solely on business functionality and offers the best economics; however, it can lock our code into a cloud vendor platform as the code is deployed to a vendor-specific runtime engine. Moreover, due to full abstraction from underlying infrastructure, concerns also exist regarding its security, controls, and predictability of the performance.

Although the number of private and public cloud FaaS providers are increasing, the emergence of open standards and architectural patterns is still evolving.

5. **Software as a Service (SaaS)**

Software as a Service (SaaS) refers to the services provided to a user for using specific applications or products running on a cloud infrastructure. It is a cloud service model in which the environment for developing and hosting applications is delivered by the service provider to customers as a service and the complete application is hosted, run, and managed by the service provider.

The application or software does not need to be installed locally on the customer's device and is accessible from various client devices through a thin client interface such as a web browser (e.g., web-based email).

The SaaS applications can be categorized into two types. The first type represents the SaaS applications to be hosted on SaaS provider's own infrastructure while in the second type, the SaaS provider hosts applications on external outsourced infrastructure (for example, Azure).

(a) **Responsibilities**: A SaaS provider manages or controls the underlying cloud infrastructure including network, servers, operating systems, storage, or even individual application capabilities. The only thing users or customers are responsible for is the configuration of the software. A customer may manage the possible exception of limited user-specific application configuration settings such as creating or federating users, managing users, access, and assigning proper access rights.

(b) **Examples**: Microsoft's Office 365, Google's Gmail, Dropbox, and Concur are some common examples. All these example products hosted in cloud with everything provided to the user other than their configuration.

(c) **Benefits, Concerns, and Considerations**: With a SaaS model, both the maintenance and support become simplified for the user since the software does not install on the user's machine and has no responsibility to maintain the application infrastructure. However, this simplicity comes at the expense of optionality, for example, users have no control on the technology selection. With a SaaS-based model, data privacy can be a concern for cloud service providers since all the data management is the responsibility of the cloud vendor.

3.1.5 Cloud Platform Models Comparison

Each of these cloud service models free developers to focus on developing significant business value while abstracting complexities from them. Any of these service models, that is IaaS, PaaS, CaaS, or FaaS can be leveraged across any cloud deployment model (private, hybrid, or public). For example, PaaS service model can be run in either a public or a private cloud. However, the abstraction level in each of the service models can be varied as shown in figure 3.5.

Highly abstracted models, for example, FaaS enable developers to focus on business projects and customers rather than configure or manage servers, which allow them to deliver their business applications faster (rapid time-to-market). However, this simplicity comes at the expense of optionality. On the other hand, less abstracted models, for example IaaS, enable developers to have much more control; however, a large proportion of their time is spent to configure and manage the underlying environment.

Each service model has its own considerations, capabilities, benefits, and tradeoffs. Therefore, an organization having a diverse portfolio of application types should consider all of these cloud service models shown in figure 3.4 to maximize the advantages and minimize the risks across their applications.

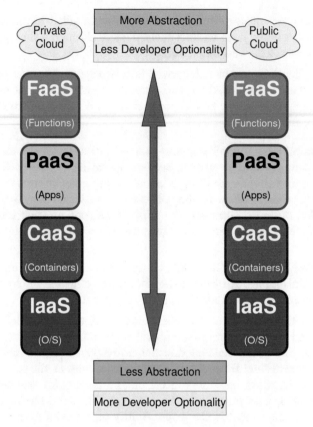

FIGURE 3.5 Cloud platform models comparison

In short, the decision to choose a specific model should be considered based on the requirements and characteristics of a given application.

3.1.6 Big Data and Cloud Computing

Cloud Computing can provide the necessary framework for processing and storing big data. A cloud can also facilitate sharing of data – a key requirement in big data systems.

Big data induces enormous challenges of processing data at high speed. As the rate of data generation is accelerating and the applications that require processing are also increasing, the intensity of these challenges is also increasing. A cloud can provide answers to several of these challenges such as availability, scalability, multitenancy, and isolation.

A cloud is an elastic model of computing, i.e., resources can shrink and grow as per the requirements. It is also based on a shared model, in which resources such as infrastructure, platform, and software are shared among users. The multitenancy environment is supported through virtualization.

3.2 VIRTUALIZATION

In this section, we will study fundamental topics related to virtualization.

3.2.1 Need for Virtualization

Virtualization could provide ease and flexibility in sharing of resources such that multiple users can share a resource. There are five fundamental reasons due to which we would need to virtualize resources [209]:

1. **Sharing**: If a resource is too large or if it is underutilized, then virtualization could provide ease and flexibility in sharing of resources such that multiple users can share a resource. For instance, modern computers are equipped with multicore processors. Virtualization can enable sharing of processors among multiple users at a time.

2. **Isolation**: Sharing of resources would require provision of isolation in order to ensure confidentiality and privacy. That is, users accessing one virtual component should not be able to access another virtual component. While virtualization would promote sharing, it would also ensure isolation.

3. **Aggregation**: Virtualization is also useful in aggregating resources. For instance, a large number of small resources can be combined to aggregate and coherently abstract one unified resource.

4. **Dynamics**: Virtualization could also be useful in migrating resources from one location to another. In the context of big data, need for migration may occur due to requirements of load balancing, workload consolidation, replication, and facilitating ubiquitous access.

5. **Ease of management**: Virtual devices are managed through software abstractions and hence are easier to manage.

Example 3.1 explains the concepts of isolation, consolidation, and migration in VMs.

VM Advantages: Isolation, Consolidation, and Migration

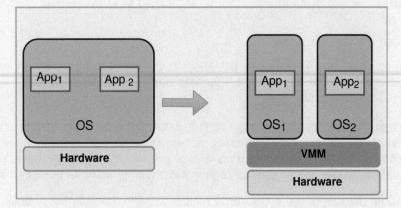

FIGURE 3.6 Workload isolation using virtual machines

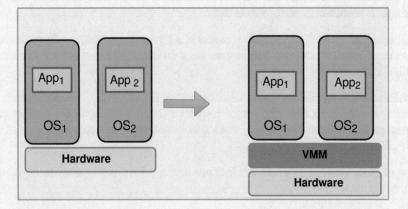

FIGURE 3.7 Workload consolidation using virtual machines

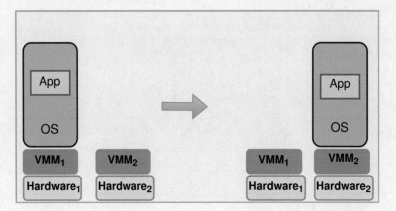

FIGURE 3.8 Workload migration using virtual machines

Example 3.1 (VM Advantages).

3.2.2 Virtualization of Resources

In a computer system, different resources can be virtualized. These include processor, operating system, storage, and network. In the context of big data systems, virtualization could be very useful in aggregating, isolating, and promoting the sharing of resources. We now explain the type of virtualization:

1. **Processor Virtualization**: Using processor virtualization, multiple Virtual Machines (VMs) could be created on a single Physical Machine (PM). A virtual machine is an abstraction of a virtualized physical machine and it mimics the complete behavior of a physical machine. With the advancements in the processor technology and multicore systems, multiple VMs can be hosted on a single physical machine. The created VMs could then be a part of a single cluster – executing a parallel task or they could perform individual tasks in isolation.

2. **OS Virtualization**: Using OS virtualization, multiple instances of operating system images and their resources are created. All instances share the same host OS kernel as the base. However, each instance has its own virtualized instance of OS resources. OS level virtualization is also referred to as containerization. In that, the OS kernel will run a single operating system and will replicate its functionality using lightweight containers.

3. **Storage**: Storage-level virtualization allows creating multiple virtual instances of a storage. These multiple instances can be used by different users individually.

4. **Network**: Network virtualization is implemented to create different virtual networks over a shared physical network. Separate virtual networks are useful in the cloud as users of different groups can share a different Virtual Local Area Network (VLAN) to ensure security and isolation.

In the remainder of this chapter, we will be focusing on process virtualization and OS virtualization. These are mainly responsible for ensuring multitenancy.

3.3   PROCESSOR VIRTUALIZATION

Processor virtualization allows creation of multiple VMs on a single physical machine. A virtual machine is a software-based abstraction of a physical machine, having its own hardware resources such as CPU, memory, hard disk, and networking. This type of virtualization is also referred as hypervisor-based virtualization as it requires a hypervisor to manage resources of multiple VMs on a single machine and ensure isolation among multiple VMs. A hypervisor is also known as a Virtual Machine Monitor (VMM).

In the literature [167], two different types of VMM are mentioned. Figure 3.9 illustrates the two types. A type 1 hypervisor (also called as bare metal or native hypervisor) is installed directly on top of hardware. Each VM may have its own guest OS. In contrast, a type 2 hypervisor is installed on top of a host OS. The OS may host other applications in access to hosting VMs. Type 1 hypervisors are predominantly used in cloud systems, primarily because they are more capable to manage clouds. They also bear low cost. Isolation and elasticity are two intrinsic properties of a cloud.

3.3.1   Intel Hardware Architecture

To understand how virtualization is handled, it is significant to understand the underlying hardware architecture. The Intel hardware processor consists of four levels of modes

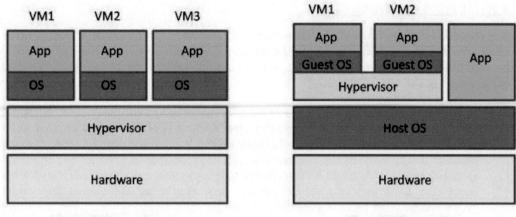

FIGURE 3.9 Types of hypervisors

(also known as rings). The highest privilege mode is at ring 0. In a nonvirtualized environment, ring 0 hosts the OS and ring 3 hosts the applications, whereas rings 1 and 2 remain unoccupied.

3.3.2 Implementing Virtualization

For virtualization, a significant question is how to execute privileged instructions. There are three important considerations and requirements for this:

1. The VMM should be able to manage all the hardware resources.

2. Privilege instructions should be handled by the VMM.

3. The overhead of VMM should be low.

These requirements may contradict each other. For instance, if all the guest binaries are executed natively then the overhead of VMM is low. However, this cannot be implemented as privileged instructions should not be handled by the guest OS.

We should make guest binaries run on the CPU as fast as possible. Theoretically speaking, if we can run all guest binaries natively, there will be no overhead at all. However, this is implausible because we cannot let guest OS handle everything. VMM should be able to control all the hardware resources. The first effort on implementing virtualization is the "trap and emulate model". Using this model, nonprivilege instructions have been executed directly by the guest OS, whereas privilege instructions initiated by the guest OS are trapped by the VMM. The VMM will emulate the trapped instruction.

When virtualization is introduced, VMM takes the role of managing resources for VMs. It is hosted at ring 0, whereas the guest OS is hosted at ring 1. The guest OS executes user-level instructions directly and privilege instructions are interrupted and translated by the VMM.

The "trap and emulate" model is limited because a few instructions are not trapped. This is because a few instructions have different behaviors in user and kernel modes.

3.3.3 Types of Virtualization

To overcome the limitations of the trap and emulate model, three types of virtualization techniques have been proposed [76, 188]. These three techniques also indicate the three generations of virtual machine evolution:

1. **Full Virtualization**: It is a software-based technique in which each VM mimics a complete abstraction of a physical machine. As a result, all the resources such as hardware, BIOS, memory, and devices are abstracted. In full virtualization, the OS remains unaware of the fact that it is being executed in a virtualized environment. Full virtualization provides complete isolation of virtual machines. Microsoft Virtual Server and VMware ESX server are the examples of full virtualization. This type of virtualization is expensive as providing a complete abstraction of a physical machine in a virtualized environment is costly.

2. **Paravirtualization**: It reduces the cost of full virtualization by providing an abstraction for only a subset of resources.

   In the paravirtualized environment, the VMM is underneath the guest OS. The guest OS is hosted at ring 0. This ensures that the OS lies above the VMM. However, it requires that the guest OS be modified to replace system calls with custom hyper calls.

   Consequently, each guest OS is needed to be modified in order to facilitate this type of virtualization. Because of this requirement, only open-source OS can be executed in a paravirtualized VM. Paravirtualization also falls in the category of software-based virtualization. Xen is a popular hypervisor, which supports paravirtualization.

3. **Hardware-assisted Virtualization**: This type of virtualization is based on hardware assistance in order to support full virtualization. Hardware-assisted virtualization enables cost-effective and efficient virtualization. Intel Virtualization Technology (VT) and AMD Virtualization (V) are well-known technologies supporting hardware-assisted virtualization.

   In the hardware-assisted virtualization, a new privilege mode, ring -1, is introduced. The VMM is hosted at ring -1, whereas the guest OS is hosted at ring 0. This allows unmodified execution of the host OS. Operation of VMM below the host OS permits efficient execution and faster context switching of virtual machines.

Example 3.2 explains the difference between the three types of virtualization techniques.

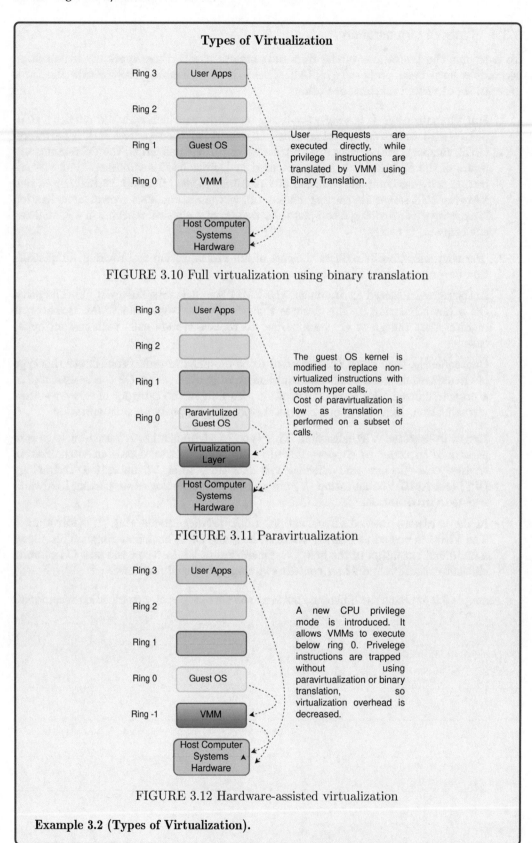

Types of Virtualization

FIGURE 3.10 Full virtualization using binary translation

FIGURE 3.11 Paravirtualization

FIGURE 3.12 Hardware-assisted virtualization

Example 3.2 (Types of Virtualization).

3.3.4 Resource Consolidation and Virtual Machine Migration

Virtual Machine Migration is a process of migrating a VM from one physical machine to another physical machine. VM migration involves migrating all the resources including memory, network, and devices. We will now study reasons for VM migration:

1. **Server Consolidation**: A VM could be migrated in order to consolidate a physical machine. For instance, two different physical machines are being operated on less than half capacity. Consequently, it becomes desirable to migrate VMs from one physical machine to another in order to conserve resources.

2. **Affinity of Resources**: For instance, in a data center environment, two VMs, which are being hosted on two different physical machines, are communicating with each other via network. As such, there is a strong network affinity between the two VMs. It would be beneficial to consolidate both the VMs on one physical machine in order to reduce network latency and improve user experience. Similarly, affinity could exist with respect to other attributes such as memory, CPU, and storage.

3. **Conserve Power**: VMs could also be migrated in order to conserve power of the data center. This includes power of servers and networking equipment references [105,359].

In a broader scope, there are two methods of VM migration.

1. **Offline Migration**: In this category, a VM is stopped before being migrated to the destination physical machine. Offline migration techniques are obsolete due to their limitations in supporting seamless migration.

2. **Live Migration**: In live migration, a VM is being copied to the destination, while the VM is in execution and serving users. This is achieved using a copy phase in which VM pages are iteratively copied to the destination, while the users are being served from the original destination. Iterative copy allows minimum interruption of users. Different variations of live migration techniques have been proposed. Readers are advised to follow literature for advanced comprehension [146].

3.4 CONTAINERIZATION

Containerization is aimed to secure a portion of a device's resources such as application, storage, or network access from other applications and systems running on the same device [288].

Containerization permits to run a multitude of processes on a single host. Each of the processes can be executed in an isolated environment. The technique is also called container-based virtualization [312].

Docker [23] and Linux Containers (LXC) [42] are the two popular platforms for containerization.

Unlike hypervisor-based virtualization, which requires hardware assistance, containers are lightweight and hardware independent. Containers can run their own operating system; however, they share the base kernel OS. Therefore, they are lighter. LXC – a popular linux-based container has its own file system and network stack. Isolation is provided through Linux cgroups and namespaces. In that, cgroups are used to manage and allocate resources, whereas namespaces are used to isolate users, processes, and files. Another important difference between hypervisor and container is that the latter cannot allocate resources on a per core basis.

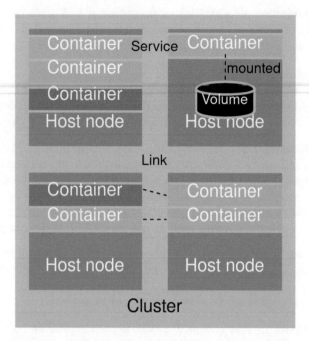

FIGURE 3.13 Cluster architecture in a container [290]

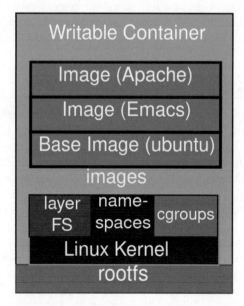

FIGURE 3.14 Docker architecture [290]

Containers (such as Docker) mount a writable file system on top of read-only file system. Through this, multiple read-only file systems can be layered together with the top most layer serving as a writeable layer. This concept is illustrated in figure 3.14.

Another major advantage of containers is that they can facilitate application clustering – a phenomenon which is used to cluster applications together. This is useful for interoperability and scalability. Figure 3.13 illustrates clustering architecture in containers.

Volumes provide persistent storage, while links are used to provide communication channel between containers. Containers run their own OS, file system, and network stack but they share kernel [312].

3.5 VIRTUALIZATION OR CONTAINERIZATION

Containers and VMs are both virtualization techniques. However, they solve different problems references [163, 166]. Containers are aimed at delivering PaaS. Their main focus is on providing interoperability and eradicating the requirements of application dependencies and installation. The main idea is based on OS virtualization principles.

In comparison, VMs are more focused on hardware-based virtualization where the aim is to address the issues of resource sharing and isolation through IaaS. Other models of cloud such as PaaS and SaaS, which utilize VMs, use a combination of preinstalled software and platform on top of hardware-level virtualization.

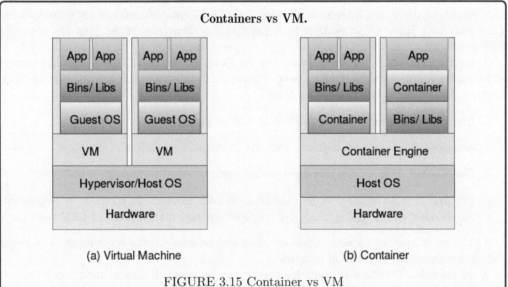

FIGURE 3.15 Container vs VM

Example 3.3 (Containers vs VM.). *Figure 3.15 illustrates the difference between a VM and a Container. Each VM instance needs a guest OS. VMs store large isolated files on their host and store the entire file system. In addition, application binaries and libraries necessary for the applications are also stored. This yields large overhead and slow startups for VMs. In comparison, a container offers lightweight virtualization. A container holds self-contained and ready to deploy applications with binaries and libraries [289].*

While isolation in VMs has been well established, container-based systems may suffer with degraded isolation [370].

Big data systems have benefited from the hypervisor-based virtualization techniques in building scalable and reliable cloud systems. Containers have emerged as a competitive technology in providing lightweight, robust, high performance, and scalable systems for big data. Studies have shown that container-based big data cloud systems may perform better than hypervisor-based cloud systems. However, performance may depend upon a number of factors such as workload, platform, and hardware resources [98].

3.6   CLUSTER MANAGEMENT

There are many cluster management solutions or container orchestration technologies, which are being used. These include Apache Mesos [213], OpenShift [297], Borg [358], Kubernetes, Docker Swarm [278], and HashiCorp Nomad. In section 5.2, we will study YARN for resource monitoring and resource scheduling in Hadoop v2. In this section, we will study Borg and Kubernetes, which are being used to manage big data systems through containers.

3.6.1   Borg

Borg has been developed by Google as a part of it's internal requirements to manage large clusters containing Linux containers [116, 358].

It caters for two kinds of jobs, i.e., long-running services and batch jobs. Of these, long-services jobs are from specific Google services such as Gmail and Google docs. They have latency-sensitive requirements, whereas, batch jobs have relaxed latency requirements. They may take from a few seconds to a few days to complete. Batch jobs are normally CPU-intensive.

Google applications and services are run on Borg. Users, which are Google developers and engineers, submit their jobs to borg. Figure 3.16 illustrates the architecture of borg. We now define a few terminologies of borg.

1. **Borg job**: A set of tasks that all run the same program.

2. **Borg cell**: It is a set of machines that are managed as a unit and runs one borg job.

3. **Borgmaster**: It is a centralized controller, which is used to manage a borg cell.

4. **Borglet**: It is an agent process that runs on each machine in a cell. It is responsible for starting and stopping tasks, failure recovery, and management of local resources.

Borgmaster receives requests from borglets and schedule tasks accordingly. For larger cells, borgmaster can operate in parallel.

Borg supports a variety of tools for cluster management. These include predicting resource requirements, configuring jobs and submitting configuration files, load balancing, auto-scaling, and machine life cycle management [116].

3.6.2   Kubernetes

Kubernetes (k8s for short) is a portable, extensible, open-source, robust, and feature-rich orchestration platform for managing containers that can operate at scale [64, 255]. It provides the platform to automate deployment, management, and scaling of containerized applications.

Kubernetes was originally developed by Google. However, its simplicity and flexibility have quickly made Kubernetes a front runner for container orchestration and cluster management. It inherited a lot of concepts and lessons learned from Google's internal large-scale cluster orchestration systems such as Borg and Omega, and was designed based on

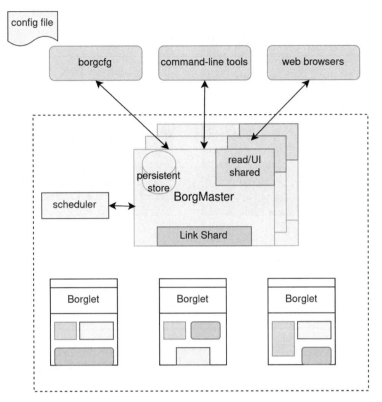

FIGURE 3.16 Borg System architecture

Google's decade-long experience deploying scalable, reliable systems in containers through these systems [116].

Kubernetes offers the following three services:

1. **Data center as a single virtual machine**: Kubernetes embraces the idea of treating our servers as a single unit and abstracts away the underlying hosting environment and how individual compute resources operate. For instance, from a collection of five servers, Kubernetes makes a single cluster that behaves like one. It allows us to deploy and run our application components without having to know about the actual servers underneath.

2. **Kubernetes as a scheduler**: When we deploy an application, Kubernetes identifies memory requirements for our container and finds the best place to deploy our application in the cluster. Instead of making the decision about how to schedule and deploy our application in the cluster, Kubernetes has a scheduler that decides automatically for us. The scheduler is optimized to pack containers efficiently.

3. **Kubernetes as an API**: Kubernetes provides a powerful set of APIs and abstractions for building distributed systems. It provides a common API for provisioning and orchestration such as provisioning storage, autoscaling, managing access etc [35].

   Kubernetes creates a unified API layer on top of the infrastructure. We can invoke commands through the REST API without worrying about the underlying infrastructure. The API layer is generic which means we can leverage the same API to install Kubernetes in any cloud provider or a data center. We can easily migrate from our

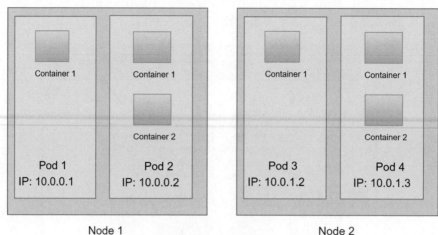

FIGURE 3.17 Pods as a collection of containers

on-premise cluster to Azure, AWS, or Google Kubernetes Engine (GKE) without risk of vendor lock-in[1].

We will now provide an introduction to some of the basic concepts (or objects) of Kubernetes and their role in the development and containerization of an application [38].

1. **Nodes**: The nodes can be either virtual machines (VMs) or physical servers.

2. **Master and worker nodes**: Kubernetes is composed of a master node and a set of worker nodes. The master node is responsible for distributing tasks to other nodes. It does not run any workload except in small clusters, e.g., Minikube[2] [277]. It schedules work across the worker nodes. The worker nodes run the actual applications we deploy.

3. **Pods**: A Pod is a collection of application containers that work as a single unit [39]. Pod is the smallest deployable artifact in a Kubernetes cluster. This means all containers in a Pod are always run on a single worker node in the cluster as shown in figure 3.17.

   Pods also share many resources between the containers. For example, containers within a Pod share the node's network and volumes with any other containers in the same Pod.

4. **Namespaces**: Kubernetes uses namespaces to organize objects in the cluster. It allows us to logically divide the cluster into smaller units of management. We can have any number of namespaces; for example, we might have one per software environment (development, testing, or production), or one per application. Objects in the same namespace share the same control access policies, authorization checks, and quotas/limits around resource usage.

5. **Labels**: A Kubernetes object such as Pods can be attached with arbitrary key-value pairs called labels. Labels are useful for organizing the Kubernetes objects. A object can have any number of labels.

---

[1]Vendor lock-in is a situation where we have a dependency on a single service provider and the migration of applications from one service provider to another is difficult or even infeasible.

[2]Minikube is an easy-to-use tool designed to run a local Kubernetes cluster in a VM on your local machine.

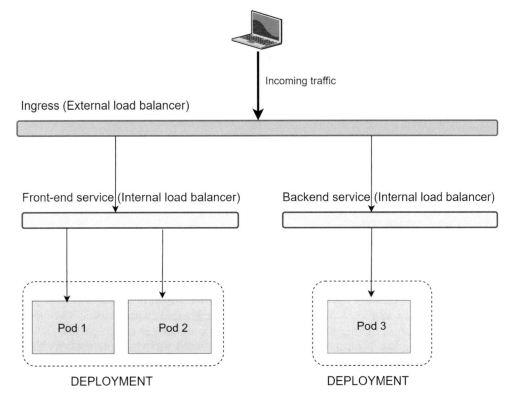

FIGURE 3.18 Deploying applications on Kubernetes

6. **etcd**: It is a key-value store which is designed to run in distributed systems. This is the database where Kubernetes stores the cluster configuration.

In general, in order to deploy an application using Kubernetes, the following objects are defined:

(a) **Deployment**: It is used to create multiple copies of an application. These copies are deployed as pods. The *Deployment* manages Pods and make sure that they are healthy. It deploys, updates, and restarts them when necessary [36].

(b) **Service**: It is an internal load balancer that routes the traffic to Pods [40].

(c) **Ingress**: It describes how the traffic should flow from outside the cluster to our *Service* [37].

Figure 3.18 explains the execution. Two layers of load balancers (internal and external) are shown in the figure. The internal load balancer is called *Service*, whereas the external one is called *Ingress*. A *Deployment* is used to creates the Pods.

Kubernetes provides a variety of options to automate deployment, scaling, and the management of containerized applications. It strives to minimal disruption or zero-down time during application update.

Kubernetes is offered by all of the major cloud providers. It has become the standard platform for building cloud-native applications[3]. There are several managed Kubernetes services being offered by cloud providers. These include:

---

[3]Cloud native applications are essentially applications that are designed from a lightweight loosely-coupled services (i.e., microservices) and utilize the unique capabilities of the cloud.

1. **AWS EKS (Elastic Kubernetes Service)**: It is the managed Kubernetes offering from Amazon Web Services.

2. **Azure AKS (Azure Kubernetes Service)**: It is the managed Kubernetes offering from Microsoft Azure.

3. **Google Kubernetes Engine (GKE)**: It is a fully managed Kubernetes service from Google Cloud.

A few of the several benefits of kubernetes include having a common API for orchestration and provisioning, greater application portability across platforms, business agility, and improved elasticity. The Kubernetes ecosystem continues to experience explosive growth with new projects being launched frequently.

3.7 FOG COMPUTING

Big data systems rely on cloud computing solutions for storage and processing. Cloud exhibits several significant features such as massive amount of storage capability, huge processing power, and central point for coordination. However, as the cloud system is at a distant location, it exhibits heavy cost of communication which is reflected in slow processing. Many big data applications such as smart traffic control require faster response time. For such applications, having a response time of a few seconds is unacceptable.

Fog computing has been introduced to cater the needs for such applications. The idea is to move processing from a distant location of cloud to nearby fog nodes. A fog layer is an intermediary layer between cloud systems and end devices such as the Internet of Thing (IoT) devices. It stores tens to hundreds of fog nodes. Data emitted from IoT devices is sent and processed on fog nodes instead of the cloud. In fog computing, since the distance between IoT devices and data processing location is reduced, response time is much lower as compared to cloud.

Figure 3.19 illustrates the main concept of fog computing. Where data are collected from IoT devices and are being sent to the fog layer [102]. The figure also shows edge devices and network core. Analytical decisions can be made at the fog layer, whereas cloud can execute the tasks of backup, feedback control, result analysis, etc [73].

3.7.1 Analysis of Fog Computing

Fog computing is an emerging platform. It reduces response time for big data systems. However, with respect to big data systems, fog computing also induces several challenges and limitations:

1. **Consistency**: As data is stored at multiple fog nodes, maintaining consistency among fog nodes is a real issue.

2. **Data Storage and Load Balancing**: A fog node has limited storage capacity as compared to a cloud. Therefore, it cannot store complete data. Decisions, that which data items are more relevant are important. Data items which are not found on a local fog node are needed to be copied from other fog nodes. Data copying could induce additional overhead.

3. **Replication**: As data is replicated across multiple fog nodes, challenges exist in reducing the cost of replication.

It is anticipated that the fog cloud integrated framework would be effective for many big data applications.

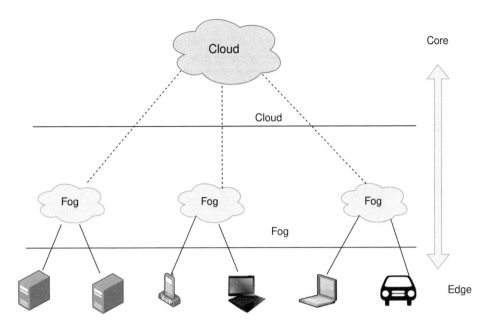

FIGURE 3.19 Fog computing

3.8 EXAMPLES

In this section, we will show a few examples for creation of cloud instances. We will also explain the process of creating container images. The purpose of these exercises is to enhance readers' learning and hands-on capabilities. In these exercises, comments are listed in italics.

3.8.1 Creating Cloud Instances on AWS

AWS is one of the largest cloud providers. It is used to provide IaaS. It utilizes public/private key pair for access.

For IaaS, storage on AWS is through S3 (Simple Storage Service). It utilizes the concept of buckets which is analogous to directory in a file system. The namespace of S3 is universal, i.e., two buckets cannot be created with the identical name. Buckets are used to store objects.

There are three ways to access AWS components. These include AWS management console, AWS command line interface (CLI), and an API (such as boto library).

Access and management through the AWS management console and AWS CLI are trivial. Example 3.4 shows a sample command to configure AWS using CLI. Comments are mentioned in italics.

Configure AWS using CLI

Example 3.4 (Configure AWS using CLI).
We can configure your AWS credentials from the AWS CLI using the following command:

```
aws configure
```

We now describe a few examples to access AWS via boto3 API.

3.8.2 Accessing AWS Using Boto Library

Boto3 is the Amazon Web Services (AWS) Software Development Kit (SDK) which allows developers to write programs that manage services like S3 and EC2 [20].

Start and Stop an EC2 instance [20]

Example 3.5 (Start and Stop an EC2 instance).

```python
import sys
import boto3
from botocore.exceptions import ClientError
instanceid = sys.argv[2]
command = sys.argv[1].upper()
client_name = boto3.client('ec2')


if command == 'ON':
Do a dryrun first to verify permissions

try:
client_name.start_instances(InstanceIds=[
    instanceid], DryRun=True)
except ClientError as e:
if 'DryRunOperation' not in str(e):
raise
Dry run succeeded, run start instances without dryrun

try:
my_response = cloud_instance.start_instances(
    InstanceIds=[instanceid], DryRun=False)
print(my_response)
except ClientError as e:
print(e)
else:


Dry run succeeded, call stop instances witout dryrun

try:
my_response = client_name.stop_instances(
    InstanceIds=[instanceid], DryRun=False)
print(my_response)
except ClientError as e:
print(e)
```

Describe an EC2 Instance [20]

Example 3.6 (Describe an EC2 Instance).

```
import boto3
client_name = boto3.client('ec2')
my_response = client_name.describe_instances()
print(my_response)
```

Reboot an EC2 Instance [20]

Example 3.7 (Reboot an EC2 Instance).

```
import boto3
from botocore.exceptions import ClientError
client_name = boto3.client('ec2')
try:
client_name.reboot_instances(InstanceIds=['
    INSTANCE_ID'], DryRun=True)
except ClientError as e:
if 'DryRunOperation' not in str(e):
print("You don't have permission to reboot
    instances.")
raise
try:
my_response = client_name.reboot_instances(
    InstanceIds=['INSTANCE_ID'], DryRun=False)
print('Success', my_response)
except ClientError as e:
print('Error', e)
```

List All S3 Buckets [20]

Example 3.8 (List All S3 Buckets).
```
import boto3
Create an S3 client
client_name = boto3.client('s3')

Call S3 to list current buckets

my_response = s3.list_buckets()
Get a list of all bucket names from the response

buckets = [bucket['Name'] for bucket in
    my_response['Buckets']]

Print out the bucket list
print("Bucket List: %s" % buckets)
```

Create an S3 Bucket [20]

Example 3.9 (Create an S3 Bucket).
```
import boto3
client_name = boto3.client('s3')
client_name.create_bucket(Bucket='my-bucket')
```

Upload a File to an S3 Bucket [20]

Example 3.10 (Upload a File to an S3 Bucket).
```
import boto3

Create an S3 client
s3 = boto3.client('s3')
filename = 'file.txt'
my_bucket = 'my-bucket'

Uploads the given file using a managed uploader, which will
    split up large files automatically and upload parts in
    parallel.
s3.upload_file(filename, my_bucket, filename)
```

3.8.3 Creating Container Images Using Docker

Docker is one of the most prominent engines for containerization. In this section, we describe examples for the use of docker. Before we proceed with examples, it is pertinent to understand the difference between a docker image and a docker container.

A docker image is an immutable file, which is used to execute code. It consists of a series of layers [23]. In that, each layer represents an instruction used to create an image. Usually, all these instructions are listed in a file called Dockerfile. Each layer except the very last one is read-only. When a docker image is executed, a container is created. A container is also termed as instance of an image. Different containers can share an image such that only the top layer is different. We now describe a few examples for accessing and managing images and containers.

List all the Container Images

Example 3.11 (List all the Container Images).
```
docker images
```

Build a Container Image

Example 3.12 (Build a Container Image).
```
Suppose that all the files which are required to build a
   docker image are in the local directory. dockerimage is
   the name of the docker image. Note the '.' means all the
   files in the current directory

docker build -t <dockerimage> .
```

Running a Container Application

Example 3.13 (Running a Container Application).
```
Redirects port 80 of the container to local port
   4000
docker run -p 4000:80 friendlyhello
```

Quitting a Container

Example 3.14 (Quitting a Container).
```
Ctrl-c
or
exit
```

Running a Container in Background

Example 3.15 (Running a Container in Background).
```
docker run -d -p 4000:80 friendlyhello
```

Attaching to a Container

Example 3.16 (Attaching to a Container).
```
docker attach <containerid>
```

Sharing your Container Image

Example 3.17 (Share your Container Image).
```
create loginid on id.docker.com
docker login
docker tag friendlyhello loginid/get-started:part1
publish image
docker push username/repository:tag
```

Delete all Images or Containers

Example 3.18 (Delete all Images or Containers).
```
Delete all Containers
docker rm $(docker ps -a -q)
Delete all images
docker rmi $(docker images -q)
```

Delete a Container Image

Example 3.19 (Delete a Container Image).
```
docker rmi image
Remove Dangling Images
docker images -f dangling=true
```

3.9 CONCLUDING REMARKS

Massive amount of resources are required to store and process big data. Cloud Computing provides flexible, scalable, elastic, and reliable model for big data processing. In this chapter, we have studied details about virtualization and containerization – the two fundamental methods of ensuring multitenancy in cloud environment. Through examples, we have also studied configuration and administration of containers.

3.10 FURTHER READING

A comparison of three types of processor virtualization is explained in references [77, 205].

Details about containers have been explained in references [267, 334].

A detailed survey on container-based cloud computing has been mentioned in references [290].

A comparison of container and VM-based hypervisor for big data applications has been discussed in [98, 289, 336]. This comparison has been more deeply elaborated in references [276, 371].

Reference [116] provides a decade of experience and a lot of lessons learned by Google from developing and operating container management systems.

Details about Kubernetes can be found in references [255] and [311]. Mobile containerization techniques have been explored in reference [288].

Performance isolation issues in container-based clouds have been discussed in reference [370].

Power-aware virtual machine migration has been discussed in references [105, 233, 359].

Details about storage virtualization techniques have been discussed in references [219, 330]

3.11 EXERCISE QUESTIONS

1. Highlight major differences between container-based cloud and hypervisor-based cloud.

2. Explain the three types of processor virtualization.

3. Explain the need of using cloud for big data systems.

4. Are multitenancy and isolation necessary for big data systems?

5. Highlight the significance of Hardware-assisted Virtualization.

6. Differentiate between Processor and OS virtualization.

7. Discuss pros and cons of fog computing for big data applications.

8. Explain different types of cloud service models.

9. What is hybrid cloud? What are the benefits of hybrid cloud?

10. Explain the difference between PaaS and CaaS service model.

GLOSSARY

Borg: Borg is Google's internal cluster management system which was developed as a part of their internal requirements to manage large clusters containing Linux containers.

Cloud: It is an abstraction of network-based (or remote) service. The service can be provided at different layers such as hardware, platform, and software. Cloud provides high availability and fault tolerance. It is based on a utility computing model in which users are charged for the services they used. A cloud is an elastic computing model in which resources can shrink and grow as per need.

Container: It is a lightweight virtual machine, which does not use any hardware virtualization. It shares the host's kernal. It includes everything (code library, dependencies, configs), which is required to run an application.

Containerization: It is a process of virtualizing OS such that multiple containers can be created on a single OS.

Docker: It is an open-source container platform for building, managing, shipping, securing, and running containers. It is a powerful and easy-to-use tool for running applications in containers.

Docker Swarm: It is a clustering and scheduling tool for Docker containers.

Database-as-a-Service (DBaaS): It is a managed database service in the cloud that provides a powerful on-demand scalable database platform.

Edge Computing: It is closely related to fog computing. It is the concept in which computing is moved from data centers to edge devices or close to the user or data sources.

EKS: It is called Elastic Kubernetes Service (EKS) which is the managed Kubernetes offering from Amazon Web Services.

etcd: It is a key-value store which is designed to run in distributed systems.

Fog Computing: It is extension of cloud computing and services that enable storage and processing to the edge of the network.

Full Virtualization: It is a type of virtualization, which involves binary translation of privileged instructions by the hypervisor.

Hybrid Cloud: It is a combination of both public and private clouds to offer the benefits of multiple deployment models.

Hypervisor: It is a software which is used to provide processor virtualization. It is used to manage hardware resources for different VMs.

Kubernetes: (k8s for short) It is an open-source, robust, and feature-rich orchestration platform for managing containers that can operate at scale. It provides the platform to automate the deployment, management, and scaling of containerized applications.

Lambda Function: It is an AWS implementation of Function as a Service (FaaS) model.

Mesos: It is an open-source cluster management framework for managing compute, memory, storage, and other resources across a cluster.

Monolithic Applications: Applications packaged as a single unit is generally referred to as monoliths. Monolithic applications are usually deployed as a single artifact. Changes to one component of the application require a new version of the whole application to be developed, tested, and deployed.

Microservices: Splitting the complex and static monolithic applications into a set of smaller, decoupled, and independent components called microservices. These components can be developed, deployed, tested, and scaled individually.

Multitenancy: It implies to the concpet that multiple users (also called tenants) can be served. Multitenancy is supported through virtualization such that multiple virtual machines can be hosted on a single physical machine.

Multicloud: It is the strategy of using the combination of services and technologies from different cloud service providers to satisfy or achieve a business objective for an organization.

OpenStack: It is a widely used framework which is used to provide IaaS.

Paravirtualization: It is a type of virtualization in which system calls are replaced with hyper calls such that these calls are sent from the guest OS to the hypervisor.

Private cloud: The network, computing, and storage infrastructure is provisioned exclusively for a single organization and is not shared with any other organizations. It may be owned, managed, and operated by the organization itself or by a third party.

Public Cloud: A public cloud is hosted, operated, and managed by a service provider from one or more data centers. The services are offered to the general public over the Internet and are typically offered on a pay-per-usage model.

Virtualization: It is a process of virtualizing resources over a physical layer. Virtualization can be implemented at different layers such as hardware, operating system, software, network, and storage. Virtualization permits multitenancy and provides isolation among multiple tenants.

Xen: It is a type of hypervisor, which supports paravirtualization.

YAML: It stands for Yet Another Markup Language, which is a human-readable text format for representing configuration-type information. YAML is a superset of JSON, which means that any valid JSON file is also a valid YAML file but not the other way around.

II

Storage and Processing for Big Data

CHAPTER 4

HADOOP: An Efficient Platform for Storing and Processing Big Data

CONTENTS

I N this chapter, we will study efficient platforms for storing and processing big data. Our main focus will be on MapReduce/Hadoop – a widely used platform for batch processing on big data. Finally, we will learn about HBase – a distributed, scalable, big data store built on top of HDFS.

4.1 REQUIREMENTS FOR PROCESSING AND STORING BIG DATA

Big data systems have been mainly used for batch processing systems with focus on analytics. Since the amount of data is quite large, special considerations are needed:

1. **Scalability**: A scalable solution is needed which can meet the growing demands of big data systems.

2. **Low Network Cost**: Cost (time) to transfer data should be low. Predominantly, time spent on computation should be more than the time spent on transferring the data.

3. **Efficient Computation**: Owing to a large amount of data, computation should be done in parallel in order to reduce time of computation.

4. **Fast and Rapid Retrieval**: As big data systems are based on the principle of 'write once read many', retrieval of data should be fast.

5. **Fault Tolerance**: Network and hardware failures are eminent. A big data storage and computation system should be fault tolerant.

The above mentioned requirements are specific to big data systems. In addition to these requirements, a big data system should provide a flexible and adaptable platform for programming and development.

Over the past two decades, big data systems have evolved on these principles. With time, their capacity and performance have also increased.

We will now discuss Hadoop, one of the most widely used big data platform, which can cater these challenges.

4.2 HADOOP – THE BIG PICTURE

Apache Hadoop is a collection of open-source software and platform for big data. The strength of Hadoop stems in from the fact that the framework can scale to hundreds or thousands of nodes comprising commodity hardware. The Hadoop framework is able to recover from issues such as node failure and disk failure. It can provide consistency, replication, and monitoring at the application layer. Hadoop has several components which are responsible for storing, monitoring, and processing at different layers. Table 4.1 lists a few major components of the framework.

Figure 4.1 illustrates a layered model of the Hadoop echo system. Each of these components have a unique feature. For instance, **HDFS** provides reliable storage for many Hadoop jobs, whereas **MapReduce** serves as the standard programming model. MapReduce performs computation jobs on the data stored by the HDFS. Both MapReduce and HDFS are combined to promote data locality – a concept in which computation is performed locally to each node where data is stored. Data locality reduces network cost. On top of MapReduce are **Pig** and **Hive** components of Hadoop. These are extensions of MapReduce, which are used for providing scripting-based access for querying and processing data. **Mahout** is a MapReduce library, which implements machine learning algorithms. **HBase** is a

TABLE 4.1 Components in Hadoop v1

Component	Purpose
HDFS (Hadoop Distributed File System)	Distributed file system that can support high-throughput for accessing data.
MapReduce	Programming platform which utilizes data stored in HDFS.
Hive	A infrastructure for querying and data warehousing solutions for Hadoop.
HBase	Is a distributed, scalable, NoSQL column family storage system built on top of HDFS.
Pig	Scripting language for accessing data stored on HDFS.
Mahout	Machine learning library that is built on top of MapReduce.
Oozie	Scheduler and workflow engine for creating MapReduce jobs.
Zookeeper	Tool to manage and synchronize configuration.
Ambari	Tool for monitoring the Hadoop cluster.
Impala	Massively parallel distributed database engine which can utilize Hadoop worker nodes for processing of queries.

NoSQL column-oriented database, which is built on top of HDFS, whereas **Oozie** is a workflow Engine for MapReduce jobs. The purpose of **Zookeeper** is to manage and synchronize configuration.

In chapter 5, we will study these components in detail.

4.3 HADOOP DISTRIBUTED FILE SYSTEM

Figure 4.2 shows the architecture of a Hadoop Distributed File System (HDFS). It provides storage for Hadoop through a cluster of nodes. Data in HDFS is stored in the form of blocks, which are distributed and replicated across the cluster. The namenode stores metadata or information about blocks, whereas data is stored on datanodes. Since there is only a

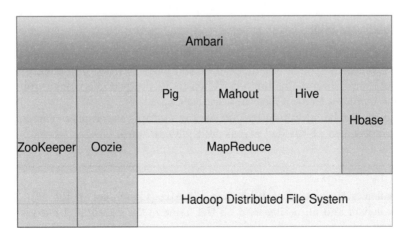

FIGURE 4.1 Hadoop echo system

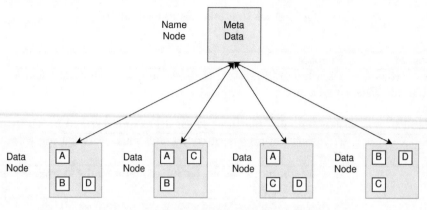

FIGURE 4.2 HDFS cluster

single namenode, performance of the HDFS cluster depends greatly upon the capacity and capabilities of the namenode.

The figure shows four blocks which are distributed across the cluster. By default, in HDFS, each block is replicated three times.

4.3.1   Benefits of Using HDFS

For big data systems, HDFS offers following advantages:

1. **Load Balancing**: As data is distributed, load on datanodes is also distributed. This allows improved performance.

2. **High Availability**: By default HDFS replicates three copies of each block. This ensures fault tolerance and high availability.

3. **Data Localization**: Replicated copies of data facilitates localized access of data, which reduces network latency.

However, HDFS entails additional cost of data storage.

4.3.2   Scalability of HDFS

Scalability of the HDFS cluster is limited by the capacity of the namenode. Since the namenode stores metadata (including namespace and block locations) in memory, its capacity to serve client[1] requests remains limited. When its memory usage reaches full capacity, its response time increases to an unbearable level [325].

This problem can be addressed by introducing multiple namespaces (namenodes) [324]. In that, namespace can be divided across multiple machines.

4.3.3   Size of Block

In HDFS, typically the size of each block is 128 MB. The choice of 128 MB is a trade off between parallelism and adjusting load on the name node. Example 4.1 explains the basis of this trade off.

---

[1]A client could be a MapReduce job, which requires access from HDFS.

Effect of HDFS Block Size

Example 4.1 (Effect of HDFS Block Size). *If the block size is* **reduced***, there will be large number of blocks, which will increase metadata. This will eventually increase load on the namenode.*
Suppose that in a cluster, 1280 MB of data is needed to be stored. For a 128 MB block size, this will lead to 10 blocks. If we reduce the size of the block to 64 MB, the number of blocks required to hold 1280 MB will be increased to 20. This will increase load on the namenode because eventually, there will be more queries about metadata. If the size of the block is **increased***, this will reduce the load on the name node. However, it will decrease the amount of parallelism as there will be more data for each data node to handle. As Hadoop is built on the concept of data localization, increasing parallelism is also significant.*

Both the size of the block and the replication factor can be customized by an administrator.

4.3.4 Cluster Management

An HDFS cluster could consist of a few thousand datanodes[2] and a single namenode.

In order to manage the cluster, the namenode periodically receives heartbeat messages from all the datanodes. A heartbeat message confirms that a datanode is alive and the blocks replicated on it are available. By default, the heartbeat messages are sent after every three seconds. If the namenode does not receive a heartbeat message from a datanode, it marks it unavailable. Further, the namenode also takes initiatives to create replicas of the blocks hosted by the failed node.

In addition to the 'I am alive message', a heartbeat message from a datanode also informs the namenode about various other statistics including total storage capacity, percentage of storage in use, and the number of concurrent connections in progress. These statistics are used by the namenode for allocating resources. An unbalanced HDFS cluster can lead to improper utilization of resources.

An HDFS cluster is unbalanced, if the number of blocks are not uniform across all the nodes of a cluster. Figure 4.3 shows an unbalanced HDFS cluster. If a cluster is unbalanced, then the namenode may initiate replica transfers to balance the load.

4.3.5 Read and Write Operations

When a client intends to read a file from an HDFS cluster, it initiates a read request to the namenode for the location of the data blocks. The namenode responds with all the replica blocks. The client then contacts the nearest replica to read the desired block.

For writing, the client requests the namenode for three replicas where the desired block can be stored. The client then writes the data to the three replicas in a pipeline mode. That is, a pipeline is created from where each node sends the request of write to its subsequent replica. Figure 4.4 explains the mechanism, where the write operation is initiated to the first replica, from where the request to the second node is initiated. Similarly, the third node receives the request from the second node. In this manner, the operation is committed only if the write has been performed on all the three nodes. If during the write operation, the pipeline is broken due to failure at any node, the client can request the namenode for an another replica.

---

[2]Konstantin Shvachko et al. [324] reported to have a production cluster of 4000 nodes

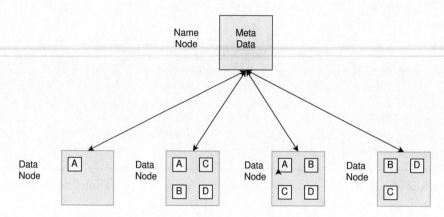

FIGURE 4.3 An unbalanced HDFS cluster

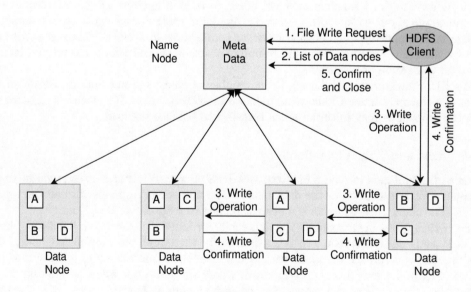

FIGURE 4.4 HDFS write operation

HDFS namenode is considered a single point of failure. Further, it has a high startup time. The bootstrapping mechanism for namenode consists of two steps [103]:

1. Reading information of the filesystem from the file fsimage. Once the information is read, transaction logs are applied and the updated information is stored as a new file system back to disk.

2. Block reports are read from data nodes to obtain information about all the known block locations.

4.3.6   Checkpointing and Failure Recovery

Since namenode is a single point of failure in HDFS, there are many enhancements and improvements to increase fault tolerance:

1. **Secondary Namenode**: A secondary namenode has been introduced. The purpose of the secondary namenode is to do checkpointing. The secondary namenode periodically reads the file system logs to provide backup of metadata. In case the primary namenode is unavailable, the secondary namenode can take over as the primary namenode. During this process, the secondary namenode does not read the file system image; however, it gathers block reports from all data nodes.

2. **Avatar Namenode**: Facebook has modified Hadoop to include an avatar namenode [103]. The avatar node is a wrapper around the namenode in HDFS. The avatar namenode consists of an avatar name and avatar secondary namenode.

   The secondary avatar node is responsible to maintain an exact replica of the primary such that in case of failure of the namenode, the secondary namenode can be replaced with minimum transition time. In this scheme, the active avatar writes all the transaction logs on Network File System (NFS). This updated information is also maintained by the secondary namenode. Thus the transition time for secondary namenode remains minimal.

4.3.7   HDFS Examples

Having studied the basic functionality of HDFS, we will now learn from a few examples which are useful to understand its operations.

A few HDFS Commands

Example 4.2 (A few HDFS Commands).
Task 1: Listing files in HDFS
```
$ $HADOOP_HOME/bin/hadoop fs -ls <args>
```

```
Where $Hadoop_Home is your home dir.
If the home directory is unknown
then type "whereis hadoop"
One can execute many unix commands in hadoop by
    using the fs option
```

Task 2: Inserting Data into HDFS

a) Create a file
```
nano testfile.txt
Write some text in the file and save it.
```

b) Create an HDFS directory
```
$ HADOOP_HOME/bin/hadoop fs -mkdir /user/
    inputhdfs
```

c) Copy the file on HDFS
```
$ $HADOOP_HOME/bin/hadoop fs -put /home/testfile.
    txt /user/inputhdfs
```

*Task 3: Retrieving Data from HDFS. The created file can be
    verified using the ls and cat commands*

```
$ HADOOP_HOME/bin/hadoop fs -ls /user/inputhdfs
```

In the next section, we describe MapReduce, a popular programming model for Hadoop.

4.4 MAPREDUCE

MapReduce [154] is a programming framework which is based on partition aggregation model. That is, a large problem with computational requirements on large data, is partitioned into smaller chunks. Each chunk is independently executed in parallel. The final result is then aggregated by combining intermediate results from each chunk.

The MapReduce framework computes the problem into two phases. During the first phase, which is also called as the **Map** phase, the data is divided into chunks. Each chunk is computed independently and concurrently on a worker node called mapper. There could be hundreds to thousands of mappers in the map phase.

The second phase is called the **Reduce** phase. In this phase, output of mappers is sent to a single node for aggregation. This process is also called as Reduction and the node performing the reduction is called as the reducer. There could be one to a few reducer nodes. MapReduce is based on the model of functional programming. That is, tasks for both mapper and reducer are specified using separate functions.

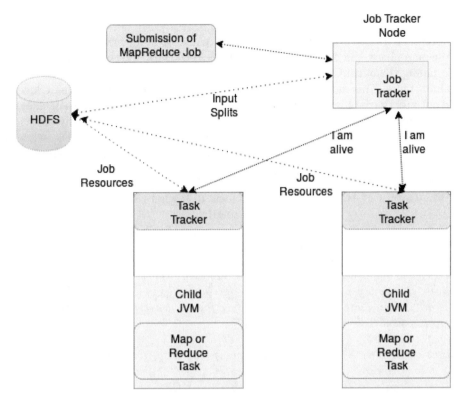

FIGURE 4.5 Execution of MapReduce job

4.4.1 MapReduce Operation

Figure 4.5 illustrates the operation of MapReduce workflow. We can notice from the figure that the input to a MapReduce program is from HDFS.

A MapReduce cluster consists of a single job tracker and many task trackers. The job tracker serves as the master node for the MapReduce cluster. It initiates and assigns tasks on worker nodes. A MapReduce job consists of a series of smaller and independent jobs called tasks such that each worker node independently executes a task. Typically, a MapReduce job consists of several mapper tasks and one to few reducer tasks. As discussed, reducer tasks are dependent on the completion of mapper tasks.

Each worker node has a special process called a task tracker. The purpose of the task tracker is to communicate with the job tracker. A task tracker executes task in an isolated environment through JVM (Java Virtual Machine). We should notice that the use of JVM allows isolation such that in case of an error or fault, the actual node remains protected.

Upon submission of a MapReduce job, the job tracker reads data from HDFS and assigns splits of data to each worker node. While assigning data splits to worker nodes, the job tracker strives to promote data localization. That is, worker nodes are preferred to be selected where data is local to the node. Data localization conserves network bandwidth and reduces data transfer time – an important factor for big data systems.

Worker nodes periodically send updates and progress of task execution through task trackers. If the job tracker does not receive an update from a specific task tracker for a certain duration, it assigns the task on another node with an assumption that the first node is unavailable. This process is called as **straggler detection**.

4.4.2 Input Output

The MapReduce framework utilizes <key,value> pairs for input output operations. For input to the map phase, the data is read from HDFS in the form of <key,value> pairs. During the map phase, the output from mappers is emitted to the local files system in the form of <key,value> pairs. This output is copied to the reducer, which performs the reduce operation and outputs the data in the form of <key,value> pairs to HDFS. The use of <key,value> pairs allows the MapReduce framework to efficiently perform many extensive tasks.

We should note that the output of mapper is written to the local disk, whereas the output of reducer is written to HDFS. We can understand the rationale behind this from example 4.3.

Why Output of Mapper is written to local disk whereas output of reducer is written to HDFS?

Example 4.3 (Output of Mapper vs. Output of Reducer). *In MapReduce, output of **Mapper** is written to disk and not to HDFS. This is because writing to HDFS is an expensive operation, which requires writing data over a network to three different replicas. Remember three is the default replication factor in HDFS. Since mapper tasks are intermediate tasks, the MapReduce framework writes the intermediate output to the local disk. In case of disk failure (or data loss), the specific mapper task can be re-executed.*

*Output of **Reducer** is generated after aggregating data from a number of mappers. This data is expected to be read many times. Since HDFS provides improved reliability and data locality, output of reducer is written to HDFS.*

A distinctive feature of the MapReduce framework is that the input to the Reduce phase is sorted by keys. The framework, while copying data from the mappers to the reducer, sorts it by keys. This operation is called **shuffle and merge** phase.

Understanding MapReduce

Example 4.4 (Understanding MapReduce). *Figure 4.6 illustrates the example of MapReduce operation for the WordCount problem.*
The Map Phase: *There are three mappers each of which processes a separate document. Mappers are shown as rectangular boxes with oasis color. The boxes also show the counting operation performed by each mapper. The output from the mapper is shown in rectangular boxes with white smoke color and dotted line. The mappers emit ¡key,value¿ pairs.*
The Shuffle and Merge Phase: *During this phase, the output of the mapper is copied to the reducer. The keys are sorted and the values are merged as array elements.*
The Reduce Phase: *The Reducer is shown as the rectangle with blue chalk color. It performs the aggregate operation over the input data. For this problem, aggregation involves adding the values with similar keys and emitting them as ¡key,value¿ pairs. The example shows the aggregate operation as well as the output. The output of the reducer is written to HDFS.*

Example 4.4 and figure 4.6 explain the execution of wordcount problem on MapReduce. A corpus of data is given in which our task is to count the occurrence of each unique word. The corpus consists of three input documents. These are processed by three mappers by incorporating the data localization concept we studied earlier. Each mapper processes a document and extracts words. These words and their interim count (which is '1' in this

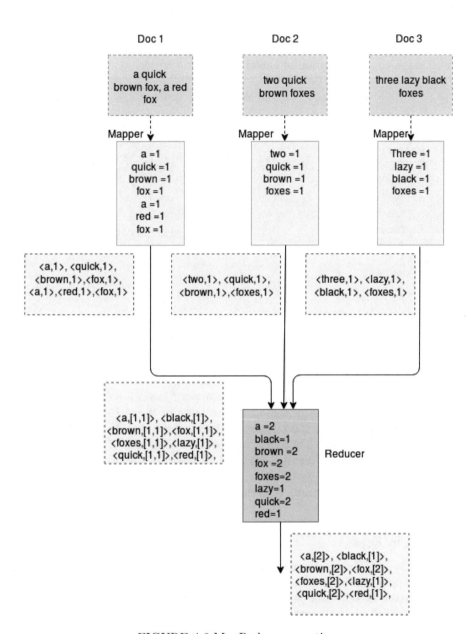

FIGURE 4.6 MapReduce operation

case) is emitted by the mappers. The data is emitted in the form of <key,value> pairs. A developer can select <key,value> pairs according to her choice. For this example, words are selected as keys and their quantities are selected as values.

These <key,value> pairs are sent to the reducer, which performs the reduce operation. For this example, the reduce operation involves aggregating the output from all the mappers.

Figure 4.10 illustrates the example of MapReduce operation for the wordcount problem. We will now learn pseudocode of the wordcount problem. Example 4.5 shows a sample pseudocode. The code has been derived from reference [245]. The word 'Emit' is a general term which refers to the operation of emitting out the <key,value> pairs.

Pseudocode for the WordCount problem [245]

Example 4.5 (The WordCount problem).
Class Mapper:
```
method Map(id a, doc d)
for all words w belongs to doc d do
Emit(word w, count 1)
```

Class Reducer:
```
method Reduce(word w, counts [c1,c2,...])
sum = 0
for all count c belongs to counts [c1,c2,...] do
sum = sum + c
Emit(word w, count sum)
```

4.4.3 The Partitioner Function

So far, we have discussed the possibility of many mapper functions and one reducer function. However, if the number of <key,value> pairs are large or if the Reduce phase is computationally extensive, then there could be more than one reducer. In this case, the number of <key,value> pairs are divided across a few reducers. The task of the division of keys is handled through a partitioner function. Figure 4.7 illustrates the process and functionality of the partitioner function.

For the load balancing purpose, a given MapReduce task could have more than one reducer.

4.4.4 Sorting by Keys

As discussed, the MapReduce framework sorts data by keys. During the execution of map phase, each mapper emits <key, value> pairs. These pairs are stored in a buffer at the mapper. When the buffer value reaches a threshold (for instance 80%) it starts spilling the data on the disk at the mapper side. Before writing the data to the disk, the data is partitioned. Within each partition, data is sorted (in the memory) by the keys. This partitioning corresponds to the specific Reducer which will handle and process the data. The sorted partitions are merged while they are being written to the disk.

In this manner, data is collected and written at the mapper side. A reducer collects data from all the related mappers. The process of transferring data from mappers to reducer is called **copying**. Since mappers may finish data processing at different times, the process of copying is executed independently and in parallel from different mappers. Once the process

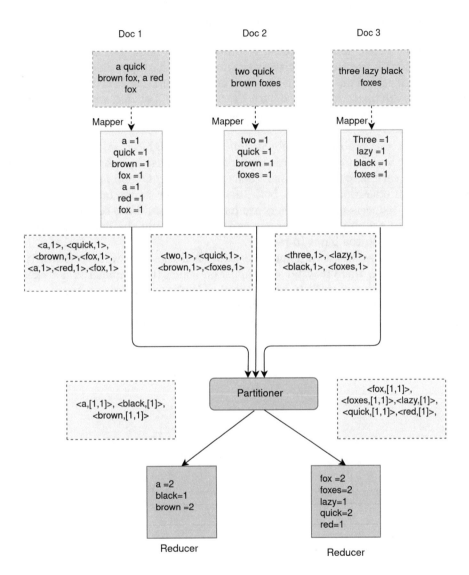

FIGURE 4.7 Partitioner function for MapReduce

of copying is finished, the data is merged at the reducer side. This merging allows a reducer to have an aggregated and sorted input from all the related mappers. The process of merging at the reducer is called **sorting** [155].

4.4.5 The Combiner Function

As discussed, the MapReduce framework employs parallelism by computing tasks using a number of mappers. Each mapper emits <key,value> pairs, which are aggregated at the Reducer. Since mappers do not perform aggregation locally, a mapper may emit a same <key,value> pair multiple times. For instance, in figure 4.6, mapper 1 emits pairs <a,1> and <fox,1> two times. Emitting the same pairs multiple times induces additional overhead in writing the output of the mapper on local hard disk. Further, it also consumes additional network bandwidth. Since both the operations, i.e., disk write and copying data over network, are slow operations, the overall efficiency of the MapReduce framework is affected.

To overcome this problem a combiner function is introduced at the mapper. The task of the combiner function is to perform local reduction. That is, reduce values with similar keys, locally at each mapper. For this reason, a combiner function is also called as a 'mini reducer'. For an operation which is both associative and commutative (e.g., addition or multiplication), reducers and combiners are interchangeable. Since combiners are optional, they should have the same input format as the reducer and the output of the combiner should also align with the input to reducer.

If a developer specifies a combiner function, then the framework executes it at each buffer spill. However, there may be some spills on which the combiner is not executed. A combiner function is guaranteed to be executed at least once for each mapper.

The task of combining can also be incorporated within a mapper. An in-mapper combiner is different than the conventional combiner as the mapper function performs local aggregation before spilling the data.

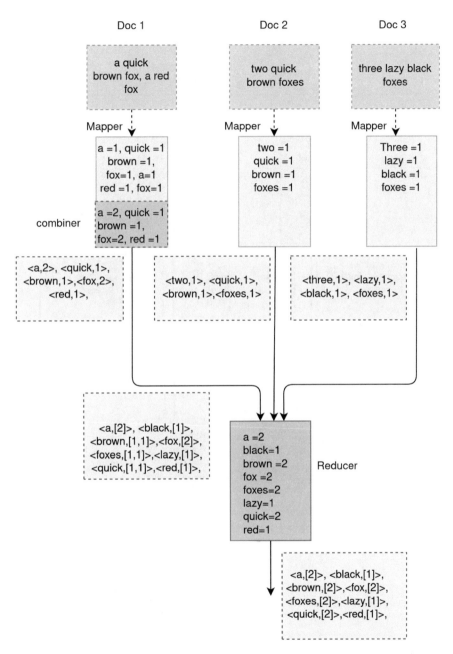

FIGURE 4.8 MapReduce: Conventional combiner

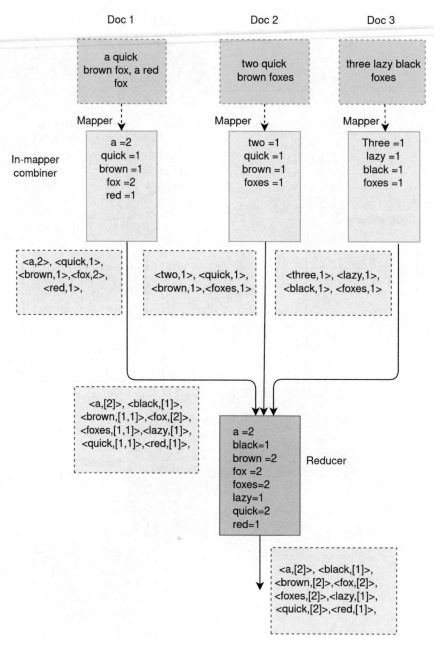

FIGURE 4.9 MapReduce: In-mapper combiner

Understanding Combiner Function in MapReduce

Example 4.6 (Understanding Combiner Function in MapReduce). *Figures 4.8 and 4.9 illustrate the execution of combiner function in MapReduce corresponding to conventional combiner and in-mapper combiner, respectively. Example 4.6 explains the difference between the two approaches.*

A Conventional Combiner

A conventional combiner is executed locally at each mapper. If a combiner function is specified by the developer, the function is called and executed by the framework before the data is spilled to the hard disk. The combiner performs local aggregation by aggregating pairs with the same keys. The aggregated ¡key,value¿ pairs are sent to the Reducer.

An In-mapper Combiner

Execution of the conventional combiner is optional. That is, even if a developer specifies the combiner function, the framework may not execute this function. To avoid this scenario, the task of combining can be integrated within the mapper code. This function requires combining using the memory. The output of the mapper is aggregated <key,value> pairs.

Conventional Combiner vs. In-mapper Combiner

The conventional combiner carries the advantage of utilizing lesser memory. Further, it adheres to the functional programming model, which is followed in MapReduce. However, the conventional combiner may not be executed by the framework during each spill. In comparison, an in-mapper combiner requires higher memory. However, it ensures that the task of combining is performed as the code (for combiner) is integrated within the mapper code.

Many organizations such as Facebook [353], Yahoo, and Adobe have implemented Hadoop-based solutions. Google has implemented a proprietary version of MapReduce, where it is used for the generation of data for production web search service, sorting, machine learning, data mining, and many other systems [154].

We will now study a few examples which will explain the use of MapReduce.

4.4.6 Counting Items

Counting Items from a list

Example 4.7 (Counting Items from a list). *We have seen an example of the Word-Count problem, where MapReduce can be used to count occurrence of words in a corpus. Similar approach can be applied to count items in a list.*

For instance, for a grocery store it is important to determine the number of items sold in a day. This information can be used to forecast sales and manage inventory. MapReduce can be used for this purpose.

Figure 4.10 illustrates the usability of MapReduce in determining number of vegetables sold in a day.

4.4.7 Secondary Sorting

MapReduce has an important feature of sorting by keys. When data is sent from mappers to the reducer, the Hadoop framework sorts the data by keys. However, the framework does

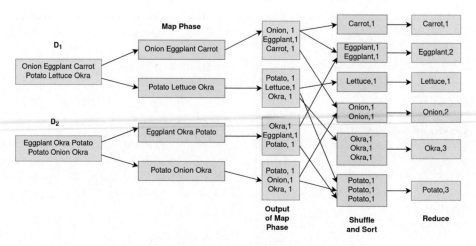

FIGURE 4.10 MapReduce WordCount example

not sort the data by values. MapReduce can be used to incorporate sorting by values, by introducing composite key. This will include integrating keys and values together as a key.

4.4.8   Inverted Indexing

Inverted index refers to a data structure, which given a term (or a keyword), would return a list of documents containing the term. It is highly useful for web search engines and other search-related assignments, where, given a keyword, related documents, and their number of occurrences can be searched.

Example 4.9 illustrates the process of computing inverted indexing through MapReduce, whereas example 4.8 shows the pseudocode for the example.

Inverted Indexing Pseudocode [245]

Example 4.8 (Inverted Indexing Pseudocode).

```
class Mapper
procedure Map(id n, doc d)
Array = new AssociativeArray
for all words w belongs to doc d do
Array{w} = Array{w} + 1
for all term w belongs to Array do
Emit(word w, posting hn, Array{w}i)


class Reducer
procedure Reduce(term t, postings [(n1, f1), (n2,
    f2), (n3,f3)])
P = new List
for all posting (a, f) belongs to postings [(n1,
    f1), (n2,f2), (n3,f3)..] do
Append(P, (a, f))
Sort(P)
Emit(term t, postings P)
```

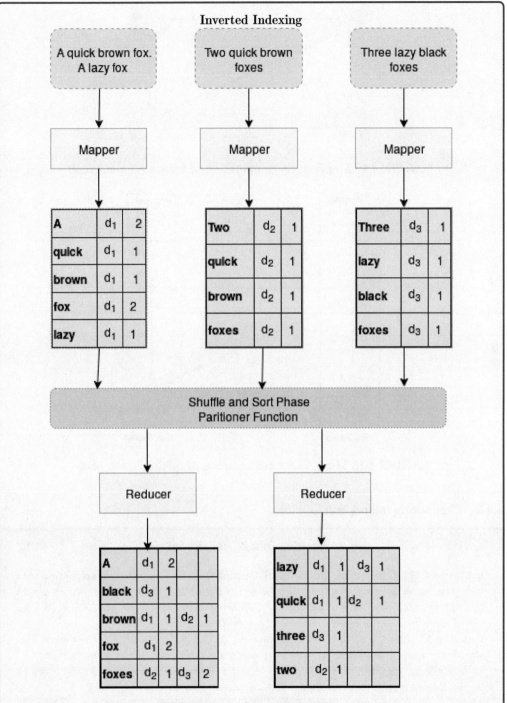

FIGURE 4.11 Inverted indexing

Example 4.9 (Inverted Indexing). *Figure 4.11 shows inverted indexing over a small corpus. Mappers emit keywords and a composite value consisting of document id and no. of occurrences as <key,value> pairs. These are combined to produce aggregated response at the reducer. In the figure, keys are represented as bold text.*

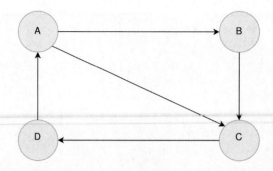

FIGURE 4.12 MapReduce. computation of inlinks – input graph

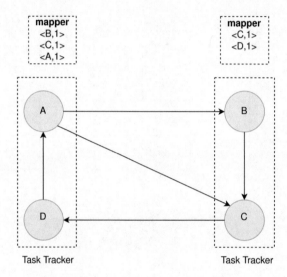

FIGURE 4.13 MapReduce: computation of inlinks – map phase

4.4.9 Computing Inlinks and Outlinks

Computing Inlinks and Outlinks

Example 4.10 (Computing Inlinks and Outlinks). *For Search engines, rank of a web page depends upon a number of factors. One of the most prominent factors in computing page rank is the number of incoming links to a web page. This is also called as inlinks. MapReduce can also be used to compute inlinks.*

Figure 4.12 shows a sample input of four webpages A,B,C, and D. The figure also shows incoming links (inlinks) and outgoing links (outlinks) for each webpage.

In figure 4.13, two mappers are created. Each mapper computes outlinks for two web pages. The mappers emit outlinks as <key,value> pairs.

Figure 4.14 shows execution of the reducer. The <key,value> pairs are sent to the reducer. The output of the reducer is the aggregated value against each URL. These values represent the inlink for the URL.

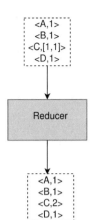

FIGURE 4.14 MapReduce: computation of inlinks – reduce phase

4.4.10 Join Operations Using MapReduce

MapReduce has been effective for batch processing of data. Using MapReduce, a large corpus of data can be processed through a distributed cluster. We should note that MapReduce is not a database as it does not ensure ACID properties. Database community has highlighted this as a limitation. However, proponents of MapReduce has re-emphasized that the focus of MapReduce has not been to support database operations but to facilitate batch processing using a large distributed cluster.

Although MapReduce is not a database, its usability has been explored to perform join operations. We now study three possibilities of implementing join operations [245]:

1. **Reducer Side Join**: We should recall from our previous study that in Hadoop <key,value> pairs from different map phases are merged and sorted during the shuffle and merge phase. In this manner, values from identical keys are accumulated together. Reducer side join operations are inspired by these characteristics.

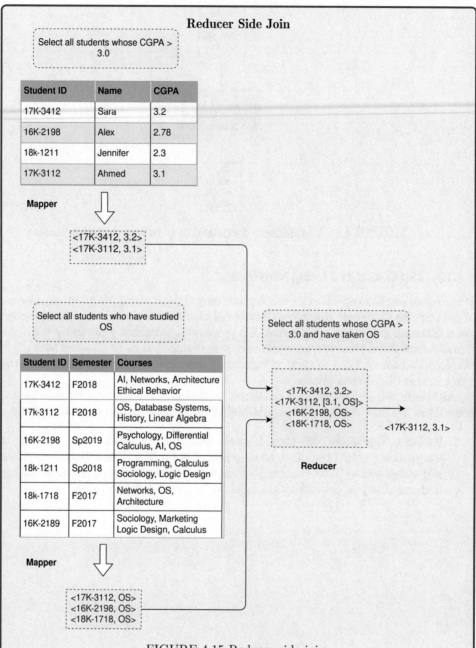

FIGURE 4.15 Reducer side join

Example 4.11 (Reducer Side Join). *Figure 4.15 illustrates the reducer side join operation on a students' dataset. The query is to Select all students who have taken the course of OS and have CGPA <= 3.0. There are two mappers. The first mapper selects the students whose CGPA <= 3.0. It emits student ID as key and their CGPA as value. The second mapper selects students and their courses. It selects student ID as the key and their courses as the value. At the reducer, students can be easily determined who have fulfilled both the criteria (i.e., CGPA > 3.00 and have taken the OS course).*

Reducer side join operations are effective in joining two related datasets. However, they may suffer from a high number of <key,value> pairs being generated. In this case, the network may become the bottleneck. Example 4.11 explains reducer side join operation.

2. **Mapper Side Join**: Mapper-side join operation can be implemented by merging the two relations (or datasets) in the map phase. The advantage of map-side join is that the overhead of a large number of keys being emitted during the shuffle phase can be avoided.

   To understand the example of Map Side join, consider that two datasets are initially sorted over the join Key. During the map phase, the two datasets can be merged and the output can be emitted.

3. **In Memory Join**: If the dataset is not sorted as per the join key and if the size of the data is small, then the process of joining can specifically be handled in the memory.

4.4.11 MapReduce for Iterative Jobs

MapReduce has been developed for batch processing. However, its use for iterative computation has also been explored. Iterative algorithms such as 'Page Rank' and 'Clustering' involves rounds of computation. Such an algorithm requires that MapReduce jobs are computed iteratively. That is, output of reducer is sent back to the mapper. This cycle of computation continues until a point of convergence is reached.

It has been observed that MapReduce has been inefficient for iterative tasks. The reason is that during the reduce phase, MapReduce writes output to HDFS. For iterative jobs, the data at the reducer is written at HDFS and then read back to the mapper as an input. Write operation to HDFS is an expensive operation as it entails transferring data over network and writing data on replicas.

Due to this reason, MapReduce is inefficient for iterative jobs.

4.5   HBASE

HBase [176] is a NoSQL storage system built on top of HDFS which is designed for storing and retrieving data for fast and random access supporting large volumes of data. It is a non-relational, open-source and distributed column-oriented data store, which is modeled after Google's Bigtable [128]. It has fault tolerance capability and it provides horizontal scalability. It is written in Java and is maintained by many engineers from diverse organizations under the framework of Apache Software Foundation.

4.5.1   HBase and Hadoop

As we discussed above, the HDFS is a highly fault-tolerant and provides high throughput access to large scale application data. However, there are following limitations with HDFS:

1. HDFS is a file-based system; it does not offer random access to data.

2. For applications where the requirement is to store structured data, the application developers find it difficult to process the data that is stored on HDFS as an unstructured flat file format.

3. Hadoop is strongly batch-oriented which emphasize throughput over latency.

TABLE 4.2 HDFS vs. HBase

Hadoop/HDFS	HBase
Provides file system for distributed storage	Provides column-oriented data store capability
Data model is not flexible	Provides a flexible schema model
Optimized for workloads with sequential reads and writes, and not for random access of files	Optimized for tabular data workloads with random reads and writes
Offline system optimized for throughput	Online system driven by low-latency
Uses a write-once and read-many-times (WORM) access model	Optimized for both read/write many, supports real time read/write random access
Mainly used for Batch processing use-cases in which data will be accessed only in a sequential manner	Used for use-cases where system needs quick random access of huge data
Data is primarily accessed through MapReduce jobs	HBase provides a command-line tool for shell support, and supports Java API, Thrift, and RESTful web service for programmatic access

To overcome these challenges, we can layer HBase over HDFS to use for applications where we require real-time read/write random access to very large datasets.

HBase is a database built on top of Hadoop and was developed to support storage of structural data, which can take advantage of HDFS and other distributed files systems. In the Hadoop ecosystem, HBase provides a persistent, structured, and schema-based data store which has the ability to store and retrieve both structured and semi-structured data for use cases where response time is critical. It is also suitable for random reads and writes and is known for high write throughput.

The HDFS gives HBase a storage layer providing availability and reliability. Although HBase primarily works with HDFS to store data but it can also work on other filesystems. Table 4.2 provides a comparison between HDFS and HBase:

4.5.2 HBase Architecture

Figure 4.16 represents the layout information of HBase. HBase implements master/slave (HMaster/RegionServer) architecture similar to HDFS. The following are the major components of the HBase architecture:

1. **HMaster**: HMaster typically runs on the Hadoop NameNode, is responsible mainly for managing the cluster state and performs administrative operations such as failover, fallback and control load balancing. HMaster is also responsible for managing Region-Servers, such as assigning regions to different region servers.

2. **RegionServers**: HBase tables are divided into small chunks, called **Regions**, which are distributed across multiple servers. The servers that host these regions are known as RegionServers. A table can have many regions across RegionServers and each Region-Server hosts several regions. The RegionServers run on the machines where DataNodes run.

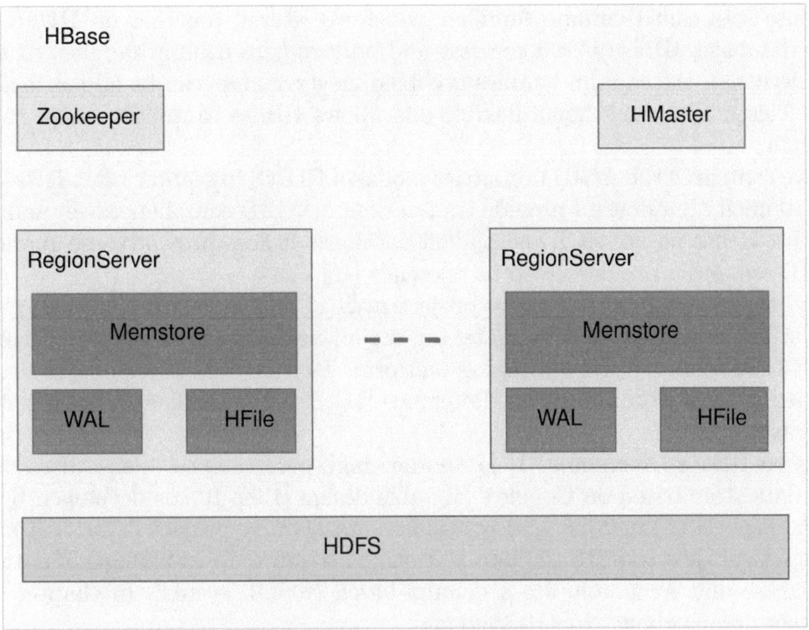

FIGURE 4.16 HBase architecture

3. **ZooKeeper**: It is a distributed coordination service for HBase cluster to provide high availability. It stores the meta information of a running HBase cluster.

4.5.3 Installing HBase

HBase can run in three different modes: Standalone, Pseudo-distributed, and Full-distributed. The first two modes provide basic access while the last one is the only mode which can be used for production environment.

1. **Standalone**: In the standalone mode, all HBase services run on a single java process and use a local disk to store tables and data. This mode doesn't require running any other external service (HDFS, Zookeeper etc.) and is suitable for exploration, testing, and local development.

2. **Pseudo-distributed**: In the Pseudo-distributed mode, all HBase services (HMaster, HRegionServer, and Zookeeper) run on a single machine but as separate Java processes. This mode uses HDFS file systems and is also suitable for testing and local development.

3. **Full-distributed**: In the full-distributed mode, an HBase cluster is set up on multiple nodes and all HBase services run under different JVMs on these cluster nodes. This mode uses HDFS as an underlying file system and is designed for use in the production environment.

4.5.4 HBase and Relational Databases

HBase tables consist of rows and columns similar to a relational database. However, HBase models data differently from the relational databases. In HBase, the columns are grouped together into sets called **column families**, which are stored together on HDFS. Unlike a relational database, HBase is schema less and only require column families to be defined up front. Although the column families are fixed, new columns can be added to a family at any time. This makes the schema flexible and allows HBase to rapidly adapt to changing requirements.

We have compared the ACID properties model of RDMS in section 1.3.2. HBase provides row-level atomicity but doesn't provide transactions or ACID compliance over multiple rows, and therefore is also not an ACID-compliant database. It does provide some guarantees and these ACID semantics are described in reference [10].

HBase became a top-level Apache project in 2010 and it is still continuing to flourish and grow which is widely used by many big organizations such as Google, Facebook, and Twitter. Facebook used it for messaging platform, Twitter used it for people searches and Apache used it for maintaining wiki. Reference [11] lists the number of organizations with their use cases.

Similar to HBase, Accumulo [1] is another high-performance open-source distributed key-value data store based on Google's Bigtable design [128]. It was developed by National Security Agency (NSA) in 2008, and became an open-source project in 2011. It uses HDFS as a storage layer, just like HBase, and is designed to store up to trillions of data.

Both Hbase and Accumulo are a column-based NoSQL system. In chapter 7, we will study further details about NoSQL systems.

4.6 CONCLUDING REMARKS

In this chapter, we elaborated on different features of Hadoop and explained why it is well-suited for big data processing. We also explained HDFS, which is a highly reliable distributed file system for storing data in a Hadoop cluster. In addition, using examples, we studied MapReduce – a fundamental component of programming in Hadoop. Finally, we discussed the Hadoop database called Apache HBase and its relationship with Hadoop. In the next chapter, we will study the Hadoop ecosystem and different tools such as Apache Pig, Hive, Impala, Sqoop, and Ambari.

4.7 FURTHER READING

Details about Hadoop and HDFS Scalability have been discussed in references [324, 325]. [154, 155] explains MapReduce in detail.

Reference [245] explains join operations using MapReduce in detail. Join operations are further explained in reference [268].

Hbase has been discussed in reference [176] and Google's Bigtable is explained in reference [128].

4.8 EXERCISE QUESTIONS

1. What are the major issues with Hadoop v1?

2. How does Hadoop detect slow progress of tasks execution?

3. What are the challenges in using Hadoop for real-time analytics?

4. Explain the rationale of writing output of Mapper to local disk.

5. Explain the rationale of writing output of reducer to HDFS.

6. Explain three types of join operations which are possible using MapReduce.

7. What are the advantages of having multiple reducers? How multiple reducers can be implemented using MapReduce?

8. What are the limitations of MapReduce in processing iterative operations?

9. Explain the pros and cons of having large block size in HDFS.

10. Explain the purpose of combiner function in MapReduce. What are the advantages of combiner function? Will combiner function be an exact replica of the reducer function?

11. Explain data localization. How does Hadoop ensure data localization?

GLOSSARY

Accumulo: It is a high-performance open-source distributed <key,value> data store based on Google's Bigtable design [128]. It uses HDFS as a storage layer and is designed to store up to trillions of data.

Ambari: It is an open-source widely used graphical management tool, which has been designed to manage and monitor Hadoop clusters.

Blocks: It is the minimum amount of data that HDFS can read or write at a time.

Chunk: It is a portion of data, which is allocated to a mapper. Chunks are computed in parallel during the Map Phase.

Cluster: It is a collection of systems that allow them to work together to either solve common computing problems or provide large storage.

Combiner: It is a process in the MapReduce model, which is used to perform local aggregation at the mapper node.

Data Locality: It is a concept employed by the Hadoop system in which compute nodes are selected based on the locality of data. This reduces time to transfer large amount of data.

DataNode: It is the worker node controlled by NameNode. It is responsible for storing application data.

HBase: It is a distributed, scalable, NoSQL column family storage system, which is built on top of HDFS and provides schema flexibility.

HDFS: It stands for Hadoop Distributed File System. It is a distributed file system designed for storing large datasets that run on commodity hardware.

Heartbeat: It is a special message in which each task tracker node periodically sends its health report to the job tracker node.

Hive: It is an SQL-like language that presents data in tabular form for Hadoop. It enables Hadoop to be used as a data warehouse by providing capability for querying and managing large datasets.

Impala: It is an open-source massively parallel processing SQL query engine designed to run on Hadoop platforms.

Job Tracker: It is a monitoring process which runs on the master and monitors the Task-Tracker applications which are running tasks at each worker node.

Mahout: It is a scalable machine learning and data mining library that is built on top of MapReduce.

Map: It is a phase in the MapReduce programming model in which each node computes independently and in parallel to other mapper nodes on a portion of data.

MapReduce: It is a widely used general-purpose programming framework for processing huge quantities of data in parallel on multiple nodes in a computer cluster.

NameNode: It is the master node which manages HDFS file namespaces and serves as a single point for all types of coordination on HDFS data. It maintains the health of each DataNode through the heartbeat mechanism.

Node: It refers to an individual system or a host within a cluster.

Oozie: It is a scheduler and workflow engine for creating MapReduce jobs in Hadoop.

Partitioner: It is a process in the MapReduce model, which ensures usage of multiple reducers. It distributes <key,value> pairs according to the specific reducer.

Phoenix: It provides a SQL layer over HBase for low-latency applications.

Pig: It is a high-level language that allows users to express their data processing and analysis operations on top of the MapReduce framework using a simple scripting language.

Reduce: It is a phase in the MapReduce programming model in which reduce operation is applied on one or a few nodes.

Secondary NameNode: It is a secondary node, which keeps a backup of active NameNode data periodically.

Straggler Detection: It is a process in MapReduce programming model in which slow nodes are detected through heartbeat messages.

Task Tracker: It is a process which runs on data nodes and is responsible for reporting the progress of tasks assigned by the Job Tracker.

Zookeeper: It is a tool to manage and synchronize configuration and is a highly available and reliable distributed configuration service.

Enhancements in Hadoop

CONTENTS

I N chapter 4, we studied fundamental topics about the Hadoop platform. In this chapter, we will learn about the Hadoop ecosystem and will study some of the enhancements which have been introduced in the Hadoop framework. To begin with, we will study the YARN ("Yet Another Resource Negotiator") framework. This will be followed by Pig and Hive, Dremel, Drill, and Impala. We will then look into specific tools and methods for moving data between external systems and Hadoop. Finally, we will learn about tools such as ambari which can be used to monitor and manage our clusters.

5.1 ISSUES WITH HADOOP

Apache Hadoop has been one of the most popular platforms for big data storage and processing. It has been used successfully across the globe. Even though Hadoop is considered as a scalable, reliable, efficient, and cost-effective solution, it is constantly evolving and the developing community is regularly contributing to improve the capabilities of Hadoop for solving big data problems.

In section 4, we studied the Hadoop architecture and learned operations of MapReduce. We also studied that how a JobTracker and TaskTrackers are used to track MapReduce jobs. The lack of a dedicated resource scheduler turned out to be a major limitation of Hadoop v1. Following are the major limitations of Hadoop 1.x:

1. **Scalability**: Large Hadoop clusters revealed some serious limitations on scalability. This is caused mainly by a single JobTracker per cluster which take cares of both job scheduling and task progress monitoring. As the size of the cluster and the number of jobs increase, the JobTracker could not perform adequately and does not able to schedule resources as fast as they become available. According to Yahoo, it highlighted serious limitations in scalability and resource utilization especially on a cluster containing more than about 4000 nodes and 40,000 tasks running concurrently. The JobTracker had to constantly keep track of hundreds of jobs and thousands of applications running tens of thousands of tasks.

2. **The Need for Non-MapReduce Workload**: Hadoop v1 was designed to run MapReduce jobs only which is useful for many applications. However, other applications such as graph processing and iterative tasks using message passing, this model does not fit well.

   It requires a separate cluster for MapReduce and other kinds of applications. Task scheduling in Hadoop v1 is not optimized to cater for heterogeneous workloads.

3. **Improved Cluster Utilization**: Hadoop MapReduce is also constrained by its distinct slots for Map and Reduce tasks. This is because slave nodes are configured with distinct Map and Reduce tasks. Since this assignment is static, a node which has been assigned to run reduce task cannot run a map task even when no reduce task is running. This limits the utilization of the cluster.

The above mentioned limitations were the motivating factors behind Hadoop v2. Figure 5.1 illustrates a layered model of the Hadoop v2 echo system. Two distinctive features in Hadoop v2 includes the introduction of YARN in order to decouple resource scheduling from MapReduce and introduction of Spark. Spark and its components are explained in chapter 6. We will now look into YARN components and its architecture.

5.2   YARN

To address the limitations of Hadoop 1.x, YARN (Yet Another Resource Negotiator) has been introduced. Its main purpose is to decouple the process of resource monitoring and resource scheduling from the MapReduce framework. It splits the resource management and job scheduling/monitoring responsibilities of JobTracker into separate daemons. Unlike JobTracker, it doesn't care about the data flow of the application and only manages resources.

With this new architecture, YARN provides a framework for managing both MapReduce and non-MapReduce tasks. It can handle tasks of greater size and complexity. It can also support simultaneous execution of different applications in a cluster (such as MapReduce and streaming applications). YARN also improves efficiency of the Hadoop framework and enhances its resource-sharing capabilities. Different distributed processing frameworks such as MapReduce, Impala, Spark, and Tez can utilize YARN.

We will now study different components of YARN:

5.2.1   YARN Components

Components in YARN not only provide finer-grained control to the end user but also offer more advanced capabilities to the Hadoop ecosystem. Core components of YARN

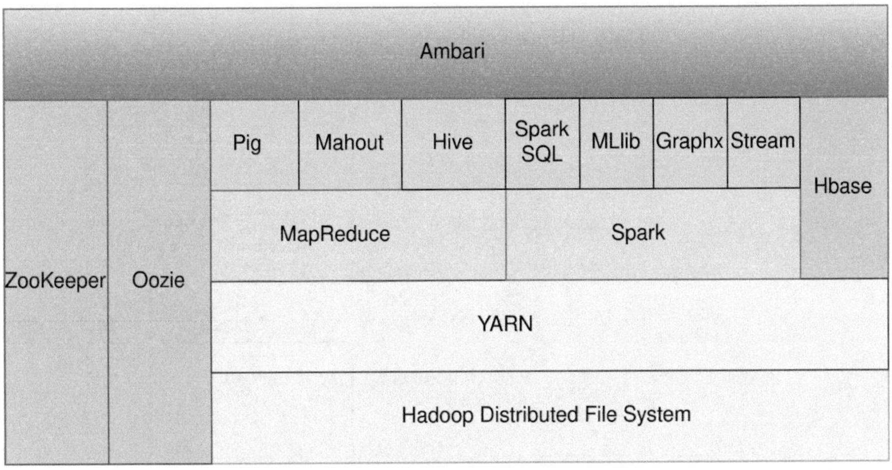

		Pig	Mahout	Hive	Spark SQL	MLlib	Graphx	Stream	Hbase
ZooKeeper	Oozie	MapReduce			Spark				
		YARN							
		Hadoop Distributed File System							

FIGURE 5.1 Hadoop v2 ecosystem

architecture includes a Resource Manager, a Node Manager, and Application Masters. Example 5.1 explains the functionality of YARN and its components.

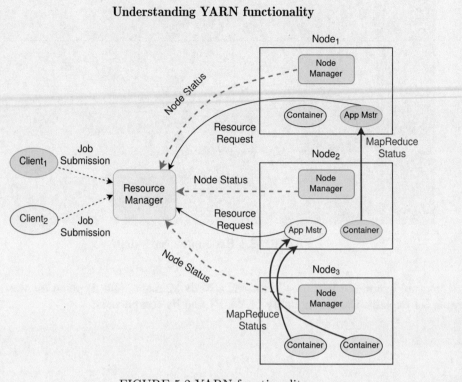

FIGURE 5.2 YARN functionality

Example 5.1 (Understanding YARN functionality). *Figure 5.2 explains the functionality of YARN and its components. The Resource Manager is responsible for monitoring the health of all the nodes in a cluster. Each worker node has a Node Manager which monitors local resources of the node and updates the Resource Manager. This information is communicated as "Node Status". In the figure, two clients are shown. Both of them submit their jobs to the Resource Manager, which assigns "App Mstr" for each application. The App Master communicates with the manager and obtains resources based on the health of nodes and needs of an application. MapReduce jobs are launched in containers to ensure sandboxing. Containers share status of MapReduce jobs to the "App Mstr".*

We will now study details of YARN components:

1. **Resource Manager**:

   The Resource Manager is a per-cluster service. It is used to monitor the health of all the nodes in the cluster and allocates resources to the applications. There are three core components of the Resource Manager:

   (a) **Applications Manager**: The Applications Manager is responsible for management of submitted applications. It executes as a service within Resource Manager which provides the following main services:

   i. Accepts the client's job submission requests as well as any application related query from the client.

   ii. Validates the application's specifications and provide the resources to run the Application Master.

    iii. Restart the Application Master in case of failure.

    iv. Monitoring the application progress. Creates and logs the runtime information related to a particular application.

(b) **Scheduler**: The scheduler is a pluggable scheduling component interface, which is responsible for resource negotiation and allocation to the applications as per the request of the Application Master. It is based on a pluggable policy plug-in and is responsible for partitioning the cluster resources among the various queues and applications. YARN incorporates following scheduling algorithms:

    i. **The FIFO (First In First Out) scheduler**: It serves application requests on a first come first serve basis. That is, any new job request has to wait until the first job runs through to completion.

    ii. **The Capacity scheduler**: An alternative to FIFO scheduler which has a very long wait time, is the capacity scheduler. It splits up the resources of the entire cluster into different queues (groups). Each queue will be configured with a predetermined fraction of the total capacity of the cluster. This assignment guarantees a minimum amount of resources for each queue. The key advantage, therefore, is that jobs of a particular category can now finish without getting stuck due to large or low-priority jobs of another category. The capacity scheduler works best for the well-known workflows.

    iii. **The Fair scheduler**: It allocates resources such that all running applications get the equal share of resources available at the cluster. Similar to capacity scheduler, application belongs to a specific queue, however, unlike capacity scheduler, all jobs make progress rather than progressing in a FIFO manner in their respective queues. This scheduler works best for unknown varied workloads.

(c) **Security**: The security component is responsible for managing access. It grants application tokens and container tokens to manage access between the application and the container.

2. **Application Master**:

The Application Master is responsible for the life cycle management of every application. It is the framework-specific process launched by the Resource Manager for each application type submitted by client that coordinates an application's execution to the cluster. Each application has its own unique Application Master which has the responsibility of negotiating for appropriate resource containers from the Resource Manager on behalf of the application itself and works with Node Manager(s) to execute and monitor tasks.

3. **Node Manager**:

The per-node Node Manager is a worker daemon that runs on each worker node in the cluster. It is responsible for managing the life cycle of the container which includes launches, monitors, and control application containers assigned to it by the Resource Manager and for monitoring their resource usage. The Node Manager registers with the Resource Manager on start-up and sends information about the resources available on the nodes. Each Node Manager periodically sends its liveliness information to the Resource Manager.

4. **Container**:

A container represents a unit of allocation resource on a single node where Application Master and application specific tasks run. There can be multiple containers on a single node in a given cluster. It is scheduled by the resource manager and supervised by the resource manager.

YARN is integrated with Hadoop v2 and is used to schedule jobs for various clients. We can find the details of the number of projects that are powered by YARN in reference [174].

5.3   PIG

Apache Pig is an important component of Hadoop. It is used for analyzing big data using scripting and easy to use language. An important characteristic of Pig is that it can incorporate parallelization and can support a very large dataset. A Pig program is written in a scripting language called **Pig Latin**.

5.3.1   Execution Scenarios and Types

Pig can be executed in two modes of operation: i.e., local mode and the cluster mode.

1. **Local Mode**: In the local mode, Pig runs on a single JVM on a local file system. This mode is suitable for small dataset.

2. **Cluster Mode**: In the cluster mode, Pig is executed on top of HDFS. Using this mode, a Pig job is translated as a MapReduce job, which is executed on top of HDFS. As compared to MapReduce, Pig offers higher flexibility at the cost of translating Pig scripts to MapReduce programs.

There are three ways of running Pig programs. These can be executed either in the local mode or in the cluster mode:

1. **Interactive Mode**: In this mode, an interactive shell called **Grunt** is used by the user. In the interactive mode, compilation, or execution is performed only when the user executes the **STORE** command.

2. **Batch Mode**: The batch mode allows a user to submit a series of pig commands in a batch mode. This mode of operation is useful if a pre-written script is used.

3. **Embedded Mode**: In this mode, a java library is used. This allows Pig Latin commands to be submitted via method invocations from a java program. This option permits dynamic construction of Pig Latin programs, as well as dynamic control flow.

5.3.2   Architecture of Pig

As Pig utilizes scripting language, it incorporates a parser and a compiler. We can understand the architecture of Pig from figure 5.3. When a pig program is submitted, the first step is to parse the program. In this phase, the program is verified for syntax checking and schema inference.

The parser outputs a logical plan, which is arranged in the form of a directed acyclic graph (DAG). A logical optimizer optimizes this execution plan and generates an optimized plan. The next step is to convert this into a MapReduce program. The MapReduce program is then optimized for improved efficiency. This optimization step may involve using combiner function to reduce <key,value> pairs. The last step is to submit the code to the Hadoop job manager.

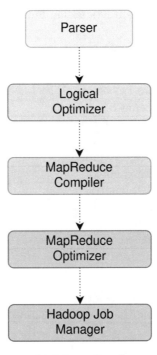

FIGURE 5.3 Pig flow

5.3.3 Optimizations in Pig

As we discussed earlier, Pig applies optimizations in two phases, i.e., logical optimizations and MapReduce optimizations [174]. Logical optimizations are mainly aimed to reduce the overhead of data transfer of shuffle phase or reduce the temporary files generated between consecutive MapReduce jobs. For this purpose, Pig utilizes various operations such as split, merge, transform, and reorder.

For MapReduce optimizations, the focus of Pig is to reduce the number of MapReduce jobs or to use combiner. A few major optimizations incorporated by Pig are mentioned below:

1. **No. of MapReduce Jobs**: A Pig script may generate a number of MapReduce jobs. If a Hadoop cluster is available, then each job may take 5 to 15 seconds to start a job. However, in case the cluster is not available then the job start time may increase. Further, MapReduce jobs may be dependent. In case of dependency, a MapReduce job may not start unless and until all the previous jobs have finished [174]. Therefore, Pig strives to reduce the number of MapReduce jobs.

2. **Key Skew**: MapReduce can speedup a pig program by running different tasks in parallel. However, during the reduce phase, it is possible that the number of keys are not well distributed. If keys are skewed then they may not be distributed to different reducers using partition function. Pig solves this problem of key skew by using skew join. Using this join operation, a key with the highest number of records is split and distributed to more than one reducer.

3. **Data Shuffling**: The amount of data transfer from mapper to reducer could consume a lot of time. The size of data can be reduced by compression or by reducing the number of <key,value> pairs emitted.

TABLE 5.1 Built-In Evaluation Functions of Pig [49]

Component	Purpose
AVG	Computes Average of numbers.
CONCAT	Concatenates two arrays. Either character or byte arrays
COUNT	Computes count of numbers.
COUNT 'STAR	Computes Count of numbers.
DIFF	A programming platform which used HDFS for accessing data.
IsEmpty	Checks if a bag is empty
MAX	Computes maximum.
MIN	Computes Minimum
SIZE	Returns number of elements
SUM	Computes Sum
TOKENIZE	Tokenize the data.

The main benefit of Pig is that it provides flexible and distributed data processing using easy to use programming environment. We will now study a sample code of Pig.

5.3.4 Running our First Pig Program

Example 5.2 shows a sample code for the WordCount problem. In the code listing, each statement is separated by a ';'. In the first statement input lines are read using the LOAD keyword. The second statement tokenizes the line to get words. As a next step, words are grouped, which are then later counted. The last statement emits the counted words.

WordCount using Pig [171]

Example 5.2 (WordCount using Pig).
```
inputlines = LOAD '/user/hadoop/hdfsinput.txt' AS
    (inputline:chararray);
inputwords = FOREACH inputlines GENERATE FLATTEN(
    TOKENIZE(inputline)) as inputword;
groupedwords = GROUP inputwords BY inputword;
wordcount = FOREACH groupedwords GENERATE group,
    COUNT(inputwords);
DUMP wordcount;
```

Pig has a strong library to provide builtin functions for many operations. Tables 5.1, 5.2, and 5.3 lists built in functions for evaluation, mathematics, and string computation respectively [49].

5.4 HIVE

Hive is a data warehousing system, which has been developed over Hadoop. Similar to Pig, the original rationale behind Hive is to develop a transition layer on MapReduce. This provides a developer to write a script for data analysis tasks. The script is translated to MapReduce tasks, and therefore exploits all the benefits of Hadoop including scalability.

TABLE 5.2 Built-In Math Functions of Pig [49]

Function	Purpose
ABS	Computes absolute value.
ACOS	Computes inverse cosine.
ASIN	Computes inverse sine.
ATAN	Computes inverse tangent.
CBRT	Computes cube root.
CEIL	Computes ceiling value.
COS	Computes cosine value.
COSH	Computes hyperbolic cosine.
EXP	Computes Euler's number e raise to the power x.
FLOOR	Computes floor value.
LOG	Computes natural log.
LOG10	Computes Log base 10 value.
RANDOM	Generates a pseudo random number.
ROUND	Computes rounded value.
SIN	Computes the sine value.
SINH	Computes hyperbolic sine.
SQRT	Computes square root.
TAN	Computes tangent.
TANH	Computes hyperbolic tangent.

TABLE 5.3 Built-In String Functions of Pig [49]

Function	Purpose
INDEXOF	Returns the index of the first occurrence of a character in a string
LASTINDEXOF	Returns the index of the last occurrence of a character in a string.
LCFIRST	Converts the first character in a string to lower case.
LOWER	Converts all characters in a string to lower case.
REGEX ˙EXTRACT	Matches a regular expression and returns index parameter of the matched group.
REGEX ˙EXTRACT ˙ALL	Matches a regular expression and returns all matched groups.
REPLACE	Checks if a bag is empty
STRSPLIT	Splits a string according to the given regular expression.
SUBSTRING	Returns a substring from a given string.
TRIM	Trims a string to remove trailing and leading white spaces.
UCFIRST	Returns a string with the first character converted to upper case.
UPPER	Converts a string to upper case.

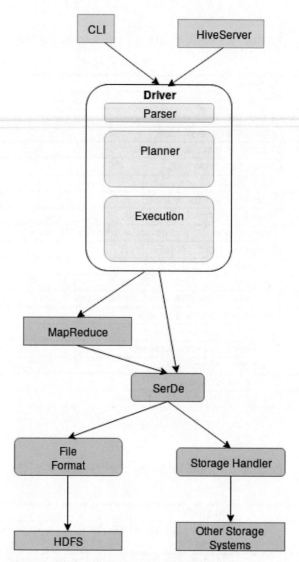

FIGURE 5.4 Hive architecture

Both Hive and Pig provide alternative interfaces to MapReduce. Hive was developed at Facebook about the same time Yahoo was developing Pig and was the first to offer a SQL-like query language, called **Hive Query Language** (HiveQL) for querying structured data stored in a Hadoop cluster.

There are two main goals for Hive [200]:

1. It should be able to provide fast storage and retrieval of data.

2. It should be able to generate highly optimized query execution plan and use the model that utilize hardware resources.

Figure 5.4 shows the architecture of Hive. We now assess the major components of the architecture:

1. **CLI and HiveServer2**: CLI and HiveServer2 (HS2) provide the two interfaces through which a user can submit her Hive statement. CLI is the command line interface which

enables a user to write the statement through command line, whereas HS2 is a process that enables multiple clients to submit their jobs (statements) to the Hive system. The HS2 server implements Kerberos [283] for user authentication.

2. **Driver**: The Driver program is responsible for parsing the statement and generating an Abstract Syntax Tree (AST). This tree contains a series of steps which are needed to be executed in the statement.

3. **Planner**: Query planner analyzes queries which are used for query processing and data retrieval. The planner assembles the operator tree to represent data operations of this query. The planner also optimizes the query for faster execution.

4. **Executor**: The executor breaks the operator tree to multiple stages represented by executable tasks.

5. **MetaStore**: Metastore stores system catalog and metadata about tables, columns, and partitions. This information is stored in an RDBMS.

6. **Data Processing Engine**: The data processing engine is responsible for executing the query. For instance, in case of MapReduce the generated task is executed as MapReduce tasks.

7. **SerDe**: It is a serialization and deserialization library which is used to serialize and deserialize data.

8. **ORC File**: Optimized Record Columnar File. It is a file format, which provides higher efficiency in reading, writing, and processing data. For instance, light weight indexes are stored within a file. Further, a single file is generated as output of each task. This reduces load on name node.

9. **Storage Handler**: A storage handler is used to process data stored in other systems. Hive implements a separate storage handler for each system. For instance, HBase storage handler is used when data is read from or written to HBase.

HDFS and Hive are both not designed for OLTP workloads and therefore, doesn't provide critical features required for OLTP. If we need OLTP features for large-scale data, we should consider a NoSQL database like HBase, which we have discussed in section 4.5. On the other hand, HDFS and Hive are best suited for batch jobs over large datasets that need to scan enormous amounts of data. Hive is also most suitable for data warehouse applications where data is relatively fixed and fast response times are not required for analyzing.

5.5 DREMEL

Dremel [264] is a large-scale platform for big data analytics, which supports interactive querying. The system is scalable to thousands of commodity machines and can perform interactive analysis in a short time.

Dremel is a columnar database. That is it stores the data in columns as compared to rows. In section 7.3.1, we discussed the difference between column-oriented and row-oriented databases.

After Google Dremel paper [264] published in 2010, it inspired a number of tools for supporting the interactive query which includes:

1. **BigQuery**: It is a product from Dremel, which is a big data analysis tool [19]. It is a petabyte scale, serverless, interactive, and ad hoc query engine that allows users to conduct analysis of large datasets.

2. **Impala**: It is an open-source, Massively Parallel Processing (MPP) query engine, which aims to provide fast, interactive queries over data stored in HDFS or Hive [28].

3. **Drill**: It is an open-source, low-latency distributed SQL query engine for interactive analysis of large-scale datasets stored in HDFS, NoSQL databases, or cloud storage [5].

4. **Presto**: It was developed by Facebook, is an open-source, distributed SQL query engine for analyzing large datasets [52]. It enables SQL access to any data source including relational or NoSQL databases, distributed object storage (Amazon S3, Google Cloud Storage), Hive, Kafka, and so on.

We will now discuss Impala and Drill in some more details.

5.6 IMPALA

Impala is a modern, open-source massively parallel processing (MPP) query execution engine [100]. It is written in C++ and is inspired by Google's Dremel [264], designed for executing low-latency queries to data stored in Hadoop.

It is built on top of HDFS and inherits the attributes of fault tolerance, parallelism, and data locality. It can be executed on many machines on an existing Hadoop cluster and provides the ability to execute queries with low-latency. It does not use MapReduce at all, instead uses an in-memory processing engine and also utilizes the data locality feature of Hadoop processing. It uses a columnar data format, similar to Dremel, for structuring data at rest.

The Impala architecture consists of following services:

1. **Impala daemon (Impalad)**: A daemon which is executed on all the worker nodes. It accepts queries from client process and orchestrates them on the cluster. A daemon can become a query coordinator if it initiates the query. Consequently, a daemon can also execute queries in fragments on behalf of other nodes. A daemon can also exploit data locality as a separate instance of daemon is deployed on each node HDFS data node.

2. **StateStore daemon (statestored)**: The Statestore daemon is responsible for disseminating cluster wide meta data to all the processes. This data is useful to implement MPP architecture. The Statestore daemon manages topic-wise membership of nodes. It sends two types of messages to nodes, i.e., *keepalive* messages to check the health of nodes and topic updates topic updates (including new entries, modified entries, and deleted entries) to all the subscribed nodes.

3. **Catalog daemon (Catalogd)**: The Catalog daemon is responsible for relay updates.

Figure 5.5 illustrates the functionality of Impala. In that, a query is sent to Impala daemon. Query planner receives the query and sends it to the query coordinator, which orchestrates it to other nodes. Query executor executes the query and fetches the results from other nodes in the calculator. It then aggregates the results and sends them back to the client. Impala can store data on HDFS data nodes.

Impala supports a subset of the HiveQL language specification, therefore most Hive queries can be executed using Impala.

Impala can utilize different components of Hadoop. For instance, similar to Hive, Impala keeps its table definitions in metastore (traditional MySQL or PostgreSQL database). This

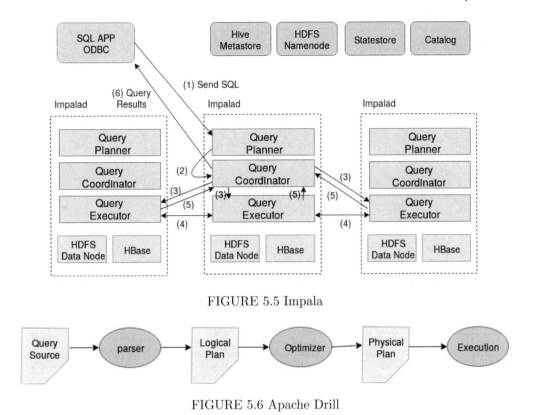

FIGURE 5.5 Impala

FIGURE 5.6 Apache Drill

permits Impala to access tables loaded or defined by Hive, provided that these have been implemented by Impala-supported tables.

Impala is well suited for use cases when we need a real-time interactive querying capability. It is also most suitable for ad-hoc query access to data in Hadoop.

5.7   DRILL

Apache Drill [5] is an open-source, low-latency query engine for Hadoop. It is a scalable and distributed system to provide interactive query services using hundreds to thousands of servers [193]. Apache Drill is inspired to respond to ad-hoc queries with low-latency and is the direct open-source implementation of Dremel [264].

The high level architecture of Drill consists of following layers:

1. **User Interface**: This layer is responsible for connecting a user with the core processing engine of Drill. The interface could be provided through different means such as command line interface, JDBC connectivity, or REST API.

2. **Processing**: This layer is responsible for processing the query distributed over multiple nodes.

3. **Data Sources**: This is the lowest level of the system. It consists of the different sources of data such as HDFS, MongoDB, Cassandra, Hbase etc.

Figure 5.6 shows the flow of query execution in Drill. It supports multiple data sources, including HDFS, HBase, and MongoDB, and various file formats such as CSV, JSON, and

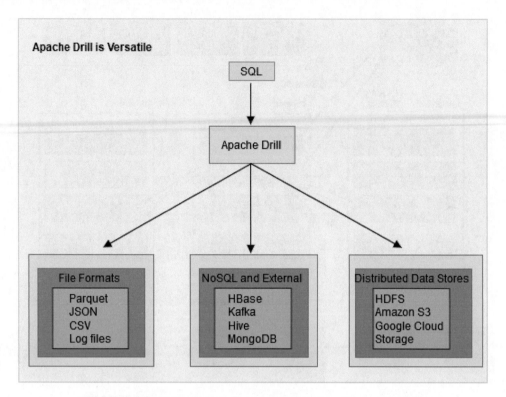

FIGURE 5.7 SQL support for various data sources with drill

Parquet as illustrated in figure 5.7. Moreover, a single query can access and join data from multiple sources. Unlike relational databases, which require users to define a schema before adding data, Drill does not require to define any schema before query execution.

Drill is easy to use and supports standard ANSI SQL syntax that allow users to query the data using standard SQL and BI tools such as Tableau or MicroStrategy. It is best suited for use cases when querying data stored in Parquet format.

5.8 DATA TRANSFER

In this section, we will introduce the tools that can be leveraged to transfer data between external systems and Hadoop. This includes importing data from external systems such as RDBMS (MySQL, Oracle, etc.) into Hadoop, and extracting data from Hadoop for loading into external systems.

Data ingestion is the process of pulling data from external source systems and transferring them to the big data systems like HDFS, Apache Hive, or Apache HBase. Data can be ingested from multiple sources for storage and further processing, and can be read from various source types, such as flat files, NoSQL systems, or relational database management systems.

Several tools are available for translating data between Hadoop and the external storage systems. Table 5.4 provides a list of Hadoop ETL and third-party tools come with the Hadoop distribution. In the context of this chapter, we will focus only on Sqoop, which is a Hadoop tool and Kafka, a third-party tool predominantly used for this purpose.

TABLE 5.4 Data Integration Tools

Tool	Description
Flume [7]	It is an open-source, distributed, reliable, and highly available service for efficiently ingesting high-volume streaming data, particularly log data, from multiple sources into data storage solutions like HDFS.
Sqoop [61]	It is a popular tool for transferring data between structured data stores such as relational databases and Hadoop. It is designed for an efficient transfer of bulk data between Hadoop data stores like HDFS or HBase, and relational databases.
Storm [16]	It is an open-source, distributed, and real-time computational framework for processing of unbounded streams of data.
Kafka [32]	It is an open-source, distributed streaming platform, widely used as publish/subscribe messaging system. It can be used to build a high-performance, real-time robust data streaming pipeline between applications.
NiFi [13]	It is an open-source real-time data ingestion tool, which enables the automation of data flow between systems in an efficient and reliable way. It is a data flow management system based on flow-based programming language that comes with an easy to use web user interface to manage data flows.
Flink [6]	It is an open-source distributed processor for stream and batch data processing. The core of Apache Flink is a distributed streaming dataflow engine which supports streaming one-at-a-time and provides fault tolerance capabilities. It has intuitive and expressive APIs available in Java and Scala.
Samza [14]	It is an open-source distributed stream processing framework that provides scalable and durable stateful stream processing. It has a simple API. It utilizes Kafka for messaging and YARN to provide fault tolerance and task scheduling.
DistCp [8]	Hadoop comes with a useful tool called DistCp, which provides an easy and efficient way to copy large amounts of data to and from Hadoop filesystems in parallel. It uses MapReduce underneath to copy in a distributed manner. We can use DistCp for use cases—for example, for disaster recovery, backups, or data migration purposes.

5.8.1 Sqoop

Originally developed by Cloudera, Sqoop [61] is an Apache Hadoop top-level project, which provides a single command line interface application. It optimizes data transfers between Hadoop and any other data stores, particularly relational databases.

Transferring data to and from any data store is a challenging and difficult job, and requires careful testing and error handling. Sqoop, however, has become a useful tool in the industry for this purpose. It is designed for efficient bulk transfer of data between Hadoop data stores like HDFS or HBase, and relational databases. With Sqoop, we can extract data from relational databases or data warehouses, process it using MapReduce, or higher-level tools like Hive and Pig, and then export the data back to an RDBMS or a data warehouse for further consumption by other clients. It supports all the leading relational database systems, such as PostgreSQL, MySQL, Microsoft SQL Server, and Oracle, and can also transfer data from a variety of enterprise data warehouses, such as Teradata and Netezza.

Since Sqoop uses MapReduce to import and perform the data processing into the Hadoop cluster, it therefore exploits the full advantage of the parallel processing capabilities of Hadoop. As a result, Sqoop provides fast data transfer performance by performing data loading tasks in a parallel manner.

Sqoop is easy and relatively quick to configure and use. It can be downloaded from the Apache site [62]. The documentation contains the detailed user installation guide as well as code and documentation. It can be installed on a user computer or on any node in our Hadoop cluster.

Having studied the basic functionality of Sqoop, we will now learn from example 5.3 some useful commands in order to understand its operations.

A few Sqoop Commands

Example 5.3 (A few Sqoop Commands).
Task 1: Sqoop version
```
$ sqoop version
```

Task 2: Getting Help
```
We can list the Sqoop tools using the following
   command:
$ sqoop help
We can also get detailed information regarding the
   specific tool like import using following
   command:
$ sqoop help import
```

Task 3: Importing Data into Hadoop
```
One important operation is import which can connect
   to any database for transferring data from the
   table of our choice directly to Hadoop. Sqoop
   gather the necessary metadata for the data
   being imported. An example of the related
   command might look like this:
$ sqoop import --connect jdbc:oracle://127.0.0.1/
   mydb --username sqoop --password sqoop --table
   exampletable
```

Task 4: Exporting Data from Hadoop
```
The other important operation is export for
   transferring data from Hadoop to the external
   data source. The export command looks similar to
   the import command but has additional options
   to support transferring data from Hadoop to a
   database.
$ sqoop export --connect jdbc:oracle://127.0.0.1/
   mydb --username sqoop --password sqoop --table
   exampletable --export-dir /exampledatadir
The export-dir option above specify the HDFS source
   directory.
```

Task 5: Importing all Tables from a Database into Hadoop
```
An example of the command to import tables from a
   database to HDFS:
$ sqoop import-all-tables --connect jdbc:oracle
   ://127.0.0.1/mydb --username sqoop --password
   sqoop
```

In summary, Sqoop is an important component and a core member of the Hadoop ecosystem. It is still one of the leading and widely used tools for import and export of data. A typical use case of Sqoop for an organization can be to import data from a production

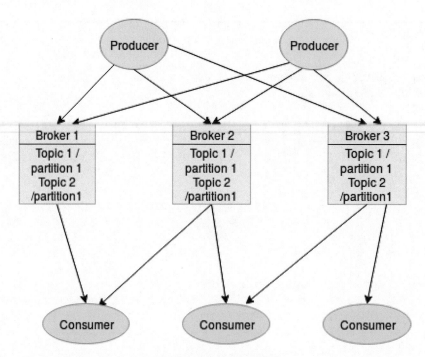

FIGURE 5.8 Kafka architecture

structured data source on an ad hoc or scheduled job basis into a Hadoop data store like HDFS, Hive, or HBase data warehouse for further processing and analysis. More information and extensive documentation on Sqoop is available at reference [61].

5.8.2 Kafka

Apache Kafka [12, 32, 229] is a distributed streaming platform. It is used to build real-time data streaming pipeline between applications. Through this pipeline, applications can produce and consume streams of data. In addition, it can also be used to develop real-time streaming applications.

In this section, we will study a few important concepts, which will help us to understand the functionality of Kafka and its usage.

1. **Messages**: A message (or record) represents a data item in Kafka. It consists of a key, a value, and a timestamp.

2. **Producer**: A producer is an entity which creates messages to the topics.

3. **Consumer**: A consumer is an entity which consumes or process messages. A consumer can subscribe to multiple topics. Consumers can poll brokers to pull messages related to topics.

4. **Broker**: In Kafka, records are stored in servers called brokers. Messages are replicated on brokers.

5. **Topic**: A topic is a collection of messages such that a group of similar messages is called a topic. A topic can have any number of consumers such as zero, one, or many.

Figure 5.8 illustrates the fundamental architecture of Kafka. It is a distributed system. It replicates messages (in form of topics) across brokers. There could be multiple brokers in a Kafka cluster. A topic may also be partitioned such that messages of a particular topic could be stored on multiple brokers. Partitioning also promotes load balancing – a key factor for performance.

Kafka supports publishing and retrieving messages simultaneously through multiple producers and consumers. Kafka also maintains consumer groups. Each group includes a set of consumers, which are working on related topics. Each consumer reads messages from a unique set of partitions.

Kafka is based on a publish-subscribe model. That is, messages are broadcast to multiple consumer groups. However, within the same group, a message is delivered and processed by a single consumer only. This is implemented such that each consumer reads from a unique set of partitions. Note that this feature is in contrast to other queuing-based systems, where a message is only delivered to the consumer which reads and pops the message from the queue.

By assigning partitions to consumers, Kafka allows messages to be processed or consumed in order. Further, it also balances load among consumers. However, the number of consumers cannot exceed the number of partitions.

Producers write data to topics which are read by consumers. Producers operate in a push mode, whereas consumers operate in a pull mode. Unless a message is pulled by a consumer, a message is stored at a broker server. Each message may have some time duration associated with it. If a message is not pulled by a consumer during that time, then it is discarded after the expiration of its time duration.

In Kafka, each partition has a set of records. Each record is uniquely identified by an offset. This identifier is used to order messages within a partition. However, this ordering is only applicable within the same partition.

Read and writes in Kafka are operated independently. A joint buffer is maintained at each broker, where producers write data at the end of the buffer. In the buffer, each consumer maintain its own offset for reading. The offset can be arbitrarily changed by the consumer as well. That is, a consumer may read messages in any sequence. Figures 5.9 and 5.10 illustrates the concept of read and write in Kafka.

In Kafka, keys can be of great significance. Messages with similar keys are guaranteed to be delivered to the same partition. Similarly, messages with similar key arrive at the same consumer.

Since Kafka provides replication and load balancing, it can be considered as a distributed file system. Each write in Kafka is acknowledged – ensuring high reliability.

Kafka is originally developed at LinkedIn and became a top-level Apache project in 2011. It is widely used as a messaging system by many organizations, such as LinkedIn [33, 227], Twitter [26], Netflix [34], and Yahoo [30]. Use cases for Kafka include log aggregation, website activity monitoring, and stream processing. Reference [31] list the number of organizations with their use cases.

5.9 AMBARI

As the size of a Hadoop cluster grew, needs for ecient monitoring arise. Apache Ambari [3, 363] is an open-source tool for monitoring and management of a cluster. It is the most popular open-source tool for Hadoop monitoring and supports the activities such as provisioning, monitoring, and managing of the Hadoop clusters. Ambari is an open framework, which can be integrated with different types of clusters including Hadoop. It uses Ganglia [261] – a distributed monitoring tool for clusters of machines.

Ambari supports the management of the Hadoop components such as HDFS, MapReduce, Pig, HBase, Zookeeper, and Hive. Figure 5.11 illustrates the fundamental architecture

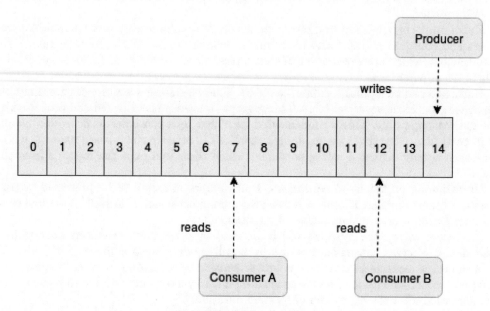

FIGURE 5.9 Kafka topics

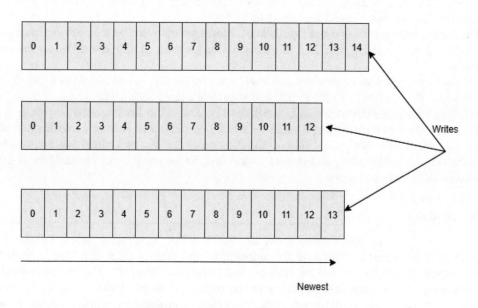

FIGURE 5.10 Write and read in Kafka

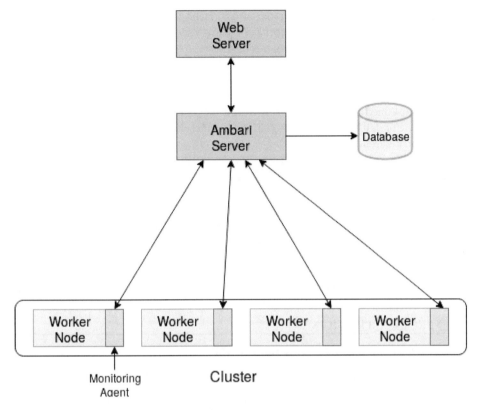

FIGURE 5.11 Ambari monitoring service

of Ambari. It consists of an ambari server, ambari web, and a few ambari monitoring agents. The main components are explained below:

1. **Ambari Agents**: The agents are deployed separately on each node of the cluster. They are responsible for monitoring different attributes such as CPU usage, RAM, and network characteristics and sending the measured attributes to the ambari server.

2. **Ambari Server**: The ambari server consists of the following components:

   (a) An **RDBMS** to store the cluster configurations. Ambari supports the popular databases such as PostgreSQL, Oracle, and MySQL.

   (b) **Nagios service** to provide alerts and notifications. This service is optional.

   (c) **REST API**, which integrates the ambari web server.

   (d) An **authorization provider** which can control user access.

3. **Ambari Web Server**: It is integrated to provide web-based management and user access. It integrates with the REST APIs provided by ambari server.

Similar to Ambari, Cloudera provides the Cloudera manager tool which performs similar functions and can be used to monitor and manage Hadoop clusters.

5.10   CONCLUDING REMARKS

In this chapter, we studied different limitations of Hadoop v1 and available features of YARN, which address these limitations. We also studied different components such as

Apache Pig, Apache Hive, Apache Impala, and Apache Drill along with their requirements. We also covered two popular frameworks for data ingestion: Apache Sqoop and Apache Kafka. We discussed their functionality, architecture, and use cases.

5.11 FURTHER READING

Pig has been explained in reference [175], whereas Pig Programming has been discussed in reference [173]. Pig Latin has been explained in reference [287]. Optimizations about Pig are explained in references [50, 174].

Reference [200] describes major advancements in Hive and how it achieves its two goals of fast data storage and retrieval and efficient query execution.

More details about YARN can be found at reference [9].

Google Dremel has been explained in reference [264]. Details about Impala are explained in reference [100]. Drill details can be found at reference [5]. [52] explains Presto in detail and reference [19] mentions detailed documentation along with all the SQL functions available to use in BigQuery SQL queries.

Details about ambari have been discussed in reference [363]. More details about Zookeeper can be found at references [201, 212].

5.12 EXERCISE QUESTIONS

1. What are the major issues with Hadoop v1?

2. Explain how YARN improves the scalability of Hadoop?

3. What are the challenges in using Hadoop for real-time analytics?

4. Describe major differences between Pig and Hive.

5. Discuss advantages and disadvantages of column-oriented and row-oriented databases.

6. What are the limitations of MapReduce in processing iterative operations?

7. Describe major differences between Impala and Drill.

8. Explain the major use of Kafka.

9. Describe and explain the usage of ambari.

10. Explain Apache Sqoop. How does Sqoop work?

GLOSSARY

Ambari: It is a widely used open-source graphical management tool, which has been designed to manage and monitor Hadoop clusters.

BigQuery: It is a petabyte scale, serverless, interactive, and ad-hoc query engine that allows a user to conduct analysis of large datasets.

DistCp: It is an open-source tool to copy large amounts of data to and from Hadoop filesystems in parallel.

Dremel: It is a distributed large-scale platform for big data analytics which supports interactive querying. It is a high-performance columnar database and can scale to thousands of commodity machines to perform interactive analysis in a short time. It inspires a number of open-source tools for supporting the interactive query.

Drill: It is an open-source, schema-free, low-latency distributed SQL query engine, which is inspired by Google's Dremel. It can be used for analysis of large-scale datasets stored in HDFS. It can also be integrated with NoSQL databases or cloud storage.

Elasticsearch: It is a highly scalable, fault tolerant, open-source real-time distributed search and analytics engine.

Flink: It is a free and open-source distributed processor for stream and batch data processing.

Flume: It is an open-source, distributed, reliable, and highly available service for efficiently ingesting high-volume streaming data. It can ingest data from multiple sources into data storage solutions like HDFS.

Hive: It is a platform built on top of MapReduce. It takes declarative SQL-like language as an input from a user and presents data in the form of tables. It reads data from HDFS and enables Hadoop as a data warehouse by providing capability for querying and managing large datasets.

HiveQL: It is a SQL-like programming language used with Hive for querying data stored in a Hadoop cluster.

Impala: It is an open-source, low-latency, distributed, and massively parallel processing SQL query engine designed to run on Hadoop platforms.

Kafka: It is an open-source, high-throughput distributed streaming platform, which is widely used as publish/subscribe messaging system. It can be used to build a high-performance, real-time robust data streaming pipeline between applications.

Kudu: It is an open-source low-latency column-oriented data store, which supports fast sequential and random access.

NiFi: It is an open-source real-time data ingestion tool, which enables automation of data flow between systems in an efficient and reliable manner.

Pig: It is a high-level framework that allows a user to express data processing and analysis operations on top of the MapReduce framework using a simple scripting language.

Pig Latin: It is a dataflow procedural scripting language, which is used by the Pig platform. It is used to perform complex operations such as joins, sorts, and filtering across several types of datasets loaded on Pig.

Presto: It has been developed by Facebook. It is an open-source distributed SQL query engine for analyzing large datasets. It enables SQL access to any data source including relational or NoSQL databases, distributed object storage (Amazon S3, Google Cloud Storage), Hive, and Kafka.

Samza: It is an open-source distributed stream processing framework that provides scalable and durable stateful stream processing with a simple API. It uses Kafka for messaging and YARN to provide fault tolerance and task scheduling.

Sqoop: It is one of the leading tools for transferring data between structured data stores such as relational databases and Hadoop.

Storm: It is an open-source, distributed, and real-time computational framework for processing of unbounded streams of data.

Tez: It is developed by Hortonworks. It is an extensible framework for YARN-based data processing applications. It is a general directed acyclic graph (DAG) execution engine, which is designed to provide high-performance and low-latency data processing.

YARN: It stands for Yet Another Resources Negotiator. It is used to centrally manage a cluster of resources.

Zookeeper: It is a highly reliable tool to manage and synchronize configuration on a Hadoop cluster.

Spark

CONTENTS

HADOOP/MapReduce has been the de-facto platform for big data computation for many years. The wide-scale popularity of MapReduce has been driven by its simple programming model and by its effectiveness in storing and processing big data. However, as big data systems continue to grow, the applications of big data evolved from batch processing to streaming. Further, continuous increase in the size of big data induced scalability challenges. Spark is motivated to address these needs. In this chapter, we will study the architecture of Spark. This will be followed by Spark programming. The chapter covers various examples in order to explain the topics.

6.1 LIMITATIONS OF MAPREDUCE

MapReduce has served as a popular platform for batch processing of big data. However, as big data applications continue to evolve, streaming applications and machine learning-based data analytics become requirement for big data processing.

Two major limitations of MapReduce become evident:

1. **Iterative tasks**: Machine Learning-based tasks require repetitive computation. MapReduce is unsuitable in such an environment because each iteration of the algorithm becomes a separate MapReduce job. This also involves writing the output of the reducer to HDFS. Since these are intermediary results, they are not required to be written to HDFS. However, MapReduce is not flexible to adapt to this modification. Consequently, iterative jobs on MapReduce induce significant overhead.

2. **Streaming-based tasks**: MapReduce has been designed for batch processing. However, streaming-based jobs require continuous processing through interactive analysis. MapReduce is not capable to handle jobs through interactive processing.

These limitations highlighted the need for a more flexible platform for processing of big data. We will now study Spark and discuss how it caters with these limitations.

6.1.1 Spark Benefits

Following are the major benefits offered by Spark:

1. **Integration of Spark with other Big Data technologies**: Spark enables users easy connection to data stores such as HDFS, Cassandra, and Amazon S3. Spark can also work with YARN as its cluster manager. In addition to YARN, Spark also supports Apache Mesos, an in-built standalone cluster manager.

2. **More Expressive**: Spark APIs incorporate Scala, which is designed to be much more concise and expressive. It allows Spark to generalize abstraction results in a small portion of the code. This increases readability and allows more expressive code.

3. **Less Code**: Big data does not mean big code. Distributed computations in Spark are similar to immutable lists in Scala that enables us to write more concise code as compared to MapReduce. Example 6.10 shows wordcount example using Spark. The example illustrates how Spark is much more concise and allows more expressive code.

4. **Performance**: The sequential read throughput when reading data from memory compared to reading data from a hard disk is always much greater. Spark's in-memory cluster computing capabilities enables us to query very large distributed dataset interactively with minimal disk I/O. This provides a substantial performance boost. This capability becomes a significant contributor to overall job execution time when an application reads and processes large volume of data.

5. **Optimization for Big Data**: As discussed earlier, many algorithms require iterations to perform the same computation multiple times. While it is easy to represent each iteration as a MapReduce job, the data from each iteration has to be loaded from the disk which results in significant performance penalty. Machine learning and graph processing applications belong to this category of applications that use iterative algorithms to iterate tens or hundreds of times over the same data. Spark in-memory computing capabilities allow these applications to run faster. Gradient-Descent is one example of such an algorithm that is repeatedly applied to the same dataset to optimize a parameter.

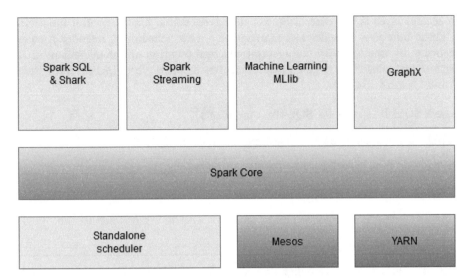

FIGURE 6.1 Spark architecture

6. **Fault Tolerance**: The probability of a node failing on any given day is always high for a large cluster of nodes. Spark provides fault tolerant capabilities by automatically dealing with failed nodes. If the node, for instance, running a partition of a map() operation crashes, Spark will automatically execute it on another node. In addition, Spark also provides capabilities to deal with slow nodes. In the situation where even if the node does not crash but runs much slower than other nodes, Spark can proactively launch a provisional copy of the task on another node, and apply its result if that finishes.

Since Spark automatically handles node failures, application developers do not have to handle such failures in their application. This feature simplifies application code.

7. **Unifying Big Data**: As evident from figure 6.1, Spark unifies several types of big data challenges and requirements, which include processing of batch data or streaming data, machine learning algorithms, and graph processing.

In summary, there are many organizations which are currently leveraging Spark for big data processing. Reference [51] lists the number of organizations with their use cases.

6.2   INTRODUCTION TO SPARK

Spark is a distributed platform, which is capable of processing large amounts of data. The core model for data representation in Spark is **RDD – Resilient Distributed Dataset**. It is the most fundamental data object used in Spark programming and is the main programming abstraction in Spark. It represents a collection of items, which are distributed across the Spark cluster. Consequently, an RDD in Spark can be executed in parallel across the cluster. RDD is immutable – i.e., it cannot be altered after they are instantiated and populated with data. RDDs use various types of elements including primitive data types (integers etc.), complex types (list etc.) as well as serialized Scala and Java objects.

Figure 6.1 shows the architecture of Spark. The first layer identifies the scheduling layer for cluster management. Spark can have its own scheduler; further, it can be integrated with other schedulers such as Mesos, YARN, or Kubernetes. This feature provides much needed flexibility to Spark.

The second layer is the core of Spark. It is responsible for the overall functionality of Spark. These functions include task management, task scheduling, memory management, fault recovery, interaction with storage systems, and creation and management of RDDs.

The third layer describes the significant features of Spark. These include SQL, Streaming, MLlib, and GraphX libraries:

1. **Spark SQL**: It is used for SQL-like operations.

2. **MLlib**: It is used for machine learning and data analytics.

3. **Streaming**: It is used for streaming-based processing.

4. **GraphX**: It is used for data visualization.

6.3 SPARK CONCEPTS

We can understand the functionality and execution of Spark through figure 6.2. A Spark program is submitted through a driver. Spark context is used to provide access to the driver program. The context can also be used to build RDDs.

Upon submission of a Spark program, the driver program creates and executes tasks on different worker nodes through executor programs. For instance, if we are running a Word-Count program, different worker nodes will count words on different data items. Results from all the worker nodes can be merged to obtain the final answer.

Spark provides programming support for multiple languages which includes Scala, Python, Java, and R supported natively by Spark. Spark also includes extended support for Clojure and other languages. However, in this book we will mainly focus our examples on Python.

Example 6.2 shows creation of Spark context. In the code, sparkapp is the name of the Spark application, whereas local denotes mode of operation.

6.3.1   Spark- Modes of Operation

Spark can either be executed as a client mode or as a cluster mode. In the former case, a Spark program is executed locally on the client, whereas in the latter case, a Spark program is submitted to a cluster. We now explain modes of operation:

1. **Local**: This is a non-distributed mode. Using this mode, Spark programs are executed locally on a single JVM. Parallelism is achieved through a number of threads. Standard options for the local mode are mentioned below:

   (a) local: single thread.

   (b) local[n]: "n" number of threads.

   (c) local[*]: as many threads as the number of processors are available.

2. **Standalone Cluster**: This is the default cluster management setup in which Spark itself manages the tasks on master and worker nodes [15].

3. **YARN**: Using this option, Spark utilizes the Yarn cluster manager. Details about YARN are explained in section 5.2.

4. **Mesos**: Spark is executed on the mesos cluster.

We should note an important point that in a local mode, there should be at least two threads in the Spark program. This is because Spark keeps separate threads for receiving data and processing data. Spark can also be used to receive data from multiple input sources at a time. In such a case, a separate thread is needed for each individual source. Same notion can be applied when Spark is executed in a cluster mode such that enough cores should be allocated to Spark so it can receive and process data simultaneously.

Example 6.1 explains Spark submit options.

Spark Submit

Example 6.1 (Spark Submit).
Using spark–submit command
```
spark-submit  --option value \
application jar | python file [application
    arguments]
```
application jar: Location of the jar file.
python file: location of the python file. For local
    mode, file should be available via local path.

Spark scripts can also be executed using shell commands. In such a case, Spark programs are written in a scripting language such as Python or Scala. The script is executed by Spark. Table 6.1 explains a few common functions.

Creating a Spark Context

Example 6.2 (Creating a Spark Context).
Creating a Spark Context
```
conf = SparkConf().setMaster("local").setAppName("
    sparkapp")
sc = SparkContext(conf = conf)
```

Example 6.3 shows creation of RDD in Spark using Python. Spark shell can be obtained using "pyspark".

Creating an RDD

Example 6.3 (Creating an RDD).
```
lines=sc.textfile("myfile.txt")
```

In this example, sc denotes Spark context. The RDD lines contain all the text in the file "myfile.txt" Example 6.4 extends the program from example 6.3 by counting no. of lines. An important point to note is that an existing RDD cannot be altered. A new RDD is created for each modification in an existing RDD.

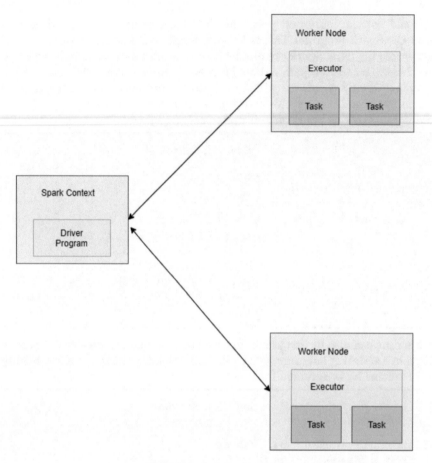

FIGURE 6.2 Spark flow

Counting no. of lines in Spark

Example 6.4 (Counting no. of lines in Spark).
Counting no. of lines
```
lines=sc.textfile("myfile.txt")
n=lines.count()
```

6.3.2   Operations on RDD

There are two types of operations in an RDD; i.e., transformations and actions.

Transformations are used to transform an existing RDD, whereas actions are used to perform action on an existing RDD. Example 6.5 highlights the difference between transformation and action.

From the example, we can learn that the filter operation filters an existing RDD – lines, for the word "Python", to create a new RDD pythonlines. The operation "count" performs a count operation on the RDD "lines" to return a number of lines. In general, actions compute a result-based on an RDD. The results are either returned to the driver program or saved to an external storage system (e.g., HDFS).

Difference between transformation and action for RDD

Example 6.5 (Difference between transformation and action for RDD).
```
lines=sc.textfile("myfile.txt")
```
Transformation
```
pythonLines = lines.filter(lambda line: "Python"
    in line)
```
Action
```
n=lines.count()
```

6.3.3 Lazy Execution

In Spark, RDDs are created in a lazy fashion. That is, they are created the first time they are used in an action. This approach allows Spark to conserve resources as Spark can compute data as it needed.

We can understand the advantage of lazy execution through example 6.6

Spark Lazy Evaluation

Example 6.6 (Spark Lazy Evaluation).
```
lines=sc.textfile("myfile.txt")

pythonLines = lines.filter(lambda line: "Python"
    in line)

first=lines.count()
```

6.3.4 Persistence

As we discussed earlier, Spark computes RDDs in a lazy fashion. This also implies that if an action on an RDD is computed more than once, then Spark will perform computation multiple times on the RDD. This behavior may lead to repetition of tasks. To avoid this scenario, Spark provides a method persist.

If the persist method is called on an RDD then Spark will store its result in the cache (of all the nodes) so that multiple calls to the RDD can be responded through cache. In this manner, the task of repetitive computation can be avoided.

For instance, let us consider example 6.7. As the method persist has been called on the RDD pythonLines, repetitive calls to the RDD will be answered through cache. The nodes that compute the RDD store the partitions. In case of a failure of a node, Spark will recompute the lost partitions.

TABLE 6.1 Spark Functions

Function	Explanation
map	Transforms an RDD. For instance, each element in an RDD can be multiplied by 2. A function in map returns only one item.
flatmap	Similar to map but gives a flattened output such that the function is applied to each element of RDD.
filter	Filters an RDD to select only contents passed as the function parameter.
distinct	Returns a new RDD with distinct elements only.
union	Returns a new RDD by creating a union of two RDDs.
intersection	Returns a new RDD by creating intersection of two RDDs.
cartesian	Computes a cartesian product of two RDDs.

Spark Persistence

Example 6.7 (Spark Persistence).
```
lines=sc.textfile("myfile.txt")
pythonLines = lines.filter(lambda line: "Python"
    in line)
pythonLines.persist()
print pythonLines.count ()
```

Spark provides multiple levels of persistence such as persistence in memory and persistence at the disk; further, persistence can also be varied from server only to server and worker nodes.

6.3.5 Spark Functions

Spark: map vs. flatmap

Example 6.8 (Spark: map vs. flatmap).
Sample Text
```
This is Big Data Systems Book
Python Scala Java
```

Usage of map function
```
mp =data.map(lambda line:line.split(" "));
mp.collect()
```
Output is as follows:
```
'This is Big Data Systems Book'
'Python Scala Java'
```

Usage of flatmap function
```
fm=data.flatMap(lambda line:line.split(" "));
fm.collect()
```
Output is as follows
```
'This','is','Big','Data','Systems','Book'
'Python','Scala','Java'
```

Example 6.8 explains the difference between map and flatmap functions. Example 6.9 explains the functionality of various Spark functions.

Spark Functions

Example 6.9 (Spark Functions).
```
RDD1={1,2,3,4,1} and RDD2={2,3,5}
```
Filter
```
RDD3=RDD1.filter(1)
```
RDD3=1,1

Distinct
```
RDD4=RDD1.distinct()
```
RDD4=2,3,4

Union
```
RDD5=RDD1.union(RDD2)
```
RDD5=1,2,3,4,1,2,3,5

WordCount on Spark

Example 6.10 (WordCount on Spark).
Type pyspark to get to the Spark shell. Use Ctrl+D to quit
1. We can get the value of the namenode by executing the following command on the shell

```
hadoop dfsadmin -report
```

2. Create an input file on HDFS file either using command prompt or using HDFS browser. This will be used as an input to the WordCount.

3. Execute the following python script on the shell..

```
myfile = sc.textFile("hdfs://name_node:8020/user/
    cloudera/input_folder

counts = myfile.flatMap(lambda line: line.split("
    ")).map(lambda word: (word, 1)).reduceByKey(
    lambda v1,v2: v1 + v2)

counts.saveAsTextFile("hdfs://name_node:8020/user/
    cloudera/output_folder/")
```
4.Check Output on HDFS

Example 6.10 shows wordcount example using Spark.

6.4   SPARK SQL

Spark SQL provides SQL-based features for accessing data either through structured or semi-structured format. It can also be used to load data from an existing data source such as Hive. SQL query can be made either inside a Spark program or using external tools or database connectors such as JDBC/ODBC. Spark SQL provides integration between SQL and Spark code written in Java/Python/Scala.

Example 6.12 shows procedure for loading data and querying data when Spark SQL is integrated with Python. In step 1, Spark SQL context is created. This step is necessary in order to call related methods on Spark SQL. In step 2, table "customers" is registered with the context. Step 3 shows the format of the select query on the customers table.

Spark SQL can also access data from the JSON format. Line 1 in example 6.12 shows the procedure of reading data from JSON file.

Spark SQL can be used to create User Defined Functions (UDF) in Java/Python/Scala. It can also be used to access existing UDF in Hive.

6.4.1   DataFrame

In Spark besides RDD, data can also be stored in a dataframe, which is conceptually equivalent to a table in a relational database. A dataframe can be constructed from different sources such as tables in Hive, structured data files, external databases, or existing RDDs. Example 6.11 shows how DataFrames can be created [53] Comments are listed in bold.

DataFrame for Spark

Example 6.11 (DataFrame for Spark).
spark is an existing SparkSession

```
dataframe = spark.read.json("example/data.json")
```
Printing contents of DataFrame to stdout
```
dataframe.show()
```

```
|age|name|

|27|Mike|
|38|Sara|
|11|Fischer|
```

Readers can get detailed information from reference [218].

Loading and querying data using Python

Example 6.12 (Loading and querying data using Python).
1. Creating Spark SQL context
```
inputctx = hiveCtx.jsonFile(inputfile)
```

2. Register the input schema RDD
```
inputctx.registerTempTable("customers")
```

3. Select customers based on the customerCount

```
topcustomers = hiveCtx.sql("SELECT ID,
    customerCount FROM customers ORDER BY
    customerCount LIMIT 5")
```

6.5 SPARK MLLIB

Spark MLlib is the machine learning library for Spark. It has been designed to run in parallel on a cluster of Spark machines. The library incorporates built-in functions for many machine learning algorithms such as clustering, classification, regression, collaborative filtering, and recommendation. It also provides various features such as developing pipelines, model selection, and tuning, feature selection, extraction, and transformation.

Spark MLlib provides the ML libraries through two different APIs:

1. **Spark MLlib**: It provides support through RDDs.

2. **Spark ML**: It provides support through dataframes.

Example 6.13 shows a sample code for K-means clustering using Spark RDD. Comments in the example are listed in bold. The data is loaded from the file input.txt. The loaded data is parsed and trained using the Spark's K-means method. The model is then tested

TABLE 6.2 Spark MLlib – Data Types for RDDs

RDD	Purpose
Local Vector	Creates a vector for strong binary values. This is useful for storing features. The vector could either be sparse or dense.
Labeled Point	A local vector to store labeled responses. These are used for supervised learning.
Local Matrix	A matrix which is stored locally in a cluster. Values are stored as sparse matrix.
Distributed Matrix	A matrix which is distributed across the cluster.

for prediction. The example also shows how the generated model can be saved and loaded. Example 6.14 shows the same task of computing K-means clustering using DataFrame [53].

The RDD-based APIs are now in maintenance mode and will not add any new features into it. Table 6.2 describes a few RDDs for MLlib.

All the new development and features will be contributed in the DataFrame-based API which is now the primary API for machine learning [45].

K-means clustering using RDD

Example 6.13 (K-means clustering using RDD).
```
from numpy import array
from math import sqrt

from pyspark.mllib.clustering import KMeans,
    KMeansModel
```

Load the data

assuming data = [0.0,0.0], [1.0,1.0], [9.0,8.0],[8.0,9.0]

```
inputdata = sc.textFile("inputdata.txt")
```

parse the data

```
parseddata = inputdata.map(lambda line: array([
    float(x) for x in line.split(',')]))
```
Build the Kmeans model for training

```
model = KMeans.train(parseddata, 3)
```
**choosing 3 leaf clustres and default values for
    maxiterations=20,minDivisibleClusterSize, and seed**

Compute and print Cluster Center

```
print("Final centers: " + str(model.clusterCenters
    ))
```

Print Cost
```
print("Total Cost: " +str(model.computeCost(
    parseddata)))
```

Predict
```
p= array([0.0, 0.0])
model.predict(p)
```

Save and load model
```
model.save(sc, "KMeansModel")
loadedmodel = KMeansModel.load(sc, "KMeansModel")
```

K-means clustering using DataFrame

Example 6.14 (K-means clustering using DataFrame).

```
from pyspark.ml.clustering import KMeans
from pyspark.ml.evaluation import
    ClusteringEvaluator
```

Load the data

```
inputdata = spark.read.format("libsvm").load("data
    /sample_data.txt")
```

Trains a K-means model

```
kmeans = KMeans().setK(2).setSeed(1)
model = kmeans.fit(inputdata)
```

Make predictions
```
predictions = model.transform(inputdata)
```

Shows the result
```
centers = model.clusterCenters()
print("Cluster Centers: ")
for center in centers:
print(center)
```

6.5.1   Pipelining

Pipelining allows to combine multiple stages into a workflow. Through this, multiple machine learning tasks can be incorporated at different stages.

Each stage in a Pipeline can either be a Transformer or an Estimator. The former stage converts a DataFrame to another DataFrame by using the transform method, whereas, an Estimator converts a DataFrame and produces a Model. It implements the fit() method.

Pipeline stages are executed in an order. Example 6.15 shows execution of ML pipeline. It has been taken from the official documentation of Spark [54].

Spark ML Pipelining

Example 6.15 (Spark ML Pipeline). *Figure 6.3 shows a pipeline with three stages. In the top row, first two stages, Tokenizer and HashingTF are Transformers. The third stage is an Estimator, which outputs Logistic Regression.*
The bottom row represents dataflow through each stage of the pipeline. Dataframes are indicated through cylinders. These show output at each stage. The tokenizer splits the input data (raw text) into words. It also adds a new column words to the DataFrame. The HashingTF transforms the words into feature vectors. These vectors are added to the DataFrame. The last stage of the pipeline, Logistic Regression, creates a model.

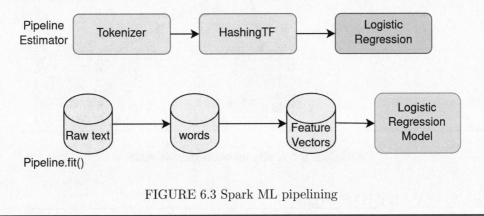

FIGURE 6.3 Spark ML pipelining

Example 6.16 shows a snippet code for ML Pipeline [54].

Spark ML Pipeline Code

```
Configure an ML pipeline, which consists of three stages:
    Tokenizer, HashingTF, and Logistic Regression

Convert input text as tokens
tokens = Tokenizer(inputCol="text", outputCol="
    words")

Convert tokens into feature vector
hashingvector = HashingTF(inputCol=tokens.
    getOutputCol(), outputCol="features")

Logistic Regression
logisticregression = LogisticRegression(maxIter
    =10, regParam=0.001)
pipeline = Pipeline(stages=[tokens, hashingvector,
    logisticregression])

Create a Pipeline
model = pipeline.fit(training)
```

Example 6.16 (Spark ML Pipeline Code).

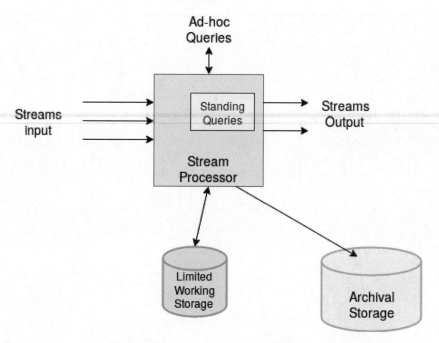

FIGURE 6.4 A stream management system

6.6   STREAM-BASED SYSTEM

Stream processing is one of the important requirements in many big data applications. A fundamental difference between a stream processing system as compared to a batch processing system is, that in the former case, either recent data or data over a specific time window is processed, whereas in the latter case, execution is performed over a large volume of data or on a large batch of data. Further, in a stream system, there is a continuous flow of data; however, the rate of flow of data may vary.

Figure 6.4 illustrates a basic stream processing system. Core of the system is a stream processor, which is responsible for computation. The processor has access to memory. Streams may be archived in the archival storage. Archived storage is only used for storage. The working storage is used to process summaries or store part of streams. It is used to answer queries related to streams. The working store could either be in the main memory or it could be in the permanent storage such as the hard disk. The former will be able to respond faster than the latter.

In stream processing, queries can be classified into two types:

1. **Standing queries**: These queries are stored and executed at regular intervals and scheduled time. For instance, for temperature reading through sensors, what is the maximum temperature recorded in a day?

2. **Ad hoc queries**: These are the queries which are needed to be answered on an ad-hoc basis. For instance, for network logs on a web server, what is the most accessed URL in the past one hour?

6.6.1   Issues and Challenges in Stream Processing

Stream processing is challenging than batch for the following reasons:

1. **Real-time Processing**: Often data in streams is delivered in real-time at a high speed. Computation over such streams requires real-time and efficient processing. Therefore, fetching large data from permanent storage or performing iterative computing could be costly. It is often important that the stream-processing algorithm is executed in main memory with little or no requirement of fetching data from the main memory.

2. **Data Input from Multiple Streams**: A stream processing system could receive data from multiple sources at a time. Even if the rate of arrival of data is low, input from multiple sources induce challenges.

3. **Scalability Limitation**: Data analytics can easily be incorporated using frameworks and languages like R, Python, and MATLAB. These frameworks generally perform well with a datasets of hundreds of megabytes or even a few gigabytes. However, the scalability becomes a bottleneck as the dataset increases and becomes too large to fit into the main memory of a single computer. These existing frameworks do not allow to scale and therefore, distributing dataset over multiple machines becomes difficult. Eventually, we may require redesigning our application from scratch using other frameworks or languages. We will need to manually figure out how to distribute our dataset over multiple nodes without the help of these frameworks.

For stream processing, we can meet the requirements of scalability and timeliness if we had access to large memory. However, as the size of data grows, meeting requirements of large memory becomes difficult. Therefore, we need to adopt efficient techniques to solve these problems.

One possible approach to solve streams is to adapt to approximation. For instance, if we can sample streams at a periodic rate over a long period of time, it is likely to capture the randomness, which will lead to an approximate and realistic answer.

6.7   SPARK STREAMING

Streaming relates to computing data analytics in real-time. Such a requirement could exist in many data analytics applications. For instance, a credit card theft monitoring system must detect possible attacks in real-time. Similarly, a weather monitoring device must detect changes in real-time.

Spark Streaming is an extension to the Spark core API designed to process streams of data. There are two streaming APIs available in Spark [59, 60]:

1. **RDD-based API**: It is used for discretized streams also known as DStreams. It is the first stream-processing framework built on top of the core Spark engine which is widely adopted in the industry and the Spark community to process large-scale data streams.

2. **DataFrames/DataSet-based API**: It is a structured streaming API, which is built on top of Spark SQL. It supports rich optimizations and provides integration with other DataFrame and Dataset code. This new streaming API introduced in Spark 2.0 which was marked as stable in Spark 2.2.

Reference [57] provides the integration guide for Spark streaming with Kafka. In this chapter, we will focus on DStreams which are RDD-based API supporting real-time data analytics using discretized streams. A DStream is implemented as a sequence of RDDs, each of which can handle data in sequence or time step.

Figure 6.5 illustrates the concept of sequence of RDDs. For instance, RDD_1 holds the data from time t_0 to t_1.

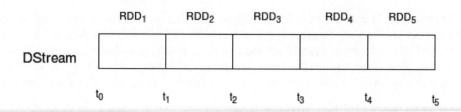

FIGURE 6.5 Spark DStream

DStreams can either be used to transform data in order to create a new DStream or to write data to output. For DStreams, data can be obtained from various input sources, such as Flume, Kafka, or HDFS, and TCP Sockets. Once the data is obtained, many Spark functions such as map, filter, reduce, and join can be applied on the streams. Further, Spark libraries such as MLlib and GraphX can also be applied on DStreams. The output of Spark streaming can either be written to a file such as HDFS or can be sent to a database.

We will now review a sample example for reading data from a stream and analyzing it using Spark StreamingContext. The StreamingContext is the entry point for a Spark Streaming application and defines the time interval by which streams of data are discretized. Example 6.17 shows Python code for reading input data from a network stream and applying wordcount operation. The stream is created with a 1-second interval.

6.7.1 Types of Transformation

Transformations on DStreams can be grouped into either stateless or stateful:

1. **Stateless Transformation**: Transformation is applied individually to each component of RDD separately, i.e., it is independent of the previous batch. Spark operations such as map and filter fall in this category.

2. **Stateful Transformation**: This transformation utilizes intermediate results from previous windows batches to compute the results of the current time slot. The transformation functions are based on sliding windows and on tracking state across time.

We can comprehend the operation of stateless transformation through example 6.17. In the example, transformation function is applied individually to each batch. Here, wordcount operation is implemented from a network source with port number 6000. At first, Spark context is created for execution on local mode with two working threads. As a second step, Spark streaming context is created with a batch interval of five seconds. That is, wordcount operation will be executed on batches of time duration five seconds. A DStream is created to receive input packets at port 6000 on localhost.

Spark Streaming from Network [58]

Example 6.17 (Spark Streaming from Network).

```
from pyspark import SparkContext
from pyspark.streaming import StreamingContext
```

Create a local StreamingContext with two working thread and batch interval of three seconds

```
spark_context = SparkContext("local[2]", "
    wordcountusingnetwork")
spark_streaming_context= StreamingContext(
    spark_context, 3)
```

Create a DStream that will connect to the local host on IP 127.0.0.1.The stream will connect to port number 6000 on the localhost

```
read_lines=spark_streaming_context.
    socketTextStream("127.0.0.1", 6000)
```

Split each line into words

```
words = read_lines.flatMap(lambda line: line.split
    (" "))
```

Apply WordCount in each batch

```
key_value_pairs = words.map(lambda word: (word, 1)
    )
wordCounts = key_value_pairs.reduceByKey(lambda x,
    y: x + y)
```

get distinct words
```
output=key_value_pairs.collect()
```

Start the computation
```
spark_streaming_context.start()
```

Wait for the computation to terminate
```
spark_streaming_context.awaitTermination()
```

The rest of the code for parsing lines to get words and counting words to complete the wordcount operation is similar to example 6.10.

We observe that example 6.17 shows two additional functions. The start function is called to explicitly start the operation on the stream. The stream operation is initiated on a separate Spark thread. The awaitTermination method is used to enforce wait on the stream to finish execution. As an optional step, a stop operation can also be applied on the stream by calling the StreamingContext.stop method.

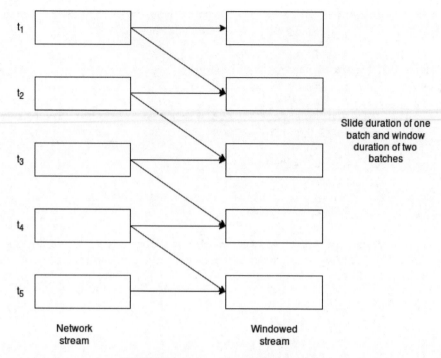

FIGURE 6.6 Spark stateful stream

In comparison to stateless transformation, which is applied to the current window only, a stateful transformation is applied using a combination of previous batches. This combination can either be computed using full session or on a windowed session.

Figure 6.6 illustrates transformation of stateful streams on a windowed stream. Here, windowed stream is computed at each time unit with computation over the previous two windows.

Example 6.18 shows an instance of computing stateful transformation over a full session. For clarity, the example only shows the piece of code necessary to execute wordcount over the complete duration. The rest of the code is similar to example 6.17.

Spark Stateful Transformation – Complete Session [382]

Example 6.18 (Spark Stateful Transformation – Completer Session).
Computing stream over a full session
```
totalCounts = wordCounts.updateStateByKey(
    updateTotalCount)
```

Example 6.19 shows computation of stream over a windowed session. The countByWindow operation performs count over the last 30 seconds of data (window length) every 10 seconds (slide interval).

The example also illustrates execution of reduceByKeyAndWindow, which performs reduction over <key,value> pairs. The first argument of the function is the reduction function, which in this case is x+y. The second argument is the inverse function x-y. The inverse of the reduction function is necessary because here computation is done by reducing the new data that enters the sliding window, and inverse reducing the old data that leaves the window.

The third and fourth arguments of the function are window length and sliding interval. For clarity, only a snippet of the code is shown. The rest of the code is similar to example 6.17.

Spark Stateful Transformation – Windowed Session [382]

Example 6.19 (Spark Stateful Transformation – Windowed Session).
Computing stream over windowed session

```
windowedCounts =
wordCounts.countByWindow(30,10)


windowedreducebykey = key_value_pairs.
    reduceByKeyAndWindow(lambda x, y: x + y, lambda
    x, y: x - y, 30, 10)
```

6.7.2 Checkpointing

Spark is a fault-tolerant distributed file system. The need of providing fault tolerance exist in stateful transformation, where a fault (such as node failure) should not lead to recomputation from scratch. For this purpose, Spark provides checkpointing – a feature which enables Spark to checkpoint the data in a reliable file system (such as HDFS). If checkpointing is enabled, recovery could easily be made using the last checkpoint.

We should note that checkpointing of data is only necessary in stateful transformations because data in the current batch depends upon the data from previous batches. Many Spark functions such as updateStateByKey () or reduceByKeyAndWindow () are used for stateful transformations.

In addition to stateful transformation, checkpointing can also be used for metadata. This includes data related to configuration and DStream operations. This information would be needed in both stateless and stateful transformations and it is useful to cater driver failures.

We can learn the process of creation of checkpoint through the example 6.20. In the example, Spark is executed in a local mode. "*" denotes to create as many worker threads as logical cores on the machine.

Spark – Creating a checkpoint [382]

Example 6.20 (Spark – Creating a checkpoint).
```
from pyspark import SparkContext
from pyspark.streaming import StreamingContext
//Get a SparkContext for execution in a local mode
sc = SparkContext("local[*]", "StreamWordCounter")

//A Streaming context is created with a batch interval of 10
    seconds

ssc = StreamingContext(sc, 10)

Set Checkpointing Directory
ssc.checkpoint(checkpointDirectory)

ssc.start()
ssc.awaitTermination()
```

In a similar context, checkpointing can be used to load the data. Example 6.21 shows that StreamingContext.getOrCreate method can be used to load data from the check point directory.

Spark – Loading data from a checkpoint [382]

Example 6.21 (Spark – Loading data from a checkpoint).
```
Get Data from the Checkpointing Directory
StreamingContext.getOrCreate(checkpointDirector,
    None)
```

6.8 GRAPHX

GraphX is the Spark library to process large-scale graphs. In this section, we will study GraphX concepts, which are specific to Spark. However, to strengthen foundation, we will also study some preliminaries about graphs. In section 7.7, we will study graph-based processing for NoSQL databases.

6.8.1 Concepts

GraphX provides graph-based processing for computation of large-scale graphs. It extends RDD concepts through a graph-based abstraction, in which a graph has properties associated with vertices and edges. In the literature, such a graph is considered as a property graph.

Example 6.22 shows a property graph with edges and vertices, whereas example 6.23 shows python code to construct such a graph using graph frames. It also shows code to perform a few basic graph operations [65].

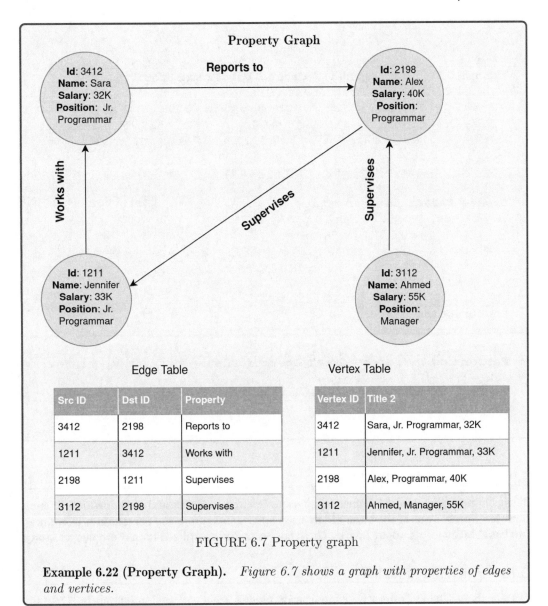

FIGURE 6.7 Property graph

Example 6.22 (Property Graph). *Figure 6.7 shows a graph with properties of edges and vertices.*

Spark – GraphX

Example 6.23 (Spark – GraphX). *Create DataFrames for vertices*
```
v = sqlContext.createDataFrame([
("3412", "Sara", "Jr. Programmar",32), ("1211", "
    Jennifer", "Jr. Programmar", 33),("2198", "Alex
    ", "Programmar",40), ("3112", "Ahmed", "Manager
    ", 55)],
["id", "name", "title", "salary"])
```

Create DataFrames for edges
```
e=sqlContext.createDataFrame([
("3412", "2198", "Reports to"),("1211", "3412", "
    Works with"),("2198", "1211", "Supervises"),
    ("3112", "2198","Supervises")],["src","dst","
    relationship"])
```

Constructing Graph
```
g = GraphFrame(v,e)
```

Performing Different Graph Operations
```
inDegreeDF=g.inDegrees
outDegreeDF=g.outDegrees
degreeDF=g.degrees
```

6.9   CONCLUDING REMARKS

This chapter introduced fundamental concepts related to Spark and explained its different libraries. Spark is one of the most widely used open-source projects. This chapter introduced fundamental concepts about Spark. These concepts can be utilized for a more deeper study.

6.10   FURTHER READING

Details about Hadoop's iterative computation models are mentioned in references [114,115].

More general details about Spark can be found in references [127, 383]. Details about Spark SQL can be found at references [56, 83, 218].

Spark programming guide can be found at reference [55] whereas Spark Streaming programming guide is explained in references [59,60]. Details about integration of Spark Streaming with Kafka can be found at reference [57].

Spark machine learning library is explained in references [46, 266]. Spark Pipelining is explained in detail in reference [348], whereas details about Spark GraphX can be found at reference [25].

6.11   EXERCISE QUESTIONS

1. What are the limitations of MapReduce in processing iterative operations?

2. What are the limitations of MapReduce in processing streamed data?

3. What is Spark? Explain its architecture.

4. Which programming languages are natively supported by Spark?

5. Explain the advantages of using Spark over MapReduce.

6. What are Resilient Distributed Datasets (RDDs)?

7. What are different modes in Spark?

8. How many JVMs are spawned in local mode?

9. What Spark Streaming is and how it works?

10. Explain the difference between stateless and stateful transformation.

GLOSSARY

Apache Spark: It is an open-source unified distributed computing engine across different workloads and platforms. It is a cluster computing system for big data.

Apache Mesos: It is an open-source cluster management framework for managing compute, memory, storage, and other resources across a cluster.

Apache Sqoop: It is one of the leading tools for transferring data between structured data stores (such as relational databases) and Hadoop.

DataFrame: It is similar to a distributed table with named columns with a schema. It is an immutable, distributed collection of data organized into rows, where each one consists of a set of columns and each column has a specific data type: integer, string, etc.

DStream: It is used for stream analysis. DStream is implemented as a sequence of RDDs, each of which can handle data in sequence or time step.

GraphX: It is Spark's graph-processing API. It is used for data visualization and implementing useful graph algorithms.

Property Graph: It is a graph which has properties associated with vertices and edges.

RDD: It stands for Resilient Distributed Dataset. It is an immutable, resilient, fault-tolerant, and distributed collection of objects, which is partitioned across the cluster.

Spark Core: It contains the Spark core execution engine and a set of low-level functional APIs for the Spark platform that all other functionality is built upon.

Spark ML: It is a Spark library for machine learning, which is supported through DataFrame-based APIs.

Spark MLlib: It is a Spark library for machine learning. It is an RDD-based API.

Spark Pipelining: It is a sequence of stages which can be used to define a workflow.

Spark SQL: It implements the higher level Dataset and DataFrame APIs of Spark and adds SQL support on top of arbitrary data sources.

Spark Streaming: It is a stream processing framework to support real-time data analytics using discretized streams (or DStreams).

Structured Streaming: It is the second-generation Spark Streaming processing engine built on top of the Spark SQL abstraction heavily based on DataFrame API with streaming capabilities.

NoSQL Systems

CONTENTS

B IG DATA systems require massive amounts of storage and this storage needs to be spread across data centers in huge clusters of commodity servers. NoSQL Systems have been specifically introduced to cater these challenges of big data systems. These databases were designed to deal with big data storage and processing demands that relational databases cannot meet. In this chapter, we will provide a detailed explanation of how NoSQL databases work and the different categories of systems that fall under this definition. The chapter covers various examples in order to explain the topics.

7.1 INTRODUCTION

In section 1.3, we discussed various types of big data systems.

Relational databases have been the primary model for database management for decades. They are still a good choice for applications that require structured data with requirements of ACID transactions. However, the need to handle massive volume of data in large scale systems has led to the emergence of NoSQL databases.

These databases are being increasingly utilized and have become an alternative to relational databases with their performance, scalability, availability, schema flexibility, and analytical capabilities.

In section 1.3.2, we discussed that as compared to the ACID properties model of RDBMS, big data systems follow the BASE model in which they relax consistency in order to achieve higher availability.

In this chapter, we will explain different categories of NoSQL database systems and will also describe their strengths and limitations.

7.2 HANDLING BIG DATA SYSTEMS – PARALLEL RDBMS

Traditionally, RDBMS systems have been sufficient and capable to handle data operations. However, as data continues to grow and data-related applications continue to be utilized, need for better systems emerge. Specifically, following requirements became significant:

1. **Data Storage**: As size of data grows, time to store and retrieve data should not be a bottleneck.

2. **Data Processing**: Processing of data should not take an overwhelming amount of time.

3. **Fault Tolerance**: High fault tolerance is desired as data should be available.

4. **Load Balancing**: Large databases need to ensure load balancing in order to provide high performance.

These requirements necessitated the need for parallel RDBMS. A parallel RDBMS is an RDBMS system with multiple processes, which can support parallel access. There are three major types of parallel databases. These types are similar to our earlier discussion in section 2.3:

1. Shared Everything

2. Shared Disk

3. Shared Nothing

Example 7.1 illustrates the difference between the three types of RDBMS.

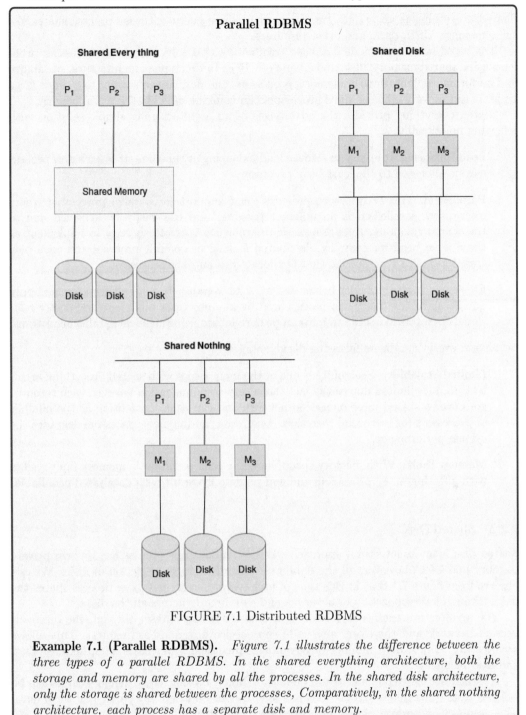

FIGURE 7.1 Distributed RDBMS

Example 7.1 (Parallel RDBMS). *Figure 7.1 illustrates the difference between the three types of a parallel RDBMS. In the shared everything architecture, both the storage and memory are shared by all the processes. In the shared disk architecture, only the storage is shared between the processes, Comparatively, in the shared nothing architecture, each process has a separate disk and memory.*

There are three major architectures for distributed database systems illustrated in Figure 7.1. We now discuss them in detail.

7.2.1 Shared Everything

Shared everything is an architectural approach where every database process shares the same memory, CPU, data, and other resources.

It is based on a single-node database architecture that solves complex processing problems using shared memory, disk, and a bank of CPUs. In this type of architecture, scalability and performance limitations of memory, processors, and data are constraint to a single large node. It can be very efficient since processors can communicate via the main memory.

Shared everything provides the advantages of an architecturally simple solution with following functionalities:

1. **Load Balancing**: It is easy to achieve load balancing at run-time since each new process can be allocated to the least busy processor.

2. **Parallelism**: This architecture provides great support for parallel processing where inter-query parallelism is an inherent property and can easily be achieved due to the shared resources. Inter-transaction parallelism is relatively easy to implement as there is no need for complex distributed locking or commit protocol and each new transaction is a new process that is allocated to another processor.

3. **Efficiency**: It also provides better design of inter-transaction parallelism for read-only queries since any query can be executed by any processor and therefore, costly relational operators like sort and join can be parallelized using classical parallel algorithms.

Shared everything bears following disadvantages:

1. **Limited Scalability**: Scalability is one of the main issues with shared everything architecture. It is limited due to the fact that every communication between each resource goes over a shared interconnection network and can cause contention as the number of processors (or resources) increases. As a result, adding new processors degrades the system performance.

2. **Memory Faults**: With memory space shared by each processor, a memory fault results with affecting many processors and can potentially result with database unavailable.

7.2.2 Shared Disk

Shared disk is an architectural approach where each database process has its own private memory and CPU; however, all the databases share the single collection of disks. We can observe from figure 7.1 that in this type of architecture, every database process shares the disks through interconnection of networks and can directly access all the disks.

The architecture enables any node to access the entire dataset through the interconnection network and therefore, any node can service any database request. This allows architecture to provide a number of advantages including lower costs, good extensibility, and load balancing.

It provides a more economical and high-availability solution, since memory faults can be isolated from other nodes and no node has sole responsibility for any particular set of data. This results in a portion of the database being available under any node failure scenario and the database continues to run when the remaining nodes are able to fill in for the failed nodes. In addition, it also provides more fluid load balancing since a query at any node can access all data on the shared disks.

Sharing peak loads across all the servers in the cluster allows each server to run at a higher CPU utilization. It allows minimum interference in the shared disk by providing each processor with enough memory, which results in better elastic scalability and extensibility. It also removes the need for re-balancing operations.

Shared disk provides the following advantages:

1. **Scalability**: It is very flexible in meeting a user's needs. In case of increase in demand, more resources (such as processors) can be added.

2. **Fault Tolerance**: Shared disk architecture improves extensibility by optimizing and minimizing the interference on the disks as each processor has its own memory. Isolation of a memory module faults from other nodes results in better availability.

3. **Load Balancing**: Load balancing feature can easily be achieved due to shared access of all data for each node.

Shared disk provides the following disadvantages:

1. **Bottleneck**: Sharing a resource over an interconnection is always a potential bottleneck, and therefore, access to a shared disk is a potential bottleneck.

2. **Increased Coordination**: It requires increased coordination effort between the processors for implementation of distributed database system protocol.

3. **Cache Consistency**: One other challenge for Shared disk is the need to coordinate and maintain cache consistency across nodes. Each node requires maintaining a consistent view of data and therefore, needs to maintain a consistent cache. Maintaining this cache consistency can incur high communication overhead among the nodes.

7.2.3 Shared Nothing

In a shared nothing architecture, each database process has access to its own private memory, CPU, and dedicated disk devices. Each node contains its own exclusive processes and subset of the database, and is responsible to maintain it. Each node is under the control of its own copy of the operating system and thus can act as a server for their own subset of data in distributed database software.

This architecture enables the simple workloads application to achieve the linear scale-up and high-availability, which provides careful partitioning and replication of data across different nodes. It also provides better design with data warehousing workloads since queries can easily be distributed over multiple nodes based on the data each node likes to process. It also yields to improve data locality.

This kind of architecture is very well suited and significantly easier to implement for kind of a system that focuses to maximize read-centric (i.e., write once read many) workloads.

This architecture allows operating with full raw memory and disk performance since the CPU, disk, memory, and all other resources are dedicated to each local server.

Shared nothing architectures offers great benefits:

1. **Reduce Conflicts**: It allows reducing interference and resource conflicts by minimizing resource sharing.

2. **High Scalability**: It offers great scalability and can easily support a large number of nodes compared to shared everything architecture.

3. **Reduced I/O Bottleneck**: This also offers a solution to the major database I/O bottleneck problem and solves the drawback of requiring each I/O to pass through a single interconnection network.

TABLE 7.1 Difference Transactional and Analytical Systems

Transactional Systems	Analytical Systems
Strict consistency is required	Consistency requirements are relaxed. Eventual consistency is desired
Data is according to a proper schema	Data may not follow a schema
Data is normalized	Data may not be normalized
Data update is quite common	Normally write once read many architecture is followed

Shared nothing clusters have the advantage of a simpler consistency model; however, the complete decoupling of all resources introduces following complexities and limitations in the architecture:

1. **Higher Coordination**: It requires a two-phase commit protocol and may need to coordinate transactions across multiple nodes. This coordination incurs complexity and potentially results with transactional performance problems.

2. **Difficulty in Balancing Load**: Load balancing becomes difficult to implement for shared nothing architecture.

3. **Limited Extensibility**: It also requires careful partitioning to ensure that the cluster workload remains balanced. This limits extensibility as adding or removing nodes from the cluster requires an expensive re-balancing.

Out of the three types of systems, shared disk and shared everything are more appropriate for parallel databases. This is because of their greater infrastructural support to provide ACID guarantees. In comparison, shared nothing architecture is a loosely connected system. The cost to ensure ACID properties may be higher due to higher communication delay.

However, as we have learned in chapter 1 that many big data systems are analytical systems and therefore they do not require compliance to ACID properties.

In the next section, we will study reasons for emergence of NoSQL (Not Only SQL) systems.

7.3 EMERGENCE OF NOSQL SYSTEMS

Data-intensive systems could either based on transactional systems or they could be based on analytical systems. Transactional systems are mainly deployed on RDBMS. They have important requirements of consistency. Data is according to a proper schema, and it is normalized. In comparison, analytical systems have relaxed requirements of consistency, data is not necessarily according to a proper format and schema, and it may not be normalized. Table 7.1 summarizes the difference between the types of systems.

When the use and applications of analytical systems emerged, it was felt that storing such data in RDBMS would be an overkill. This is because many such systems have write once and read many architecture.

Analytical systems are more likely to utilize shared nothing architecture. In such systems, a query can be divided across multiple hosts. A prime objective of such systems is to provide fault tolerance by supporting uninterrupted execution of service. They also have relaxed requirements for distributed locking and commit. As analytical systems are more appropriate for data-intensive applications, two types of platforms can be adopted:

1. Parallel Databases with shared nothing architecture.

2. NoSQL systems, which are distributed and non-relational data storage systems.

In databases relying on shared nothing architecture [282, 342], a table is horizontally divided across multiple nodes. The division can be implemented either in a round robin manner or through hashing of indexes. Distributing indexes is beneficial for distributed query processing gives advantages of distributed query processing and heavy storage. Results of queries from individual nodes are merged and shuffled to process final results. These databases have fast retrieval capabilities, which are aided through advancements in indexing such as B-trees.

In comparison, NoSQL systems such as MapReduce [154], Hadoop, MongoDB [140], and Cassandra [234] do not support a descriptive SQL language for query processing. The storage is normally provided through a distributed storage, which is spanned across a large number of machines.

The lack of strong consistency in NoSQL (which are also referred to as MR-like) systems has been debated in the research community. NoSQL systems appeared to be inspired from the CAP theorem [111], which states that out of the three characteristics of consistency, availability, and no partition, only two can be achieved at a time by a distributed system. However, in a blog, Abadi [74] highlighted some potential problems in the CAP theorem. Abadi argued that it is not necessary that consistency be compromised only to achieve availability. Instead, consistency may also be compromised for latency.

7.3.1 Column-Oriented vs Row-Oriented Databases

A database can store data in two ways, i.e., row-wise and column-wise. Column-oriented databases store their data in a columnar fashion which we will discuss in section 7.6. Columnar databases can provide faster operations for analytical systems where data from specific columns is required to be read or analyzed. Comparatively, row-wise databases can provide improved results where read operations are spread on multiple columns or write operations are frequent. Example 7.2 illustrates the difference between these two types.

7.3.2 Types of NoSQL Systems

NoSQL systems have provided well established platforms for big data. They can be represented as following four types:

1. Key-value Database

2. Document-oriented Database

3. Column-oriented Database

4. Graph Database

We now discuss these four types in detail.

Understanding Difference Between Column-Oriented vs Row-Oriented Databases

Example 7.2 (Column-Oriented vs Row-Oriented Databases).

ID	Name	City	Age
1	Michael	Chicago	27
2	Sara	London	30
3	Ahmed	Karachi	29
4	Vishanti	Mumbai	28
5	Xiang	Beijing	25

Representation using Row-oriented

1,Michael,Chicago,27;2,Sara,   London,30;3,Ahmed,Karachi,29;4,Vishanti,   Mumbai,28;5,Xiang,Beijing,25

Representation using column-oriented

1,2,3,4,5;Michael,Sara,Ahmed,Vishanti,Xiang;Chicago,London,Karachi,   Mumbai,Beijing;27,30,29,28,25

Column-oriented or Columnar databases are useful for aggregation type of queries. For instance, let us consider if the average of "Age" is required to compute. Then for column-oriented databases, the "Age" column can be read and average can be computed. Comparatively, for a row-oriented database, data will be first collected row by row and then the aggregate function will be applied.

Further, for columnar databases, since the data type for each column is same, we can get better compression results. This will lead to faster query processing.

In comparison, row-oriented databases are useful when data is required to be read from multiple columns. They are also useful for transactional systems, where new rows are frequently added to the database.

7.4   KEY-VALUE DATABASE

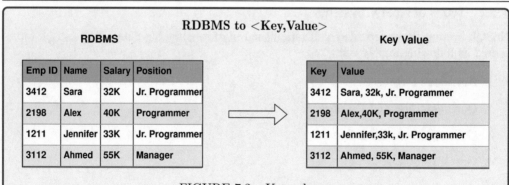

FIGURE 7.2 <Key,value>

Example 7.3 (RDBMS to <Key,Value>). *Figure 7.2 shows <key,value> pairs related to an RDBMS.*

A key-value database is one of the simplest NoSQL databases. Data is represented as a collection of <key,value> pairs. It works by storing buckets of <key,value> pairs in a logical way in which all relevant data relating to an item are stored within that item. A key can have a dynamic set of attributes attached to it. It has an ability to store an enormous number of records with extremely low-latency and provides all the maintenance and failover services.

Example 7.3 shows how an RDBMS system can be represented as a key-value system. In that, primary key (unique key) of RDBMS has been mapped as a key in the key-value storage, whereas all the other columns have been mapped as values.

7.4.1 Strengths

There are numerous advantages of a key-value database:

1. It provides a simple mechanism to store and represent data.

2. It has scalability as it does not require data from multiple tables. A key-value database can scale easily as compared to an RDBMS.

3. It can handle truly massive amounts of network traffic.

4. It can handle a massive number of records and large volume of state changes per second with millions of simultaneous users through distributed processing and distributed storage.

5. A key-value database has built in redundancy. That is, there are no single points of failures and the database can handle the failure of storage nodes without bringing down the whole application.

6. It is programmer friendly and can be accessed easily through API.

7.4.2 Limitations

Key-value databases have a few limitations. These are described below:

1. It does not have the richness of a query language similar to SQL and does not support range queries.

2. The values in the key-value database are opaque to the database which means that we cannot index and query by the fields of values.

3. Transaction guarantees are generally available in the context of a single key put in a <key,value> store.

4. A relational database uses integrity constraints to prevent invalid data and ensure that data at the lowest level have integrity. It means that data that violate integrity constraints cannot exist in the database. However, a key-value database typically does not support these constraints.

5. In comparison with other NoSQL databases, it provides a simple and limited set of operations.

7.4.3 Use Cases

We will now study a few use cases for key-value databases. A key-value database is best applicable in following scenarios:

1. For on-demand, high-end, large-scale, data.

2. For storing indeterminate form of data which cannot be easily stored in relational databases. For instance, HTML pages normally have different structures with optional headers, tables, and images. A key-value database does not require a schema, and can therefore store this kind of data.

3. For modeling rich and complex data that cannot be easily modeled in an RDBMS.

4. <key,value> pairs are useful for data where the relationship among multiple subsets does not exist. For instance, bank, account, and transaction are all related and can be saved in relational databases for a single application. On the contrary, log files and cached application data is not related to each other. However, this data is required to be stored for an application. Storing these unrelated data types in a key-value database would be easier since no relations are ever going to be modeled between them.

5. When large datasets are required to be stored. Such datasets are easier to be stored in key-value databases as these can easily be spread out across multiple servers.

6. For rapid and agile development.

7. When aggregate information is to be computed. For instance, counts, sum, and similar kind of operation on normalized data. Similarly, finding most popular items, votes, ratings, session data, some statistics are a few useful examples.

8. For applications which needs easier and simpler storage and retrieval. This is because it is easier to store and retrieve data from <key,value> pairs.

Some examples of this type of databases are Redis [121], Riak [90], Amazon DynamoDB [332], and Voldemort [126].

7.4.4 Amazon DynamoDB

As an example of key-value databases, we will study Amazon DynamoDB [332]. It is a distributed key-value storage with important features of scalability and availability.

1. **Components of DynamoDB**: DynamoDB has following important components:

   (a) **Tables**: Data is stored in tables. Each table consist of items.

   (b) **Item**: A table may have zero or more items. Items in DynamoDB are in many aspects similar to what columns in RDBMS.

   (c) **Attributes**: Items have values, which are represented as attributes. Nested attributes are also possible.

   DynamoDB is schema-less, i.e., in a table, different attributes are possible for two different data items. However, each item in a table has a unique identifier, which is denoted by primary key.

   We can better understand these concepts through example 7.4

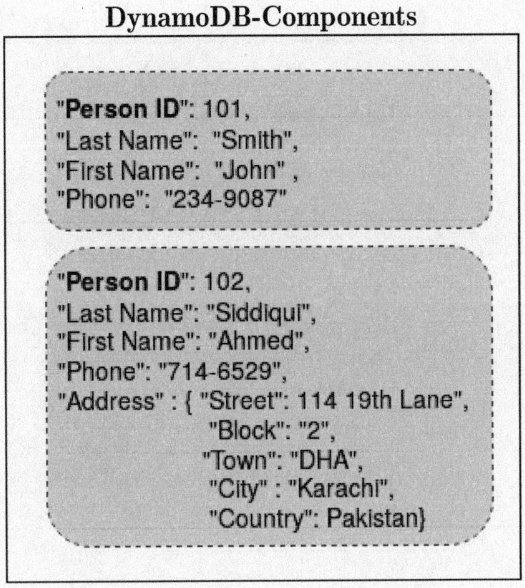

DynamoDB-Components

"**Person ID**": 101,
"Last Name": "Smith",
"First Name": "John",
"Phone": "234-9087"

"**Person ID**": 102,
"Last Name": "Siddiqui",
"First Name": "Ahmed",
"Phone": "714-6529",
"Address" : { "Street": "114 19th Lane",
             "Block": "2",
             "Town": "DHA",
             "City" : "Karachi",
             "Country": Pakistan}

FIGURE 7.3 DynamoDB

Example 7.4 (Components of DynamoDB). *Figure 7.3 illustrates different components of DynamoDB. The People's table has two items. Both of them are uniquely identified by a primary key. The second item has an additional address field, which is nested and contains many attributes.*

A simple primary key with one attribute also serves as a partition key for DynamoDB. Partition key is used to compute a hash function which determines the actual placement of physical storage where the item will be stored. In DynamoDB, a composite primary key is also possible. In that, two attributes are used as a primary key. The first attribute serves as a partition key, whereas the second attribute serves as a sort key. All items with the same partition key are stored together in the location in the order defined by the sort key. Example 7.5 illustrates the concept of composite key in DynamoDB.

2. **Read Operations**: DynamoDB supports two types of read operations. An eventually consistent read and a strict consistent read. When a read operation is initiated in DynamoDB, by default an eventually consistent read operation is performed. This implies that the read operation may not return the most recent data; it may return stale data, which could be 20 seconds stale. Strictly consistent read may not be available for some data.

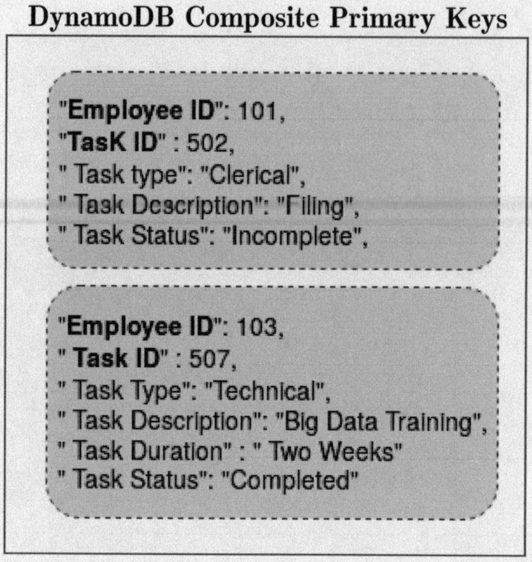

DynamoDB Composite Primary Keys

"**Employee ID**": 101,
"**TasK ID**" : 502,
" Task type": "Clerical",
" Task Description": "Filing",
" Task Status": "Incomplete",

"**Employee ID**": 103,
" **Task ID**" : 507,
" Task Type": "Technical",
" Task Description": "Big Data Training",
" Task Duration" : " Two Weeks"
" Task Status": "Completed"

FIGURE 7.4 DynamoDB – composite primary keys

Example 7.5 (DynamoDB Composite Primary Keys). *Figure 7.4 illustrates the concept of composite primary keys in DynamoDB. Two items have been shown. Both have a composite primary key, consisting of Employee ID and Task ID.*

3. **Write operation**: In Amazon DynamoDB, writes are strictly consistent. In general, data is replicated along three different nodes in a partition. When a read operation is requested, the query is first written to a leader node from where it is propagated to the other two nodes. A confirmation message is only generated when all three nodes confirm the write operation.

7.5 DOCUMENT-ORIENTED DATABASE

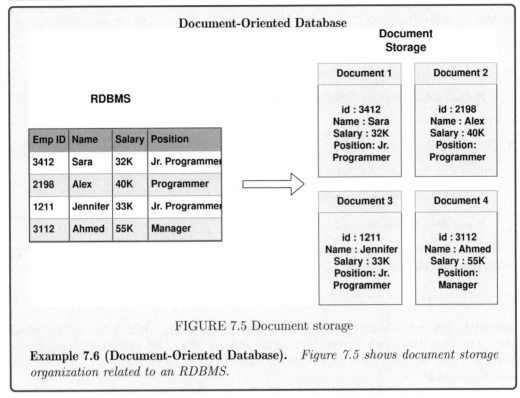

FIGURE 7.5 Document storage

Example 7.6 (Document-Oriented Database). *Figure 7.5 shows document storage organization related to an RDBMS.*

A document-oriented database extends the concept of a key-value database by employing flexible data structures, which do not require predefined schemas. These databases store records as "documents" and support nested and complex structure documents to define subcategories of information. For a document database, the basic atomic stored unit is a document.

There are a few major differences between document databases and key-value databases. First, a document database organizes documents into related sets called **collections**. This is similar to the concept of tables. A document itself is analogous to a row in a relational database. In comparison, a key-value database stores all <key,value> pairs collectively in a single namespace. Secondly, the data values in a key-value database are opaque to the store, whereas the data values in a document-oriented database are transparent to the store.

7.5.1 Strengths

Document databases can offer the following advantages for the users:

1. The price of scaling out with a document database is much less, compared to a SQL database.

2. Since the data is transparent to the store, these databases can index the fields of documents which allows the user to query not only by the primary key but also by a document's contents.

3. Provides the ability to do extremely rapid application development.

4. Schemaless, completely free to define the contents of a document.

7.5.2 Limitations

Besides the powerful query engines and indexing features, there are few limitations:

1. This database is not suitable for business transaction application.

2. It does not offer joins across collections.

3. It does not offer any referential integrity support.

7.5.3 Use Cases

Document databases are a great solution for many use cases including:

1. When data is heavily document-oriented and makes more sense.

2. When data is unstructured.

Some well-known examples of document databases are MongoDB [86], Couchbase [112], and CouchDB [241].

7.5.4 MongoDB

MongoDB is a non-relational, open-source, NoSQL database, which relies on document storage to store data. This implies that all the data in MongoDB is stored in documents. MongoDB provides a few services of relational databases such as sorting, secondary indexing, and range queries.

MongoDB is a scalable database which relies on scaling out. This means that more computing nodes can be added easily.

1. **Data Representation**: As discussed, MongoDB is a document-style database. Document-style is analogous to the concept of row in RDBMS. Documents in MongoDB are stored in JavaScript Object Notation (JSON) format [140]. In MongoDB, a **Collection** is a group of documents. This is analogous to a table in RDBMS.

Document Storage in MongoDB

Example 7.7 (Document Storage in MongoDB). *In this example, we will learn some of the valid and invalid styles of representing <key,value> pairs in MongoDB documents.*

```
{"Student" : "John, Smith"}.
```

Here, the document contains a key "student", with a value "John Smith".
Multiple <Key,Values>:
Multiple keys in a document can also be included but they must be unique. For instance, following is a valid representation:

```
{"Student" : "John, Smith", "City": "Cleveland
    "}
```

Duplicate Keys:
Duplicate keys are not allowed. For instance,

```
{"Student" : "John, Smith", "Student": "John,
    Smith"}
```

Case-Sensitive:
Keys are case-sensitive. Therefore,

```
{"Student" : "John, Smith", "student": "John,
    Smith"}
```

are valid <key,value> pairs.

---

2. **Indexing and Sharding**: MongoDB supports indexing of data for fast query processing. Documents are indexed according to keywords for faster access and retrieval.

Understanding Sharding

Example 7.8 (Understanding Sharding). *In a DBMS, sharding (or index sharding) is the process of splitting a database across multiple machines. Sharding is the process of splitting the data into small chunks and storing them into partitions such that each partition stores a few chunks. The process is also called as* **partitioning**. *Sharding increases scalability of the system as more data is possible to be stored. It also enhances speed of execution as parallelism can be incorporated.*
As the size of dataset grows, sharding can be incorporated to distribute the data across multiple nodes and meet scalability requirements.
Using sharding, data can either be divided horizontally or it can be divided vertically. Vertical sharding implies that a table is divided across columns, whereas, horizontal sharding means that data is divided into rows. Vertical sharding is more efficient for data searching and querying as data is divided into columns. By dividing data across different machines more data can be stored.
Manual process of sharding can cause challenges. This is because as size of the cluster grows data is needed to be handled dynamically.

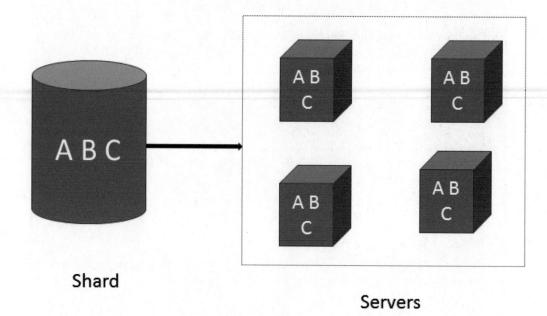

Shard

Servers

FIGURE 7.6 MongoDB – replication [139]

MongoDB incorporates auto-sharding, through which a MongoDB cluster can split data and re-balance automatically. The automatic sharding feature provides following benefits [250]:

(a) Automatic balancing of data.

(b) Scaling out with minimal down time, i.e., new hosts can be added.

(c) Replication to avoid single point of failure.

(d) A robust failover mechanism to avoid downtime.

A **shard** consists of one or more servers that contains the subset of data that it is responsible for. For instance, if we had a cluster containing data of 100,000 users, one shard may contain data of 20,000 users. If there are more than one servers in a shard then a shard may also contain replicated data.

MongoDB uses keys (also called as **shard key**), which can be any field or combination of fields. For partitioning, a shard key is specified which specifies fields upon which data will be distributed. Because of shard key, chunks can be described as a triple of $<$collection, key$_{min}$, and key$_{max} >$.

Maximum size of a chunk is 200 MB. Once a Chunk grows to a maximum size of 200 MB, it can be split into new chunks.

We can get the basic idea about the architecture of MongoDB replication from figure 7.6. A shard containing data "ABC" is represented as a cylinder, whereas, data is replicated across multiple servers, which are represented as cubical boxes.

To evenly distribute data across shards, MongoDB may transfer chunks of data from one shard to another shard. The data which may be copied depends upon the key of data selected.

```
{"ID" : K001-12 , "Name" : "Abdul", "DoB" : 15-12-2000}
{"ID" : K002-12 , "Name" : "Ahmed", "DoB" : 18-11-2000}
{"ID" : K003-12 , "Name" : "Anisha", "DoB" : 15-12-2000}
{"ID" : K001-11 , "Name" : "Bob", "DoB" : 18-11-2000}
{"ID" : K002-14 , "Name" : "Christine", "DoB" : 15-12-2000}
{"ID" : K004-13 , "Name" : "Jeniffer", "DoB" : 18-11-2000}
{"ID" : L001-11 , "Name" : "Kim", "DoB" : 15-12-2000}
{"ID" : L002-10 , "Name" : "Li Hao", "DoB" : 18-11-2000}
{"ID" : L002-11 , "Name" : "Melissa", "DoB" : 15-12-2000}
{"ID" : P002-10 , "Name" : "Otiquo", "DoB" : 18-11-2000}
{"ID" : P001-12 , "Name" : "Paul", "DoB" : 15-12-2000}
{"ID" : K004-12 , "Name" : "Ravinder", "DoB" : 18-11-2000}
{"ID" : P004-12 , "Name" : "Salman", "DoB" : 15-12-2000}
{"ID" : P005-12 , "Name" : "Sam", "DoB" : 18-11-2000}
{"ID": P006-12 , "Name" : "Wing", "DoB" : 15-12-2000}
{"ID": K005-12 , "Name" : "Xue", "DoB" : 18-11-2000}
{"ID": K006-12 , "Name" : "Zafar", "DoB" : 18-11-2000}
{"ID": K006-12 , "Name" : "Zuli", "DoB" : 18-11-2000}
```

FIGURE 7.7 Sharding in MongoDB

MongoDB automatically balances data across all shards. Each shard contains multiple ranges in order to reduce the amount of transferred data. We can consider a range as a collection of keys such that each shard could contain multiple ranges.

To understand the whole scenario of data splitting and auto-sharding, let us consider example 7.9, which is based on a database of students containing their IDs, Names, and DoB (Date of Birth).

Auto Sharding in MongoDB

Example 7.9 (Auto Sharding in MongoDB). *In figure 7.7, there are 18 records. Let us suppose if the data is sharded in to three shards such that names in the range [A-J]^a are in shard 01, [K-R] in shard 02, and [S-Z] in shard 03. This division provides balanced load in each shard. Now let's suppose if the number of records increases such that both shard 01 and shard 02 have 12 records each, whereas the number of records remain unchanged in shard 03. Since the total records are now 30, a naive way is to move two records from shard 1 to shard 2 and then four records from shard 2 to shard 3. In this manner, six records are to be moved. As an alternative, if another shard is to be added, then in total eight records (four each from shard 1 and shard 2) can be moved such that shard 1 and shard 2 will contain eight records each, whereas shard 3 and shard 4 will have seven records each.*

In order to reduce the amount of data transfer, another approach is to define multiple ranges in shards. In this manner, multiple ranges can be stored in each shard. So instead of [A-J], shard 1 can have two chunks [A-G] and [H-J]. The size or the range of the chunk can be adjusted on need basis. In this case, two records from shard 1 can be directly moved out to shard 3. Similarly, chunks at shard 2 can be divided in this manner, two records each from shard 1 and shard 2 can be moved to shard 3. Thus we can observe that the total number of records to be moved can be reduced to 4 records.

---

^aHere "[' and ']" denote inclusive bounds

MongoDB supports auto-sharding. The cluster manages the splitting of the data and rebalancing automatically. This removes some of the administrative headaches of manual sharding.

7.6 COLUMN-ORIENTED DATABASE

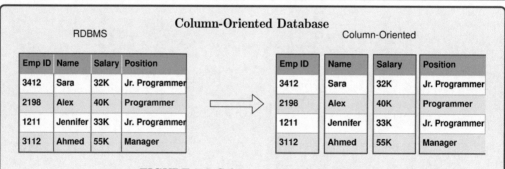

FIGURE 7.8 Column-oriented database

Example 7.10 (Column-Oriented Database). *Figure 7.8 shows column-oriented organization related to an RDBMS.*

A column-oriented database stores its content by column as opposed to by row and serializes all of the values of a column together. A columnar database aims to efficiently retrieve or write data from hard disk storage in order to speed up the time it takes to return a query.

7.6.1 Strengths

Column-oriented database can offer the following advantages:

1. Because the data stored in columns is typically similar and the columns are stored adjacent to one another, the compression algorithms make use of this similarity of adjacent data for highly data compression and help storage capacity to be used more efficiently.

2. The compression of data can greatly enhance the performance by reducing the disk I/O for reading large amount of repeating values. This improves query performance by greatly reducing the I/O required to execute analytical queries.

3. A Columnstore index achieve high query performance on aggregation queries such as AVG, SUM, MAX, MIN, and COUNT. This is due to the fact that the number of hard disk seeks are reduced as compared to row-based databases.

4. Column-oriented databases are more efficient for inserting a single column values at once as this can be written efficiently without affecting any other columns for the rows. This is in contrast with row-oriented databases which are more efficient for writing a new row if all of the column data is supplied at the same time.

5. The quick searching, scanning, and aggregation abilities of column-oriented database storage are highly efficient for analytics.

7.6.2 Limitations

The column-oriented databases has following limitations:

1. Column-oriented databases are not useful for systems that require ACID transactions. They are significantly slower at handling such transactions.

2. Write operations such as INSERT or UPDATE are relatively slow in comparison with row-oriented or row store databases due to the number of disk seeks required to insert or update a row. Writing to a row requires seeking to each column for an insert or multi-column update in contrast to a row-oriented database where the entire row can write at once.

3. Column-oriented databases are not useful for systems with wildly varying queries.

7.6.3 Use Cases

Column-oriented databases are designed for use cases such as:

1. Column-oriented database are more suited for data warehousing applications and it is how they are utilized presently in the industry.

2. Column-oriented database may also be utilized for online analytical processing (OLAP) systems.

3. Column-oriented database may perform much better when writes are uncommon and usage involves small set of column retrieval and column aggregation. They can speed up analytical queries of the data by reading only columns which need to be read.

Cassandra [234], HBase [176], and Amazon SimpleDB [125] are popular examples of column-storage databases.

TABLE 7.2 RDBMS vs Cassandra Notations

RDBMS	Cassandra
Database	Keyspace
Table	Column Family (CF)
Primary Key	Row Key
Column Name	Column Name
Column Value	Column Value

7.6.4 Apache Cassandra

In this section, we will study about Cassandra, which is a column-based distributed NoSQL data storage developed by Facebook.

Cassandra has been developed to meet the storage needs of Inbox search at Facebook. The feature allows Facebook users to search for messages in their Inbox. The requirement was to scale the system with the increase in number of users and to provide high throughput with billions of writes per day. Since Facebook users are scattered around the globe, an important requirement was to replicate data across various data centers in order to reduce access latency.

1. **Data Model**: A table in Cassandra can be distributed across various nodes. Data model of Cassandra consists of keys and values. Each attribute is stored as a key, where the value represents the actual value corresponding to that key. Cassandra implements a flexible approach in which there may be few optional values in data so some rows may have more attributes as compared to other rows.

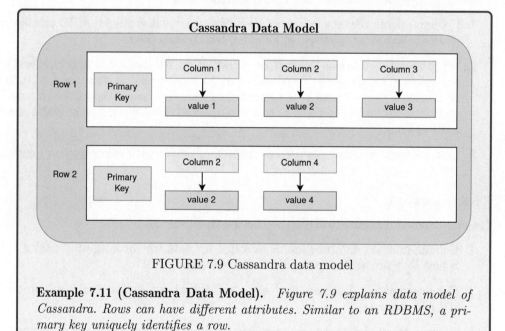

FIGURE 7.9 Cassandra data model

Example 7.11 (Cassandra Data Model). *Figure 7.9 explains data model of Cassandra. Rows can have different attributes. Similar to an RDBMS, a primary key uniquely identifies a row.*

Table 7.2 explains different notations for Cassandra.

Cassandra partitions the data using consistent hashing. Using this method, each hash value is mapped to a distinct Cassandra node. We should recall from our fundamental concepts of hashing that in consistent hashing, nodes are organized in the form of a circle. To find the mapping location of a data item, its hash value is used to find the first node which maps the item. Scalability is achieved by adding more nodes in a circle. Upon addition of a node, a portion of data items are remapped. The number of data items which are needed to be remapped are determined using the two neighboring nodes of the new node.

By employing consistent hashing, Cassandra achieves scalability.

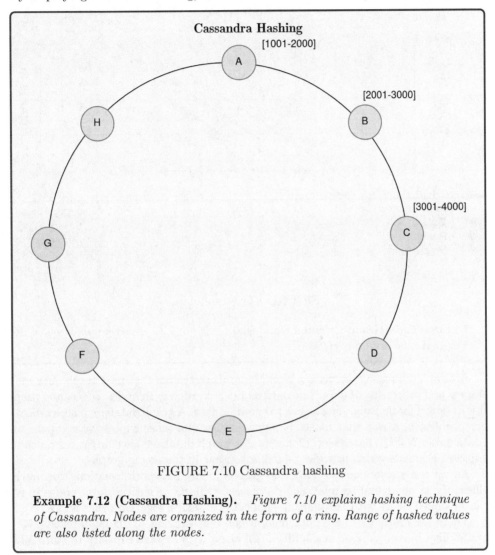

FIGURE 7.10 Cassandra hashing

Example 7.12 (Cassandra Hashing). *Figure 7.10 explains hashing technique of Cassandra. Nodes are organized in the form of a ring. Range of hashed values are also listed along the nodes.*

In Cassandra, the primary key is used to determine a hash value. For this reason, the primary key is also called as the **partition key**. If the primary key consists of composite entities, then the first component is used to determine the partition.

2. **Replication**: Cassandra replicates data items to achieve high scalability and durability. Each data item is replicated N times, where N is the replication factor defined in the system. Each key has a coordinator node, which ensures that the data item is distributed to the remaining N-1 replicas.

7.7 GRAPH DATABASE

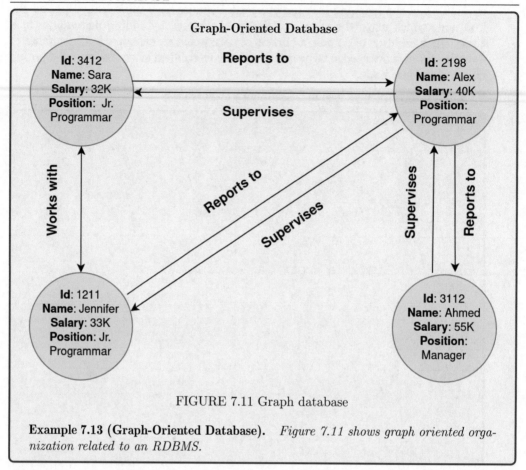

FIGURE 7.11 Graph database

Example 7.13 (Graph-Oriented Database). *Figure 7.11 shows graph oriented organization related to an RDBMS.*

A Graph database systems is a NoSQL database system that uses graph data model for storage and processing of data. The data model is a graph with nodes, edges, and properties. It is designed for lightning-fast access to complex data. A graph database enables us to model our problem in a way that makes it much simpler and more expressive compare to other relational or NoSQL databases. Elements of a graph database have direct reference to their adjacent elements which provides added advantage in traversing graphs.

As we can see in example 7.13, the graphs model real-world relationships much more efficiently as compared to relational databases. Objects or entities form nodes in a graph can be added easily with relationship connections linking together other nodes.

There are graph database implementations that provide ACID guarantees [272], high-availability, horizontal read scalability [326] along with storage capacity to store billions of entities.

7.7.1 Strengths

The strength of graph databases are as follows:

1. Graph databases have the ability to store various types of graphs: undirected graphs, weighted graphs, hypergraphs, etc.

2. Graph data models performs a good job when creating rich and highly connected data to represent the real world use cases and applications.

3. They have the ability to efficiently manage highly connected data and complex queries irrespective of the size of dataset.

4. The underlying model of graph database provides the functionality of graph theory and can easily handle complex and flexible data models.

5. Graph databases are optimized for local graph traversals and provides exceptional performances for local reads by traversing the graph.

6. Graph databases are very good for storing entities and the information about the relationships between these entities.

7.7.2 Limitations

Besides the numerous advantages, there a few limitations of using graph databases:

1. Graph databases are not the best solutions for applications of very large volumes of data or for updating sets of data.

2. The strength of a graph database is in traversing the connections between the nodes and generally require all data to fit on one machine. However, this becomes the limitation for graph database scalability. Also, many off-the-shelf graph databases are also not horizontally scalable. Therefore, applications for graphs have limited usage for large volume application.

3. Because data is connected by nature, scaling a graph becomes more difficult compared to other NoSQL databases. Scaling graph data by distributing it across multiple machines is not easy. Similarly, relationships that span across nodes make graph distribution much more difficult.

4. Graph databases are more suitable for visualization and understanding relationships instead of storing transactions. For instance, using a graph database to store transactions of a grocery store is not viable. However, a graph database can effectively capture and present a customer's spending patterns.

5. Large graphs can be partitioned to be deployed over a distributed cluster. However, partitioning a graph sometimes is not easy because of the factors including high network latency, access patterns in the graph, and real-time evolution of the graph.

7.7.3 Use Cases

Graph-based systems are increasingly used to store and process big data. Graph theory has been effective and significant in many problems across various domains. Graphs can be applied to many real world applications. Social networks such as Facebook, Twitter, and LinkedIn can be represented as graph-based systems, where each profile (or a user) denotes a vertex and their relationships are edges of the graph. Similarly, the World Wide Web is the biggest representation of a real graph, in which each URL denotes a vertex and the outlinks of the URL are edges of the graph.

Other applications such as employee-task relationship, shortest path from one location to another, and flow management for an oil pipeline are also represented as graphs.

TABLE 7.3 Usage of Graph-based Databases

Applications	Usage
Social Networking	These applications allow organizations to identify direct and indirect relationships between people, groups, and activities. Graph databases are typically go-to database for social networking by making it simple to discover how a person is connected to another person within a group or an organization. Many large and successful social networks organizations use graph databases at their core, which allows to quickly traverse through a social graph and return query results at a high-speed.
Recommendation Systems	A recommendation system helps users by providing suggestions for their products or services based on user behavior or preference. Graph databases are naturally well-suited for building recommendation engines. These databases have the ability to make an effective recommendation. Although relational databases can be used to represent such kind of data structure, graph databases are actually built to solve this kind of problem and widely used in regards to performance and maintainability.
Authorization and Access Control	A graph database has the ability to manage access to content and manage relationships between users, groups, assets, and collections. It can traverse millions of relationships per second to execute queries in milliseconds and can access lookups over large and complex structures.

Some of the most common graph database use cases are mentioned in table 7.3. In addition, graph database is a great solution for many other use cases including the following:

1. Query performance and responsiveness are generally main concerns with regard to the data platforms for many organizations. Applications like online transactional system or enterprise web applications typically require to response the user queries in milliseconds. However, as the size of the dataset increases, the joins operation becomes more challenging and the query performance deteriorates. Apparently, graph databases have no such penalties and turn complex joins into fast graph traversals by scaling query times and maintaining millisecond performance irrespective of the overall size of the dataset. Therefore, if application has joint pain, that's another indicator that graph databases will be a better choice and solution to a complex data model in a relational database.

2. A graph database is best used for exploring data that are structured like a graph, tree, or a hierarchical and the relationships between entities are significant. Graph data also useful for application domain having complex data and highly connected model, for example social network, healthcare, real-time logistics etc.

3. Graph databases are also useful for applications which require a lot of graph-centric querying. For example, they work best for analyzing queries like how closely things are related, how many steps are required to get from one point to another etc.

4. Graph databases are also fit good for data visualization including how things are connected together. Analyzing relationships between people in social networking sites such as in Facebook, Twitter, and LinkedIn are typical use cases for graph databases.

A few of the well-known examples of graph database are Apache Giraph [305], Neo4j [362], OrientDB [351], HyperGraphDB [204], and AllegroGraph [72].

7.7.4 Apache Giraph

Apache Giraph [138] is a distributed system for graph processing. Input to Giraph could be from any text file or source such as HDFS. Input is in the form of tuple consisting of <vertex, edges, and relationships>.

Large graphs G<V,E,R> incorporates **Vertex Partitioning**, i.e., graph is partitioned with respect to vertices. This is contrary to the **Edge Partitioning** approach in which a graph is partitioned with respect to edges.

For computation, Giraph relies on Bulk Synchronous Parallel (BSP) mode of operation. The BSP model is used in many graph processing systems such as Pregel [258, 374] and GraphHP [132].

Using this model, large scale computation is decomposed into a series of iterations. Each iteration is termed as a *superstep*. Each *superstep* involves computation on multiple worker nodes. After each superstep, worker nodes exchange messages for synchronization. The message exchange involves receiving value from neighbors and updating own value based on the value received from the neighbor. The updated value is also sent to the neighbors, which becomes available to them in the next iteration. At the end of the message exchange, each worker node can decide to be active or halt its state.

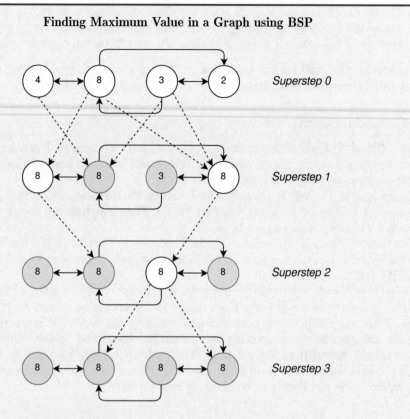

FIGURE 7.12 Supersteps to determine maximum value

Example 7.14 (Finding maximum value in a graph). *Figure 7.12 illustrates an example of finding maximum value in a graph consisting of four nodes. Solid arrows indicate neighbor relationship, whereas dotted lines indicate communication. Shaded node indicates that a node has decided to halt. A node can become re-active after deciding to halt.*

7.8 CONCLUDING REMARKS

NoSQL systems have emerged as an alternate to RDBMS systems. The main focus of these systems is to achieve targets of scalability and availability, while facilitating data analytics. In this chapter, we have studied four types of NoSQL systems. We have also studied examples, strengths, limitations, and case studies for each of them. New NoSQL systems are being developed to cater emerging needs of big data systems of flexibility, scalability, and analytics.

7.9 FURTHER READING

A survey of NoSQL systems is presented in reference [190]
    Details about Cassandra can be found in reference [234].
    Details about different graph-based systems is explained in references [138, 306].
    NoSQL systems have been compared with document storage systems in reference [239].

Document storage system Riak has been explained in reference [385]. Riak and Redis have been compared in reference [90].

MongoDB has been discussed in detail [86, 140, 141].

Couchbase has been explained in reference [112]. CouchDB has been explained in references [82, 241].

HBase has been discussed in reference [176], whereas Amazon SimpleDB has been discussed in reference [125].

Details about Graph-based systems can be found in respective references. Apache Giraph [138, 259, 305, 306], Neo4j [362], OrientDB [158, 221, 351], HyperGraphDB [72, 96, 204], and Allegrograph [24].

7.10   EXERCISE QUESTIONS

1. Differentiate between RDBMS and NoSQL databases.

2. Explain why a graph database will yield lower performance when it is deployed over a distributed cluster?

3. Describe how a bulk synchronous parallel mode is useful for graph databases?

4. Explain why RDBMS are suitable for transactional systems?

5. Is it possible to ensure ACID guarantees for analytical systems?

6. Describe how column-oriented databases are useful for aggregation?

7. Explain strengths and weaknesses for <key,value> storage.

8. Explain scenarios where document-oriented databases are useful.

9. Describe deriving factors behind popularity of NoSQL systems.

10. Explain how MongoDB performs sharding?

11. How Cassandra achieves scalability?

GLOSSARY

ArangoDB: It is an open-source, highly available, scalable, and multi-model database that can handle key-values, graphs, and JSON documents.

Cassandra: It is an open-source column-based distributed NoSQL data storage initially developed by Facebook.

Column-Based System: It is a type of NoSQL system in which data is organized in columns instead of rows.

Document Based System: It is a type of NoSQL system in which data is organized in the form of documents.

Edge Partitioning: It is a graph partitioning method in which a graph is partitioned on edges.

Graph Based System: It is a type of NoSQL system in which data is represented as a graph. Nodes represent the data items, whereas edges represent relationships between them.

Key-value: It is a type of NoSQL system in which data is stored in the form of <key,value> pairs.

MongoDB: It is an open-source NoSQL document-oriented database supports automatic sharding and MapReduce operations.

NoSQL: (aka "not only SQL") It is a data storage system in which data is stored differently than traditional relational form and provide flexible schemas.

SQL: Structured query language; It is a language for accessing and manipulating data from relational databases.

Sharding: It is a process of distributing a database over multiple nodes.

Shared Nothing Systems: It is a type of cluster arrangement in which participating nodes do not share anything; neither the memory nor the storage.

Shared Disk Systems: It is a type of cluster arrangement in which participating nodes share common storage.

Shared Memory Systems: In such a system participating nodes are arranged in the form of a cluster such that they share memory.

Vertex Partitioning: It is a method of partitioning large graphs in which a graph is partitioned on a vertex.

NewSQL Systems

CONTENTS

N EWSQL databases are designed for specific applications relying on different underlying mathematical models while offering unique benefits. In this chapter, we will provide a detailed explanation about NewSQL systems and its types. The chapter also includes a few case studies of NewSQL systems. Various examples are also included for explanation.

8.1 INTRODUCTION

In section 7, we have studied NoSQL systems. A NoSQL system is generally optimized to meet the scalability needs of big data. Scalability is achieved at the expense of consistency such that eventual consistency techniques have been implemented. Such models are suitable for OLAP (Online Analytical Processing). However, with the increased usage of big data systems, use of OLTP (Online Transaction Processing) systems have also increased. NewSQL systems are a kind of big data DBMS which provide consistency requirements of DBMS and are capable to meet scalability requirements of big data.

These databases are a set of new relational databases that provide improved performance while incorporating the use of the SQL language. These systems intend to promote the same performance and scalability improvement of NoSQL systems, while meeting the relational and ACID (Atomicity, Consistency, Isolation, Durability) compliance of traditional databases. In this chapter, we will study generalized architecture of NewSQL systems and will also study their prominent types.

8.2 TYPES OF NEWSQL SYSTEMS

In the literature, three broad categories of NewSQL systems have been defined.

1. **New Architectures**: This category of NewSQL systems are built on a new DBMS which is constructed on a shared nothing architecture. Distributed shared nothing ar-

chitecture facilitates many desirable features such as multi-node concurrency control, distributed query processing, fault tolerance through replication, and flow control.

NewSQL systems in this category manage their own primary storage through in-memory storage or disk. As the DBMS is managing its storage through its custom engine, it can manage and implement its replication strategy. Further, queries are sent to the data (replicas) instead of data being sent to the query engine. This reduces network traffic and also allows rapid execution.

2. **Sharding Middleware**: Sharding splits a database into multiple smaller portions. This splitting is done row-wise such that each shard has a large number of rows. Shards are stored across a cluster of single-node DBMS instances. Each shard runs the same DBMS and only has a portion of the overall database. Further, shards are not meant to be updated or accessed individually. The middleware consists of two components. A centralized component and a client component. The former coordinates transactions and manages loads across shards. Depending upon the requests, it also decides about data placement and replication. In comparison, the client component is placed at each DBMS node that communicates with the middleware. This component is responsible for executing queries on behalf of the middleware. Both the centralized component and the client component combines to form an integrated DBMS.

3. **Cloud Computing**: NewSQL databases can also be handled through cloud computing platforms. An organization does not need to maintain the DBMS on its privately available hardware. The Database-as-a-Service (DBaaS) provider could maintain and manage the configuration.

8.3   FEATURES

We will now study a few significant characteristics of NewSQL systems which enables them to achieve ACID compliance while ensuring high-speed and scalability [292].

1. **Main Memory Storage**

   In this approach the entire DBMS is stored in the main memory. This approach enables certain optimization. As the data is only stored in the main memory, the DBMS can safely commit transactions without going through the hassle of updating them on disk. Thus, these systems can get better performance. Example 8.2 explains the concept of storing databases larger than the size of memory.

   > **How a DBMS with size greater than main memory is handled?**
   >
   > **Example 8.1 (NewSQL systems with large main memory requirements).** *NewSQL systems having size greater than the main memory can be handled. For such systems, a subset of DBMS (which is not expected to be accessed anymore) is evicted and written to the persistent storage. Through this, a DBMS with a larger footprint can also be executed. Generally, an internal tracking system can be used to identify which tuples are not being accessed anymore.*

2. **Partitioning**

   NewSQL systems utilize partitioning to distribute large size data over multiple partitions. To ensure consistency, NewSQL systems mainly utilize multi-version concurrency control (MVCC). In that, whenever there is an update on a transaction, a new version of the tuple is created in the database. This allows a tuple to be updated by a transaction even if another transaction is updating the same table. MVCC also permits read-only transactions to execute without blocking on writes.

3. **Concurrency Control**

Concurrency control system provides means of maintaining concurrency among all the partitions. Two schemes for concurrency control exist. A centralized controller which can coordinate query updates among all the shards. This scheme limits the scalability as too many requests at a time or increasing number of concurrent requests will increase coordination requests at the controller. An alternate approach is to build a decentralized system. In that, each node maintains the state of transactions that access the data that it manages. In order to execute concurrent transactions, nodes are required to coordinate with each other.

How MVCC is useful in a distributed database?

Example 8.2 (Multi-Version concurrency control in distributed databases). *MVCC or Multi-Version Concurrency control allows to maintain multiple versions of an object in a distributed database, while minimizing the need of maintaining locks. For instance, a write operation on an object creates a new immutable version. A read operation at a timestamp returns the value of the most recent version prior to that timestamp. Write operations doesn't need to be blocked. Proper timestamps are needed to be maintained.*

---

4. **Secondary Index**

For faster searching, NewSQL systems utilize secondary indexes. A normal DBMS is partitioned on primary indexes. Partitioning on the secondary indexes allows faster searching. If the system resides on a single node then secondary indexing is trivial. However, if the system is distributed then partitioning could be challenging. Two approaches are used to coordinate searching on secondary indexes, a centralized coordinator approach and a distributed approach. Example 8.3 explains the two mechanisms.

How secondary indexes are arranged in NewSQL systems?

Example 8.3 (Maintaining secondary indexes in distributed databases). *Two approaches can be used for storing secondary indexes:*

(a) **A centralized controller***: If a system is equipped with a centralized controller then secondary indexes can be stored on both the controller and the shard nodes. Only a single version of indexes is maintained.*

(b) **A distributed scheme***: An alternate approach is to distribute indexes and replicate them on multiple nodes. Each node only stores a portion of indexes. This enhances failure recovery but also increases overhead as a query needs to be propagated to multiple nodes.*

5. **Replication**

Distributed databases maintain large number of replicas for load balancing and user localization. A fundamental challenge in distributed database systems is to have an efficient update mechanism among all the replicas.

There are two fundamental approaches for maintaining consistency among replicas in NewSQL systems:

(a) **Active-active approach**: In active-active approach all the replicas are immediately updated upon execution of a query. This approach guarantees strict consistency; however, it incurs higher overhead and delay in update transactions.

(b) **Active-passive approach**: In this approach, there is a master replica for each object. For updates, only the master is updated first. The master node then distributes the update to other replicas.

Most of the NewSQL systems use the active-passive approach. They follow non-deterministic concurrency control scheme. This implies that queries on the replicas may get executed in a different order. This is due to the fact that replicas may experience several factors such as network delays, cache stalls, and clock skew. This step requires additional coordination among replicas.

There are a few deterministic NewSQL systems. These include H-Store [214] and VoltDB [343]. These systems guarantee that transactions execute in the same order among all the replicas. Such systems have consistent states among all the replicas.

6. **Crash Recovery**

Crash recovery mechanism refers to the process of recovering from a failure. Normally, this refers to failure recovery for the master node. When the master node fails, another replica can take over as a master. When the master is alive-back, it has two options for recovery:

(a) **Checkpointing and logs**: The first mechanism is to recover from the last checkpoint and then apply all the logs of the update. This mechanism requires that all the logs are needed to be maintained.

(b) **Copying from the Replica**: In this approach, the master node gets a copy from a replica node. This approach is also useful if a new replica is needed to be initiated.

8.4 NEWSQL SYSTEMS: CASE STUDIES

In this section, we will study a few examples of NewSQL systems. This will help us in better understanding about the execution of these systems.

8.4.1 VoltDB

In VoltDB, data is distributed across partitions [343, 360]. In addition, stored procedures (such as SQL Scripts) are also partitioned. Each stored procedure is a transaction. Each transaction in VoltDB is executed in its own thread. This minimizes the individual latency for each transaction, where latency is measured from the time when the transaction begins until processing ends. Since each transaction has its own thread, there is no need for locking.

Example 8.4 explains the partitioning mechanism of VoltDB, whereas example 8.5 explains execution of stored procedures.

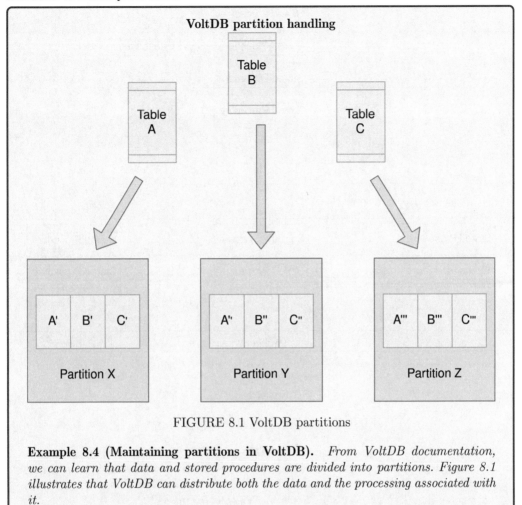

FIGURE 8.1 VoltDB partitions

Example 8.4 (Maintaining partitions in VoltDB). *From VoltDB documentation, we can learn that data and stored procedures are divided into partitions. Figure 8.1 illustrates that VoltDB can distribute both the data and the processing associated with it.*

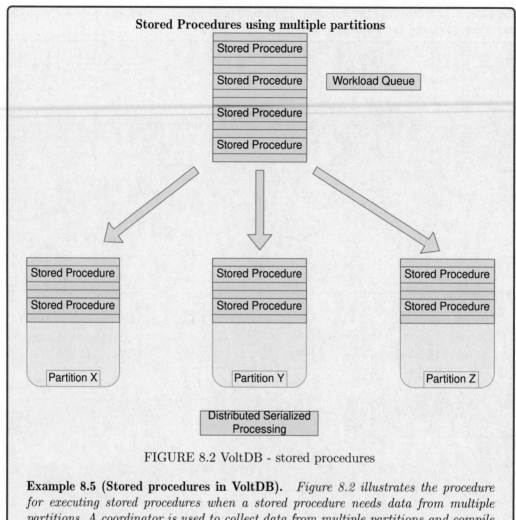

FIGURE 8.2 VoltDB - stored procedures

Example 8.5 (Stored procedures in VoltDB). *Figure 8.2 illustrates the procedure for executing stored procedures when a stored procedure needs data from multiple partitions. A coordinator is used to collect data from multiple partitions and compile aggregated result. This may slow down the VoltDB operation.*

8.4.2 NuoDB

NuoDB is another useful NewSQL system [113]. It is based on Peer-to-Peer (P2P) architecture. Each peer follows a two-tier architecture. A transaction processing layer (also known as Transaction Processing Engine or TE) and a storage layer (also known as Storage Engine or SE) . The two layer approach separates transaction processing and storage.

Out of the four desirable ACID properties, Atomicity, Consistency, and Isolation are handled by the transaction processing layer, whereas durability is handled at the storage layer. The transaction processing layer is in memory, which is responsible for managing transactions. The storage management layer is responsible for ensuring durability.

Durability is achieved by making data durable on commit. The storage layer also provides access to data when the TE does not find data in the memory. This is considered as a cache miss. A set of peer-to-peer coordination messages are used. Separating transaction and storage layers provides fast transaction processing.

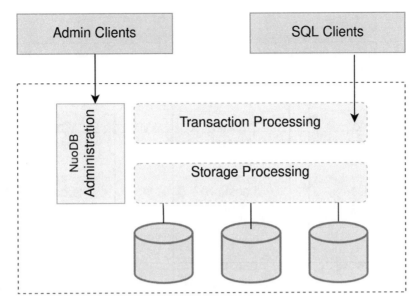

FIGURE 8.3 NuoDB architecture

In a NuoDB system, all processes are peers. This means that there is no need to have a single coordinator. It also eliminates single point of failure.

TEs are responsible for accepting SQL client connections. Further, they are also used for parsing and running SQL queries against cached data.

All processes, i.e., SEs and TEs, communicate through a P2P protocol. When a cache miss is observed by a TE, it contacts its peers to fetch the data. This could either be another TE with data in its cache or an SE with access to data.

NuoDB employs Brokers, which are peer processes responsible for management. Each physical node, which executes the database service runs a broker service. A Broker is responsible to start and stop NuoDB services and monitoring processes health. It is also responsible for configuration management. Brokers coordinate with each other to have a global view. Figure 8.3 illustrates the architecture.

8.4.3 Spanner

Spanner is an open-source, fault-tolerant, and globally distributed database, which provides the features of a relational databases such as SQL queries and ACID transactions with the horizontal scaling capabilities of a non-relational database. Figure 8.4 shows the architecture of Spanner. It consists of multiple zones. Each zone has a zone master, a location proxy, and one to thousands of spanserver. The zone master assigns data to spanservers. Clients connect to the spanservers for data retrieval. Proxies are used to locate spanservers inside zones. Placement driver is responsible to move and replicate data in order to balance load and maintain locality across zones, whereas universe master provides a console that is used for interactive debugging across all zones [148].

There are some important features of Spanner, which helps it in achieving ACID guarantees at a wide-scale [110].

1. **Replication**: Replication decisions are controlled by applications at a fine-grain level. An application can decide replication factor based on following characteristics:

    (a) **Read Latency**: How far data is from the users to control read latency?

    (b) **Write Latency**: How far replicas from each other to maintain write latency?

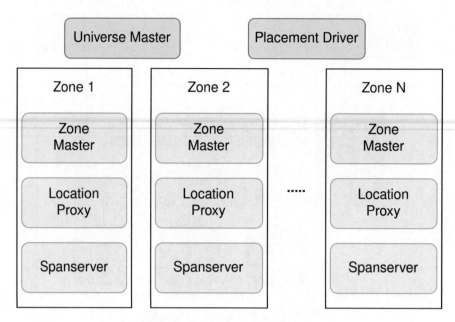

FIGURE 8.4 Spanner architecture

(c) **Other Attributes**: How many replicas are maintained to control durability, availability, and read performance?

2. **External Consistency**: External consistency implies that transactions appear to execute in a serializable manner. It will appear that if all transactions are executed sequentially, although they may have executed across multiple servers over multiple data centers. The system guarantees that if a transaction "A" commits before another transaction "B" starts, then A's timestamp of commit will be smaller then B's timestamp of commit.

3. **Global Consistency**: Global consistency implies that all replicas of the database are consistent.

4. **TimeStamps**: Spanner has TrueTime API, which enables it to assign globally meaningful timestamps to transactions. Spanner depends on TrueTime to generate monotonically increasing timestamps. These are used to generate proper timestamps for write transactions without the need for global communication. Further, they are also used for read operations.

8.4.4   HRDBMS – NewSQL System for Data Analytics

HRDBMS is another NewSQL system, which is inspired by MapReduce. It consists of a two-tier architecture. Metadata is stored at coordinator nodes which are responsible for query planning, while data is stored at worker nodes. HRDBMS also implies a query optimizer, which prepares a query plan according to the statistical data available. The query plan is submitted for execution. Results from the query are collected at the coordinator node which sorts and aggregates the query. In HRDBMS, a query is optimized to reduce cost of execution, while queries are executed on the model of Map/Reduce. While the former is useful in achieving higher speed, the latter is beneficial in improving scalability.

HRDBMS bears many distinct characteristics for performance enhancement. Foremost, HRDBMS omits the reduce phase. We should recall that in the reduce phase, output is written to HDFS, whereas the output of the map phase is written to the local disk. By omitting the reduce phase, HRDBMS can utilize a series of map phases to be executed with low cost. In such a manner, relational operations can be performed. While data is shuffled between map phases, it is not sorted. Shuffle in HRDBMS only ensures that data with similar keys is sent to the same node for processing including joins and aggregation.

Data in HRDBMS is stored in local disk. Coordinator nodes contain information about the stored data. The first map phase is always executed on the node where data is stored, which allows data to be read efficiently.

The Optimizer in HRDBMS utilizes query execution information to build efficient workflows. Shuffle is the most costly step in HRDBMS. The number of shuffles are reduced by efficiently partitioning the data.

HRDBMS is inspired to support relational operations while meeting the high scalability demands. However, it lacks fault tolerance, which are inherent large scale big data systems.

8.5   CONCLUDING REMARKS

NewSQL systems have emerged to provide transactional assurances for database systems at a wide scale. They possessed increasing scalability and assurance to meet ACID guarantees and perform real-time analytics. They provide a comparable alternate as compared to NoSQL systems, which have relaxed requirements of consistency and higher scalability. NewSQL systems such as S-store [123] have also been used for streaming analysis. NewSQL and NoSQL systems can together be used to provide hybrid solutions as well.

8.6   FURTHER READING

Details about Google Spanner can be found at references [110, 148].

NuoDB is explained in reference [113], whereas VoltDB is explained in reference [343]. Other NewSQL systems [185] such as MemSQL [130] and HRDBMS [84] can also be explored.

A performance comparison of NewSQL systems has been presented in reference [220].

8.7   EXERCISE QUESTIONS

1. What are the major issues which drive the popularity of NewSQL?

2. How does in-memory NewSQL systems maintain databases with size larger than the system memory?

3. What is MVCC? How is it used by NewSQL systems?

4. Describe the failure recovery mechanism for NewSQL systems.

5. Explain how VoltDB handles partitions?

6. Describe how external consistency is maintained by Spanner.

7. How secondary indexing is useful for NewSQL systems?

8. What is meant by sharding? How is it useful for NewSQL systems?

9. Most of the NewSQL systems are based on a peer-to-peer architecture. Explain how P2P architecture could be useful as compared to a centralized architecture?

10. Explain how stored procedures are handled in VoltDB?

GLOSSARY

ACID Guarantees: Atomicity, Consistency, Isolation, and Durability are the four important attributes of a DBMS.

Broker: It is a management service which runs on each physical node executing the NuoDB system.

Clock Skew: The term is referred as the deviation of time among different nodes of a distributed system.

CockroachDB: It is an open-source, globally distributed, horizontally scalable, and ACID-compliant database. It provides high-availability and fault tolerance, and supports distributed SQL transactions.

Concurrency: It is a process of executing multiple computations at a time.

Database-as-a-Service (DBaaS): It is a managed database service in the cloud that provides a powerful on-demand scalable database platform.

Indexing: It is a method of optimizing performance of a DBMS by minimizing the number of disk accesses required when a query is processed. Indexing is supported through a data structure technique which is used to quickly locate and access the data in a database.

In-Memory Database: It is a type of database system which maintains and retrieves data from memory for faster execution.

Load balancing: It is a process of distributing load or data across different replicas in order to balance load across them.

MemSQL: It is a high-performance in-memory distributed database that provides high availability, fault-tolerance, and ACID-compliant relational database management. It is a cloud-native NewSQL database that is massively scalable across various geographic regions.

Online Analytical Processing (OLAP): It is a type of system which is used for analytical processing of the system.

Online Transactional Processing (OLTP): It is a type of system which is used to process transactions. Normally, it guarantees ACID properties.

Replica: It is a backup-node which is used to maintain replication and load balancing.

Zone: It is a unit of execution in Google Spanner.

III

Networking, Security, and Privacy for Big Data

Networking for Big Data

CONTENTS

B IG DATA systems require high throughput and effective means of data transfer in order to process data efficiently. In this chapter, we will study numerous network-related technologies, which are being incorporated by big data systems to fulfill these requirements. We will also discuss several issues and challenges encountered in this regard. Network performance of a system would depend upon end-to-end network paths. However, for simplicity, we will restrict our focus on networking within a cluster (or a data center), as this is considered more relevant for the processing of big data [378].

9.1   NETWORK ARCHITECTURE FOR BIG DATA SYSTEMS

In order to understand network requirements for big data systems, let us first envision the network architecture of these systems. As discussed in chapter 2, a big data system will be deployed on a cluster. This cluster could either be setup on a public cloud, or it could reside locally on a private cloud. In either way, a cluster mimics the controlled environment, which is necessary to execute big data systems.

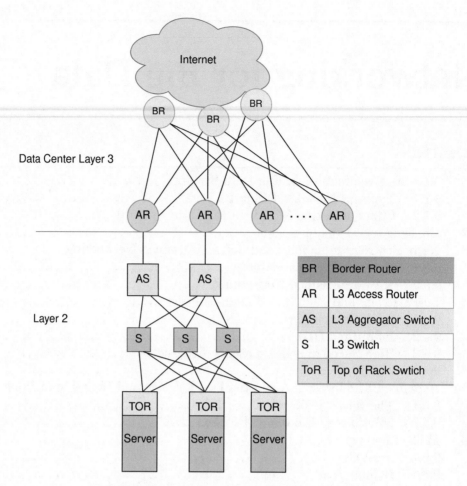

FIGURE 9.1 Data center architecture [145]

In section 3.1.2, we studied data center architecture. Figure 3.2 is redrawn as figure 9.1. It illustrates a typical data center architecture. In a data center, hundreds to thousands of machines (called nodes or hosts) are installed. These nodes are organized into racks.

Worker nodes are organized at the edge layer. Data from the edge layer is aggregated through the aggregator switch. At the top, is the core layer, which is supported through border router and provides an interface of the data center with the outside world. In a typical data center, there could be one to tens or hundreds of clusters.

Figure 9.2 illustrates a sample cluster which consists of numerous racks of servers. Each rack may contain tens of servers and a Top of Rack (ToR) switch. These are considered at the edge layer in the data center. Data from these racks is aggregated through aggregated switches, which is then sent to the IP router. We should note that servers in a cluster are organized in the form of a virtual LAN (VLAN). This allows consistent routing policies throughout the servers in a cluster. We will revert back to routing when we will discuss Software-Defined Network (SDN).

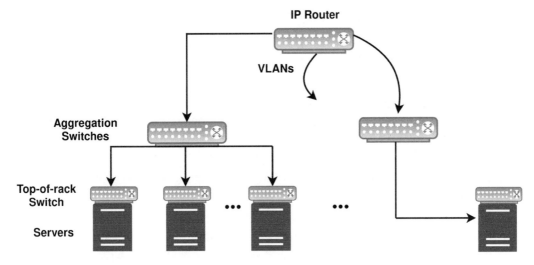

FIGURE 9.2 Cluster architecture

9.1.1 Types of Network Traffic

In order to understand network operations in big data systems, it is important to discuss types of traffic. Normally, big data systems consist of three types of traffic. These include data aggregation/partitioning, bulk transfer, and control messages [365]. We will now briefly study the three types of traffic:

1. **Control Messages**: These are latency-sensitive messages, which are used to send time-sensitive information such as cluster control or to detect abnormal activity or configuration updates. For instance, a head node could send *are you alive* messages to all the worker nodes in a cluster on a routine basis. These messages are sent to detect node failure and to inquire the availability of resources. Similarly, routing updates can be sent for network optimization. In case of Hadoop and YARN, heartbeat messages can be considered as control messages. In general, control messages have low data-rate and the latency-sensitive requirement can be met through Ethernet.

2. **Aggregation**: This type of traffic is most common for big data systems. For instance, MapReduce-like systems has a normal pattern for aggregation. We should recall from our study in chapter 2, how a task is distributed and aggregated. A task is submitted to the head node, which splits it into smaller tasks and distributes it among worker nodes. The worker nodes compute the smaller task and send the results back to the head node, where the partial results are aggregated to compute the final result. Partition and aggregation systems are used in many big data systems such as search engines and querying systems.

3. **Bulk Transfer**: This type of traffic is usually required either for maintenance or for management of a data center. Objectives for bulk data transfer could include replication, fault tolerance, recovery, and data migration. The size of data traffic could be huge, involving petabytes to zettabytes of data. Generally, such type of transfer does not have critical requirements of timeliness.

9.1.2   Communication Models in Big Data Systems

Big data systems desire high bandwidth for efficient communication. In general, following communication models exist in big data systems [186]:

1. **One-to-One**: This is a fundamental traffic model in which data is transferred (or messages are communicated) between two hosts on a one-to-one mapping. High network throughput is desired for this purpose. An efficient one-to-one communication system would yield effective several-to-one and all-to-all support. Examples of the one-to-one model include VM migration, data backup, and hotspot mitigation.

2. **One-to-Many** This type of traffic pattern is desired when data is copied from one host to many other hosts. For instance, by default, data is replicated in a distributed file system (such as GFS [177] and HDFS [324]).

3. **One-to-All**: This type of traffic patterns include patterns in which data is transferred from one host to all the other hosts in a cluster. Examples of such traffic models include data broadcast, system upgrade, and transfer of application binaries.

4. **All-to-All**: In such a model, each host transfers the data to every other host in the cluster. Such type of traffic model is common in MapReduce [154], when during the reduce phase data is shuffled across many servers [186].

9.2   CHALLENGES AND REQUIREMENTS

In section 9.1.2, we discussed different traffic models for big data systems. We now describe a few significant requirements for these systems:

1. **Flexibility and Adaptability**: Big data systems may contain heterogeneous applications with varying requirements. An adaptable and flexible solution is needed which can meet the requirements of these applications.

2. **Low-Latency and High-Speed Data Transfer**: Communication latency should be low. If large amount of data is needed to be transferred, efficient mechanisms for data transfer should be employed. Network should not become a bottleneck due to network transfer.

3. **Avoiding TCP Incast – Achieving Low-Latency and High Throughput**: Big data systems have varying requirements of traffic. For instance, control messages require low-latency, whereas bulk data transfer requires that the throughput remains high. A big data network is vulnerable to congestion and packet loss as well. In addition, big data systems may suffer from TCP Incast problem, where throughput of the network may decrease abruptly due to sudden increase in packet loss. The TCP Incast problem has been described in section 9.5.

4. **Fault Tolerance**: In a big data network, there should be enough redundant network resources, as failure in the network could induce huge delay.

Table 9.1 shows challenges and their corresponding solutions discussed in the chapter. In the remaining sections of this chapter, we will study different solutions to meet these requirements and challenges.

TABLE 9.1 Network Challenges and Their Solutions

Challenges and Requirements	Solutions
Flexibility and Adaptability	Network Programmability and Software-Defined Networks
Low-Latency and High-Speed Data Transfer	Edge Computing, InfiniBand, and Low-Latency Ethernet
Avoiding TCP Incast	Data Center TCP (DCTCP)
Fault Tolerance	Fat-tree and BCube

9.3 NETWORK PROGRAMMABILITY AND SOFTWARE-DEFINED NETWORKING

In this section, we will learn different benefits and features for Software-Defined Networks – a widely used paradigm for flexibility and adaptability.

9.3.1 Network Programmability

In big data systems, applications could have varying demands of network bandwidth and connectivity. Therefore, network programmability and adaptability is a key consideration in designing networks for big data systems.

1. **Significance**:

   Significance of network programmability can be understood from example 9.1.

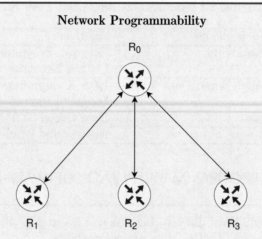

FIGURE 9.3 Network routing

Example 9.1 (Network Programmability). *Network statistics are utilized to allocate network resources in data centers. For instance, consider figure 9.3, where three routers R_1, R_2, and R_3 are connected to R_0. In case of congestion in link from R_0 to R_1, traffic can be diverted through link R_0-R_2. This diversion is only possible if network-level characteristics are periodically collected and analyzed. These techniques are implemented in various schemes such as c-Through [364], Helios [165], and OSA [131]. However, just relying on network level routing is not sufficient for efficient performance [365]. This is because applications may have conflicting or supplemental requirements. In such cases, application-aware routing decisions are needed to be made.*

Let us consider the figure again. Suppose that the link R_0 - R_1 is not available due to failure. Further, assume that bandwidth in the link R_0-R_2 and R_0-R_3 is 100 Mbps and 200 Mbps respectively. Now let us assume that there are two applications A and B which are sending data through R_0. Both these applications have different bandwidth requirements. By smartly assessing the bandwidth requirements, the aggregator switch, i.e., R_0, can send the application with high bandwidth requirements to the link R_0-R_3 and the data of application with lower bandwidth to the link R_0-R_2. Since requirements of applications may change over time, network programmability is significant in providing a dynamic and adaptive system.

2. **Benefits**:

Network programmability promotes application-awareness – a key requirement for big data systems. In order to leverage the need of network programmability in big data systems, we will now see a few examples where application awareness could be beneficial:

(a) **Load Balancing in Cassandra**: Cassandra incorporates sharding through which load is automatically balanced across different nodes. In order to implement load balancing, the Cassandra framework may automatically initiate bulk data transfer. Application awareness could be highly useful in this context such that high priority jobs can be prioritized, whereas load balancing tasks can tolerate some delay.

(b) **Reduce task in Hadoop**: Application-awareness could be greatly beneficial for Hadoop. In that, when reduce jobs are assigned to nodes, data is shuffled and aggregated from a large number of mapper nodes. If application and network requirements are known, a network could be optimized to reduce bulk data transfer and reduce the number of hops.

(c) **Task assignment in Hadoop**: In Hadoop, data locality is considered while assigning tasks. That is, tasks are assigned to the nodes where data is placed. However, if for any reason, it is not possible to assign tasks to the nodes where data is placed, then Hadoop scheduler strives to schedule tasks to nearby nodes. Network programmability could be very useful in this context as cost of data movement could be reduced by carefully computing network paths.

9.3.2 Software-Defined Networking

We have studied that network programmability is a useful feature for big data systems. Programmability allows network policies and decisions to be controlled centrally at the software layer.

We will now study Software-Defined Network (SDN), a dominant framework for providing network programmability.

1. **Significance**:

   Figure 9.4 illustrates the comparison between a traditional network vs an SDN-enabled network. In a traditional network, forwarding devices (switches or routers) are used to forward packets. Each device can execute its own policy. This implies that control logic or control plane is integrated with each switch. In comparison, in an SDN, a centralized controller provides the control logic. The rules and policies about the forwarding decisions are made by the centralized controller, whereas switches are mere forwarding devices.

   In an SDN, the control plane is separated from the data plane. That is forwarding decisions are made by the centralized controller (control plane), whereas forwarding actions are made by switches (data plane), which seek commands and instructions from the controller. Upon arrival of a flow of packets, a switch checks for the available set of rules for the flow. If it doesn't find any rule for the flow then it checks with the controller about the rule for the flow.

   Figure 9.5 shows the working model where numerous switches are connected to a controller. The controller can communicate from applications to make application-aware decisions. In an SDN, there are two categories of communication, i.e., communication between the controller and the switches, and communication between the controller and applications. Both these types of communications are handled through software or Application Programming Interface (API). Northbound API is used for communication between the controller and the application, whereas, southbound API is used for communication between the controller and forwarding devices.

   Use of a centralized controller provides greater flexibility as policy decisions and forwarding updates can be centrally controlled through software. Similarly, application-aware decisions can also be made with greater ease. However, a centralized controller is vulnerable for a single point of failure. To cater this issue, SDN has evolved from a single controller to a centralized control plane with multiple controllers. Multiple controllers allow fault tolerance, as in case of a non-availability of a controller, backup controllers are available. Backup controllers induce challenges of maintaining consistency.

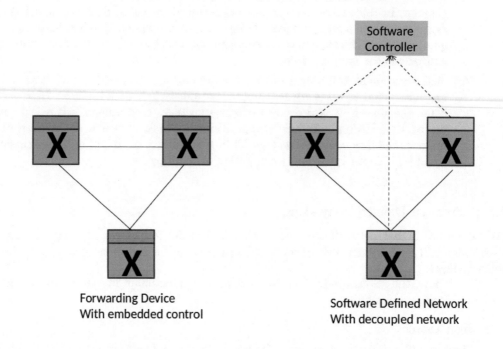

FIGURE 9.4 SDN vs traditional networks

2. **Important Features**:

Following are the four prominent features of SDN:

(a) The control and data planes are decoupled. This decoupling allows adaptability and flexibility.

(b) The decision to forward packets are made on flows instead of destinations. Flow-based decisions allows greater flexibility and application-specific routing. This improves the efficacy of the network.

(c) Control logic is centralized. This implies that the network can be controlled centrally. Routing rules, firewall policies, and decisions to forward flows can all be controlled through a centralized controller or network operating system (NOS).

(d) Network is programmable; i.e., software applications can run on top of the NOS, which interacts with the underlying data plane devices.

These features can greatly enhance performance and utilization of a network.

3. **Benefits**:

SDN can benefit cloud data centers meeting Service Level Agreement (SLA) for big data applications. SLAs for big data applications include many attributes such as processing time, data transfer time, security, and bandwidth etc. SDN can help in meeting these SLAs by efficiently selecting routes in order to optimize network efficiency. SDN can also be used for optimizing network bandwidth utilization. Big data applications

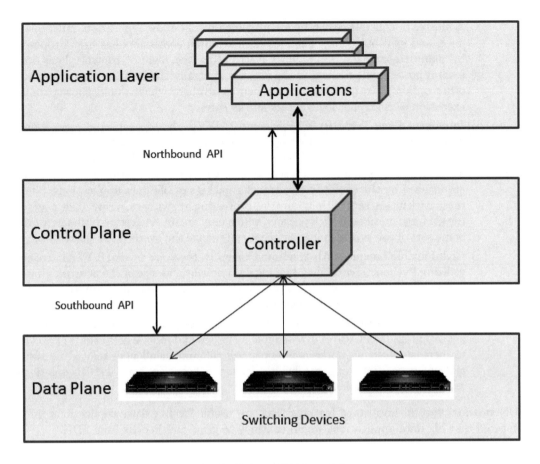

FIGURE 9.5 SDN model

can have diverse traffic, ranging from streaming applications to file transfer. Meeting SLA requirements for different types of applications can be challenging. SDN could promote flexibility and adaptability by allowing application-specific traffic engineering.

For big data systems (such as Hadoop), data locality is essential to reduce network-transfer cost [300]. A prime requirement for data locality is to have a global knowledge of the network. SDN can take advantage of having global knowledge to promote data locality and reduce network transfer time. In such a way, Hadoop jobs can be scheduled to promote data locality. Eventually, this would lead to reduced job completion time in Hadoop.

4. **Open Issues**:

Although SDN can be exploited to handle networking issues related to big data but there are many open challenges which are needed to be addressed [150]:

(a) **Scalable Controller Management**: Controllers in big data applications often require frequent flow table updates and involve a large amount of data transfers. In general, current controllers can only have capacity of 8000 entries for flow table [230]. This is insufficient for big data applications. As big data systems are being increasingly used, need for scalable and robust controlling mechanisms are growing.

A cluster of controllers can be set-up which would allow replication, fault tolerance, and load balancing. The idea of distributed controllers has been proposed by many researchers. This allows distributing the logic of control plane over several hosts, while managing the network centrally through the controller. Another option is to incorporate multicore controllers which would allow parallel execution of controller logic across all the cores.

(b) **Intelligent Flow Table/Rule Management**: While the separation of control and data planes in SDN has simplified management of network, it has also increased processing requirements for the controller. In an SDN-compliant big data system, forwarding tables and rules are sent to the switches in the network. These tables are utilized by the controllers to transfer packets of big data applications. Since these packets are sent without any pre-processing at switches, a controller may receive a large number of such packets, which may create congestion in the network. Some sort of pre-processing at switches can reduce the overhead at the controller.

(c) **High Flexible Language Abstraction**: Currently, there are several SDN controllers utilizing Python, Java, and C. In a big data network, as size of the network grows, heterogeneous controllers may be employed. In such a scenario, a unified abstractive language is needed to support programmability for big data networks.

(d) **Wireless Mobile Big Data**: With advancements in wireless technologies and Internet of Things (IoT), use of SDN-enabled wireless and mobile networks is expected to increase. Such networks may encounter different challenges related to availability, connectivity, and bandwidth. In such a scenario, capable SDN solutions are needed to be explored.

SDN provides several important features that are useful for big data applications. It is expected that big data applications would continue to grow and benefit from SDN.

9.4 LOW-LATENCY AND HIGH-SPEED DATA TRANSFER

Big data systems require low-latency and high-speed data transfer. Traditional bus-based network systems are incapable to transfer data at high-speed due to several limitations. The bus is shared by many I/O devices in a system. An arbitration mechanism is used to facilitate sharing. As the speed of the bus is increased, the effects of arbitration overhead are also increased. This reduces the capability of the bus to facilitate long transfers with high-speed. System Bus is considered slow and unreliable. In this section, we will briefly discuss edge computing concepts for reducing latency. We will also study a few methods for high-speed data transfer. These are broadly categorized in two sections, i.e., InfiniBand (IB), and Data Center Ethernet (DCE) or Low-Latency Ethernet (LLE).

9.4.1 Edge Computing

Edge computing refers to the computing technologies and platforms that bring computation and storage closer to the location of need. In chapter 4, we have studied Hadoop. It incorporates edge computing by localizing computation at the point of storage. Mobile computing is another example of edge computing where a mobile device computes and stores data instead of sending it to the cloud. In section 3.7, we have studied fog computing, which is another example of edge computing. While edge computing can reduce data access latency, it can increase computation time if data is large [375]. This is because edge devices may not have extensive computational power as compared to the cloud. Since overall latency include latency of access as well as latency to compute data, computation over edge may not always yield lower latency.

9.4.2 InfiniBand (IB)

InfiniBand (IB) is currently a popular standard for small to medium size HPC clusters running commodity hardware [293]. The main goal of the IB architecture is to facilitate high-speed network transfer through low-latency and high bandwidth.

IB protocols has several variations such as Single Data Rate (SDR), Double Data Rate (DDR), Quad Data Rate (QDR), Fourteen Data Rate (FDR), and Enhanced Data Rate (EDR). All these types provide speeds at different levels. For instance, as per the current standards, QDR can provide speed up to 40 Gbps, whereas FDR can facilitate communication up to 56 Gbps.

In addition to increasing the serial data rate, it is possible to combine multiple parallel lanes into a data bus in order to achieve high-speed [156]. We will now study different characteristics of IB:

1. **Features and Protocol**:

   To achieve high-speed data transfer, the IB architecture supports several features such as Remote Direct Memory Access (RDMA) and operating system kernel bypass.

   Two types of Application Programmer Interface (APIs) are supported in InfiniBand: One-side and two-sided. We now discuss these features and the APIs in detail:

   (a) **OS Kernel Bypass**: This feature allows an application running an IB to provide user-level message exchange. These messages are passed directly between user space applications and the network adapter, bypassing the kernel. These are normally implemented as Send and Recv operations. Since each Send operation requires a matching Recv, these are often referred as *two-sided* operations [99].

   (b) **Remote Direct Memory Access (RDMA)**: Using the RDMA technology, a device can directly access the memory of the remote host – bypassing the need of interrupting the CPU. When an application needs to send a packet, it pins a region of memory and registers it with the Network Interface Card (NIC). The application also completes the mapping of virtual to physical memory through the page table. Once the region is registered, the NIC can directly access the memory of the remote host without interrupting the CPU. A complete queue for sending and receiving packets is maintained by the NIC. RDMA does not require maintaining the complete network stack and an NIC can copy packets from user space directly without going through the CPU. This bypasses the need of relying on context switch. Apparently, the latency is much lower as compared to traditional TCP-based transfer. RDMA-based operations are often considered as *one-side operations*, as they do not involve remote host CPU. These include read, write, and atomic operations [273]. In that, read and write operations allow read or write data from the remote memory of another machine. Similarly, atomic operations such as fetch-and-add and compare-and-swap allow remote memory access atomically.

   Two-sided operations are much slower as compared to one-sided operations due to their requirements of a matching receive operation [242].

2. **Architecture**:

   The architecture of the InfiniBand system is divided into following three layers:

   (a) **InfiniBand Verbs Layer**: The verbs layer provides lowest level access to Infini-Band system. Data transferred through verbs is completely bypassed from OS, i.e., there are no intermediate copies in the OS. The verbs layer incorporates a queue pair model which implements communication end points. Work requests are placed on a queue pair which are then processed by the Host Channel Adapter (HCA). A completion queue is maintained to store notifications for the completion of work. The process of completion is detected through polling or interrupts.

(b) **InfiniBand IP Layer**: The purpose of the IP-based layer is to provide support for communication with traditional socket-based systems. A driver is provided for this purpose, which is responsible for communicating over socket API. For such communication, the InfiniBand adapters appear as traditional socket-based devices such as ib_0, ib_1, and so on. It is often referred as IP-over-IB or (IPoIB). It supports both the unconnected datagram protocol as well as the connected protocol. Of the two types of protocols, the latter is considered more reliable.

(c) **InfiniBand Sockets Direct Protocol**: The Sockets Direct Protocol (SDP) emulates TCP sockets stream semantics. SDP is layered on top of IB message-oriented transfer model. The SDP protocol achieves high-speed without requiring modifications to existing socket-based applications. For smaller messages, buffered mode transfer is implemented, whereas for large messages, RDMA-based transfer is incorporated. The use of RDMA allows SDP to offer improved performance than IPoIB. However, as RDMA is not utilized for all messages, performance in SDP is lower as compared to the performance of verbs.

InfiniBand has been a popular framework for high-speed networks. The RDMA feature has been instrumental in providing high-speed. Owing to its efficiency, the IB systems have been deployed by many HPC clusters.

9.4.3 High-Speed and Low-Latency Ethernet

Although IB has been very effective in reducing communication latency, its wide-scale adoption is limited; partly because Ethernet has been a dominating protocol for conventional PC-based systems. In order to converge high-speed networks over Ethernet, several variations of Ethernet have been proposed. Low-Latency Ethernet (LLE) is a consolidated term used to refer types of protocols and standards which can facilitate high-speed traffic over Ethernet. In this context, two related terms Data Center Bridging (DCB) or Data Center Ethernet (DCE) are commonly used. The former is a suite of standards from IEEE that enables convergence in a data center, whereas the latter has been used in a similar context by Cisco. DCB or DCE commonly refers to the set of protocols used for data center storage, networking, and Inter Process Communication (IPC) [271]. We now explain a few prominent protocols used in this context.

1. **iWARP**:

    Internet Wide Area RDMA Protocol (iWARP) is another protocol used to provide for high-speed data connection. Similar to IB, it also utilizes RDMA to achieve low-latency and high bandwidth. However, this is achieved over Ethernet. There are three key iWARP components that deliver low-latency [203]:

    (a) **Kernel Bypass**: This feature removes the need for context switching from kernel-space to user-space and allows an application to post commands and write messages directly to the server adapter. This is in contrast to traditional message transfer where messages are transferred from user-space to kernel-space through context switch.

(b) **Direct Data Placement**: Using Direct Data Placement (DDP), data can be copied directly from the server adapter's receive buffer to the application buffer. This is achieved through RDMA. DDP eliminates the need of intermediate operations which would otherwise be required to copy data to an application buffer and conserves time and memory bandwidth.

(c) **Transport Acceleration**: In a traditional system, the processor maintains substantial connection information and resources for maintaining network stack information. This includes connection context and payload reassembly. This overhead increases linearly with the speed of the wire. Using iWARP, this information is maintained at the network controller. This feature frees up processor resources and it is now available to process other applications.

2. **Fibre Channel over Ethernet**:

Fibre Channel over Ethernet (FCoE) allows integration of fibre channel and ethernet. This is achieved through encapsulation and decapsulation of the fibre channel frame over the ethernet frame. FCoE can achieve speed of 10 GBPS or higher. The technology could be useful for many big data applications requiring high bandwidth and low-latency. As many data centers may have both fibre optic and ethernet, the FCoE technology solves convergence issues as well [284].

3. **RDMA over Converged Ethernet (RoCE)**:

RoCE (RDMA over Converged Ethernet) is an Ethernet-based implementation of RDMA. Instead of InfiniBand-based Adapters (IBA), it requires RDMA-based Ethernet Adapters. RoCE is considered less expensive with wide applicability due to its convergence with Ethernet. In comparison, IB provides higher speed for data transfer [199]. RoCE has been integrated with IB-supported hardware by various vendors such as Mellanox. In traditional IB systems, packet drops are rare. When an out of order packet is received at the receiver, the packet is discarded and a negative acknowledgment (NACK) is sent to the sender. Upon receipt of NACK or timeout, the sender retransmits all packets that were sent since the last acknowledged packet. This methodology is well suited for lossless systems such as InfiniBand because packet loss is rare. However, for RoCE (when RDMA is integrated with Ethernet), it yields slower performance because packet loss may occur frequently in Ethernet [274]. RoCE implements congestion control mechanisms such as ECN (Explicit Congestion Notification) [323]. Using ECN, sending rate can be reduced if the queue at the receiver approaches congestion. The sending rate can be restored if the queue has more capacity to accommodate packets.

4. **Soft RoCE**:

To emulate the RDMA system, Soft-RoCE, a software-based version of RoCE, has also been released. It bypasses the requirement of having an RDMA-enabled Ethernet network adapter. Using Soft-RoCE driver, InfiniBand-based RDMA support can be incorporated in the Linux OS. An Ethernet adapter-based system can either connect with a hardware RoCE adapter-based system or with a Soft-RoCE-based system. Since the implementation is based on a software and hardware infrastructure is not required, Soft-ROCE is unlikely to achieve the performance of traditional RoCE-based systems [157].

For large-scale clusters, inter-node communication is significant. High bandwidth is desired by many big data applications. For instance, in MapReduce, a large number of <key,value> pairs emitted by the map phase are aggregated at the reducer. Similarly, in a search engine, a query could be executed in hundreds to thousands of nodes in order to fetch the results. These examples highlight the significance of high inter-node bandwidth in a cluster.

In general, there are two modes of providing high-speed bandwidth in a cluster:

(a) Specialized hardware and communication protocol can be incorporated to implement high-speed network. Examples of such setup include InfiniBand and Myrinet. They can provide high bandwidth with high-speed at a larger scale. However, these mechanisms are expensive and may require special considerations for compatibility with existing commodity networks.

(b) The second option is to deploy commodity Ethernet switches and routers to implement a high-speed interconnect for clusters. This approach carries the advantage of ease of integration with existing networks without the modification of operating systems and hardware. However, the performance may degrade with the increase in number of nodes in the cluster.

9.4.4   iSCSI

iSCSI (Internet Small Computer Systems Interface) is a protocol for linking data storage facilities [254] through Storage Area Network (SAN). It is one of the most widely used protocols for remote data storage access. It encompasses two major protocols to facilitate access. Small Computer System Interface (SCSI) protocol is used for accessing storage and TCP is used for networking transport access. It enables applications like data mirroring, remote backup, and remote management. Such features allow a big data system to have management and data recovery features in case of catastrophic events. These are specifically needed for mission critical systems such as business and banking data.

The iSCSI protocol supports many kind of interconnects between a server and remote storage. These include Parallel SCSI bus, fibre channel, and RDMA. Of these, parallel SCSI bus suffers from the limitation that it can only have a few meters distance between the server and the storage device and the number of storage devices are limited to 16. Alternatively, SCSI devices can be connected via fibre channel which increases the allowable distance and the number of devices. In this context, Fibre Channel-Arbitrated Loop (FC-AL) [159, 222] can attach up to 126 nodes. Since multiple FC-ALs can be connected, the number of disks could be considerably large. However, fibre channels do not solve the distance problem and access to the SCSI device remains confined to LAN.

Traditional TCP-based solutions for network access solves the distance issue and allows access to remote storage locations. However, the speed of data transfer remains limited. The main reason for the slow speed is due to out-of-order arrival and reassembly of TCP segments. This reassembly is required because iSCSI header is not likely to be present in every TCP packet. Thus TCP packets are stored and reassembled such that data can be placed in iSCSI buffers. Reassembly wastes memory bandwidth and CPU cycles and affects the overall speed [29].

iSCSI can also utilize RDMA technique for access protocol [310, 314]. iSCSI Extensions for RDMA (iSER) is a generic term used for this purpose [124]. iSCSI can exploit direct data placement from RDMA to achieve higher speed. Using DDP, need for intermediate operations for data transfer is eliminated and data is copied directly to an application buffer. RDMA Write, RDMA Read Request, and RDMA Read Response Messages are used for data as well as control messages for the iSCSI data-type.

9.5 AVOIDING TCP INCAST – ACHIEVING LOW-LATENCY AND HIGH-THROUGHPUT

In the previous section, we have discussed various methods for facilitating high-speed Internet. Measures such as InfiniBand and RoCE increase speed of data transfer while increasing throughput and decreasing latency.

9.5.1 The Incast Problem

Another major requirement is to mitigate the effect of TCP Incast. It is one of the most significant network-related issues which occurs in big data systems. The issue is mostly common in partition/aggregate types of systems, where response from a large number of servers is aggregated to formulate a result. Incast occurs when data packets from these large number of servers are queued and bottlenecked at the aggregated switches. As the size of the response exceeds the capacity of the switch, data packets start to drop. Figure 9.6 illustrates the scenario where a user submits a search query. The query is distributed to hundreds of servers. Response from these servers is expected to be received at the client. However, as there are a large number of packets being received rapidly at the adjacent switch, the accumulated size of packets exceeds the queuing capacity of the switch. Consequently, the switch starts to drop packets.

TCP Incast is frequent in data centers as compared to Wide Area Network (WAN) because Round Trip Time (RTT) in data centers is low and the response from a large number of servers gets accumulated quickly at the network switch which is adjacent to the querying server. Further, as the typical value for TCP Retransmission Time Out (RTO) is 200 msec, packet loss is detected considerably late as compared to the RTT. Consequently, a large number of packets are needed to be retransmitted.

The Incast problem increases queuing delay in flows. Due to retransmissions, it also decreases application-level throughput. Specifically, this problem affects computing paradigms in which distributed processing cannot progress until all parallel threads in a stage complete. For instance, applications such as Web search, distributed file systems, advertisement selection, and other MapReduce-type applications can suffer from the incast problem.

9.5.2 Solutions to the Incast Problem

Researchers have explored several solutions to the Incast problem:

1. **Large Buffer in Switches**: One possible solution is to increase the size of the buffer in switches. In this way, a large queue can be maintained and packet drop can be decreased. However, large queue increases the cost of switches and does not have a significant impact on packet drop [136].

2. **TCP's Minimum RTO**: In TCP, Retransmission Time Out (RTO) is the time during which a sender must wait to receive an acknowledgement before re-sending a packet to the receiver. A large value of RTO avoids unnecessary retransmission of packet and increases TCP throughput; however, it slows down a system as packet loss is detected late. In comparison, a small value of RTO reduces the packet loss detection time at the cost of reducing the system throughput. As big data systems are connected via high-speed networks in a cluster environment, a low value of RTO seems appropriate in many cases. Many researchers have performed experiments demonstrating the effectiveness of low value of RTO. Typically, RTO of 1 ms has been found to be effective. Decreasing TCP RTO may reduce latency; however, it may decrease throughput due to the possibility of a large number of retransmissions.

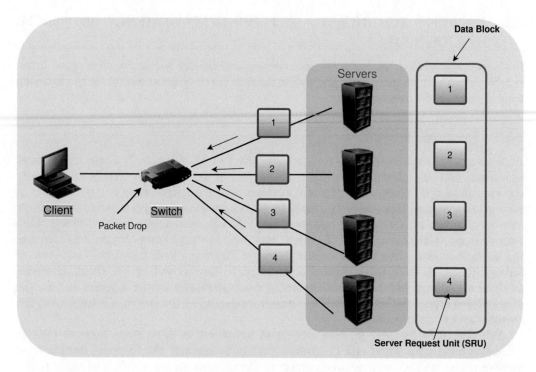

FIGURE 9.6 TCP Incast

3. **DCTCP**: Data Center TCP is a variation of TCP, which employs explicit congestion notification. Using ECN, a switch can mark packets if its queue exceeds a predefined threshold. This marking is then utilized by the recipient to notify the sender about the possibility of congestion at the switch. The sender can then adjust the sending rate to avoid packet loss. DCTCP carries the advantage of providing low- latency and high-throughput.

9.6 FAULT TOLERANCE

For medium to large scale clusters and data centers, cost of networking could scale up rapidly. As the number of hosts increase, pricing for interconnection also increase. One way of reducing the cost is to oversubscribe the network. Over subscription implies that full capacity bandwidth communication may not available to all the hosts all the time. For instance, for 1 Gbps, a ratio of 1:5 implies that at most 200 Mbps is available for host to host communication at a time.

While oversubscription reduces the cost, it also decreases the efficiency of the network. Therefore it is desirable to have high fault tolerance in the network. We now discuss Fat-tree and BCube – two popular architectures for achieving high fault tolerance.

9.6.1 Fat-Tree

The fat-tree architecture has been motivated to increase fault tolerance in data centers. A fat-tree is a general-purpose interconnection that is effective in utilizing high-speed interconnect bandwidth. Hosts (or nodes) are connected in a tree-like structure in a manner such that link bandwidth increases when upward from leaves to root. That is, as we traverse from

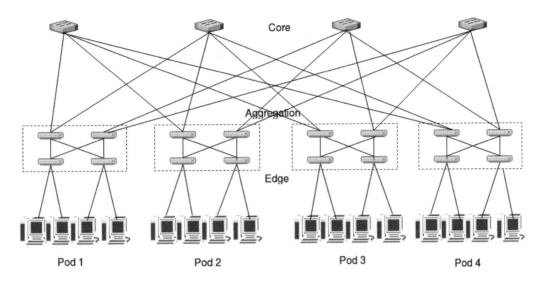

FIGURE 9.7 Fat-tree

end hosts to core of the network, bandwidth of the network increases. This characteristic reduces network congestion [246].

A typical fat-tree architecture is shown in figure 9.7. We can learn from the figure that if a host wants to send a message to another host then there are multiple paths available.

A unique feature of a fat-tree is that for any switch, there are same number of edges going down to the siblings of the switch as the number of parents going up to its parent in the upper level. In comparison to the traditional tree in which the link bandwidth is fixed, a fat-tree has increasing bandwidth when traverse upwards from leave to root. In this manner congestion problem is mitigated. In a fat-tree, leaf nodes represent processors whereas internal nodes are switches. Fat-tree also employs commodity hardware in order to reduce the cost.

9.6.2 BCube

BCube is a network architecture that takes a server-centric approach [186]. It is based on a modular data center, in which the data center is considered as portable module which can be deployed easily. The BCube architecture has servers as well as switches. Each server has multiple ports and switches that connect to a fixed number of servers. Figure 9.8 shows a sample BCube architecture with both servers and switches.

BCube can be connected recursively with $BCube_0$ simply being n servers connected to an n-port switch. $BCube_k$ is constructed with n $BCube_{k-1}$ having n^{k-1} switches each connecting same index server from all the BCube $_{k-1}$.

With 8-port mini-switches, it can support up to 4096 servers in one $BCube_3$ [186].

Both BCube and fat-tree utilize redundancy to achieve high fault tolerance. There is a high cost of fault tolerance. This can be mitigated through commodity hardware.

9.7 CONCLUDING REMARKS

Big data Systems require extensive networking solutions to support transfer of large data with low-latency. In this chapter, we have studied different mechanisms to cater network-related problems and issues for big data systems. These include flexibility and adaptability,

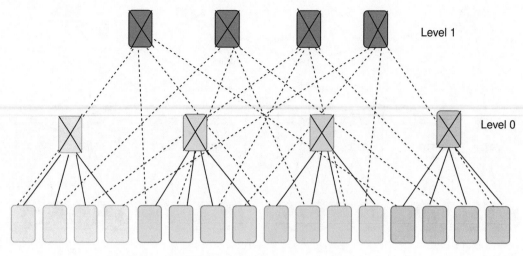

FIGURE 9.8 BCube architecture

high-speed data transfer, dealing with TCP Incast, and high fault tolerance. To provide an effective networking solution for big data is a challenging task. New challenges and solutions are being emerged.

9.8 FURTHER READING

Network requirements for big data have been discussed in references [150] and [379].
    Effect of SDN in big data has been discussed in reference [275].
    Edge computing has been explained in many research papers in references [195, 375].
    Data Center Network Topologies have been discussed in various papers [237, 377, 381].
    Data Center TCP (DCTCP) has been discussed in references [79, 80, 134, 381].

9.9 EXERCISE QUESTIONS

1. Describe why flexibility and programmability are important for big data systems?

2. Explain the significance of high throughput for big data systems.

3. Explain Software-Defined Network. How is it useful for big data systems?

4. Explain how RDMA is useful for big data systems?

5. How is InfiniBand different from Ethernet?

6. What benefits does SDN provide in terms of flexibility and adaptability?

7. Explain TCP Incast.

8. Explain DCTCP. How does it solve TCP Incast?

9. Explain how fault tolerance is achieved in data centers?

10. High-speed network incurs high cost. Do you think this is justified for all big data systems?

GLOSSARY

Bulk Transfer: It is a type of network traffic, which is usually required either for maintenance or for management of a data center.

Control Messages: These are latency-sensitive messages, which are used to send time-sensitive information such as cluster control or to detect abnormal activity or configuration updates.

Direct Data Placement: It is a technique through which data can be copied directly from the server adapter's receive buffer to the application buffer. DDP is built upon the RDMA protocol.

Fibre Channel over Ethernet (FCoE): It is a network technology that enables Fibre Channel communications to run directly over Ethernet.

InfiniBand (IB): It is a type of high-speed connection link, which is used in HPC systems. It facilitates high-speed network through RDMA.

RCaP: It is also referred as an RDMA-Capable Protocol. It is a generic term used to refer protocol stacks that provide the Remote Direct Memory Access (RDMA) functionality, such as iWARP and InfiniBand.

RDMA over Converged Ethernet (RoCE): It is a type of network, which delivers many advantages of RDMA while using the Ethernet-based implementation instead of InfiniBand-based Adapters (IBA).

Remote Direct Memory Access (RDMA): It is a technique to copy data directly to the remote server's memory.

Software-Defined Networking: It is a technique of implementing a network in which control plane is separated from data plane in order to have a more flexible and adaptive control of the network.

Security for Big Data

CONTENTS

S Ecurity is an important operational requirement for big data systems. A secured system is expected to provide trustworthy and uninterrupted access to users. The purpose of this chapter is to assess security requirements, identify challenges, and elucidate security-based solutions for storage and processing of big data systems.

10.1 INTRODUCTION

In order to understand security requirements and solutions, let us first discuss what is meant by security.

The term security in big data can be defined as collective means and measures to safeguard the service layer, data storage, processing, and networking against malicious attacks such as theft, leakages, undesired access, and improper computational output [349, 386]. Figure 10.1 illustrates four layers of a big data system. However, it is understood that implementation of a big data system varies for different systems. For instance, big data storage server may have a negligible role in computation. Similarly, a standalone big data server will have minimal implementation of the networking layer.

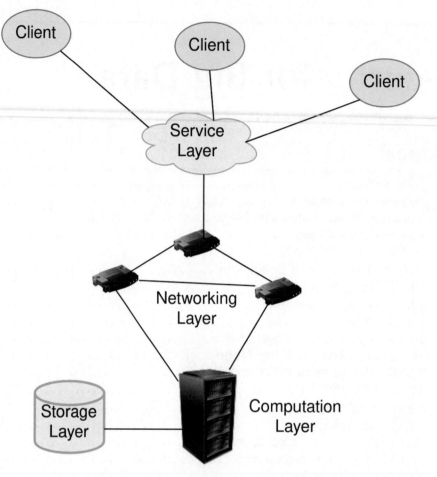

FIGURE 10.1 Big data-layered architecture

We will now assess a few important requirements of security.

10.2   SECURITY REQUIREMENTS

We outline the following important security requirements for a big data system:

1. **Service Availability**: A big data system should have high availability in order to meet its core operations. For instance, a video server should be able to provide video access to users. Similarly, an analytical system should have uninterrupted service of analytics.

2. **Confidentiality and Integrity**: The system should ensure confidentiality and integrity of data as well as of messages. The former term implies that confidential data should not be accessible to any other entity, whereas, the latter term requires that data and message integrity should be maintained such that fabrication or modification with false intent should be implausible and easily detectable. While confidentiality requirements may vary from one system to another, integrity requirements exist for all the big data systems.

3. **Protection Against Intrusion**: A big data system should have a strong protection from intrusion such that the possibility of launching attacks should be minimal.

4. **Ensuring Privacy and Protection Against Data Leakage**: The system should adhere to privacy of users. It should also ensure that data should not be leaked or stolen from the system.

The above mentioned four requirements should be met at all the layers of a system [215].

10.3   SECURITY: ATTACK TYPES AND MECHANISMS

Normally, attacks happen due to some **vulnerability** in the system. A vulnerability is defined as an opening or a weakness in the system, which can be exploited to launch an attack [320].

If a vulnerability is unknown, it is termed as a **zero-day attack**. An **attack vector** can be considered as a series of actions or operations launched by an attacker.

In terms of big data security, an **adversary** is an entity who has malicious intent and aims to induce security attacks. When the adversary becomes successful in launching an attack, she is termed as an **attacker**.

10.3.1   Attack Types

In a big data system, attacks can be of different types. These are mentioned below:

1. **Espionage**: An action where adversary spies classified or confidential data. The main goal here is to retrieve information that would not otherwise be available.

2. **Data Theft**: An action which involves the theft of confidential data.

3. **Denial of Service**: Also called as a **DoS attack** – an attack which degrades or denies core service operation of a system. For instance, a storage system will be unavailable to provide storage access if it encounters a denial-of-service attack. When the attack is launched through coordinated multiple sources, it is called a **DDoS (Distributed Denial Of Service) attack**.

4. **Fabricated Message**: A fake message, which is induced by an adversary into the system to either implicitly or explicitly induce false information.

An attacker can either be an insider or can be an outsider. The former implies that the attacker is from within the organization. In comparison, in the outsider attack, the attacker is an external person.

In order to launch an attack, an attacker needs access to the system. Access can either be physical or it can be through software. A software, which gives access to an attacker, is also known as **malware**. Table 10.1 summarizes the methods of access along with their description [161].

Once the access is granted, attack can be launched by exploiting vulnerabilities.

10.3.2   Attack Methods

We will now study different methods for launching attacks on big data systems [202, 232].

1. **Network Flooding**: A large number of messages are sent to the victim, which becomes unable to respond to legitimate requests, leading to a denial-of-service attack. There could be different types of attack messages such as connection requests, service requests, or arbitrary network messages [129]. **Example:** Denial of Service.

TABLE 10.1 Means to Gain Access for Launching an Attack

Access Method	Means and Description
Login-based access	An adversary can either steal user credentials or she can launch a brute force attack.
Code Injection	An adversary can inject malicious code through some Physical or remote access mechanism. For instance, using an infected USB or hijacking a user's click to download malicious code. It is important to note that person using the USB or downloading the code may not be the intruder.
Network Connection	An adversary can either intercept the network connection or exploit network-based vulnerabilities (such as DNS) to get access to the system.

TABLE 10.2 Types of Malware

Type	Description
Virus	It must be triggered by the activation of the host such as human activity.
Worm	It does not require activation through host. It can self-replicate and execute itself.
Rootkit	A malicious code that provide remote access to the target host without being detected.
Trojan-horse	A malware which disguises itself as a normal program.
Spyware	A malicious program that spies a user activity without being detected.
Adware	A type of malware which automatically displays advertisements.
Ransomware	A software which holds resources of the system while demanding some ransom.
Downloader	A malicious code or software that downloads and installs additional malware code to perform exploitation on the infected system.

2. **Malware**: A malicious code is injected in a system through some means. In table 10.1, we studied various mechanisms to get access. Malware could lead to different types of attacks such as data theft, DDoS, and Espionage. There could be different types of malware. These are summarized in table 10.2. **Example:** Denial of Service, Espionage, Data Theft, Fabricated Messages.

3. **Botnet**: An adversary can inject malicious code in a computing system and control the system remotely. This is called **bot** (derived from robot). A network of bots is created when an attacker is able to control many nodes. A botnet can be used to launch an attack on a target system as well. Botnet can also lead to a flooding attack.

   One of the most notable botnets that hit millions of devices, especially Internet of Things (IoT) appliances, and caused major outages in previous years was the Mirai botnet. The adversary were able to successfully compromise millions of devices to perform massive DDoS (Distributed Denial Of Service) attacks against very famous service providers including GitHub, Netflix, PayPal, Twitter, and Reddit. **Example** Denial of Service, Espionage, Data Theft, Fabricated Messages.

4. **DNS (Domain Name Service) Attack**: An attacker exploits vulnerabilities in the DNS entries of a system to make the DNS server holding the DNS information unavailable. Consequently, the big data system becomes unavailable. **Example:** DDoS.

5. **Man-in-the-middle Attack** : An adversary can intercept and fabricate communication between two communication end-points. **Example:** espionage, fabrication, DDoS, and Data Theft.

6. **SQL Injection Attack**: Malicious SQL statements are executed to extract sensitive information from a database. This is specifically true if the database is configured incorrectly [189]. **Example:** DDoS and Data Theft.

7. **Clickjacking**: An adversary can hijack user clicks through different measures such as sending spoofed emails, or malicious links. A malware is installed on the system which can be used to launch different attacks such as botnet [318]. **Example:** Data Theft, DDoS, and Espionage.

8. **Drive by Download Attack**: An adversary can initiate download of malicious malware. This can be initiated through clickjacking. **Example:** Data Theft, DDoS, and Espionage.

9. **Cross-site scripting**: An attacker can initiate execution of malicious script through embedded HTML. **Example:** Data Theft, DDoS, and Espionage.

10. **Data Breach**: An adversary can access to confidential data from the system. This can be accessed to various means such as malware, man-in-the-middle attack or even misconfiguration of the system. **Example:** Data Theft, DDoS, and Espionage.

11. **IP Prefix hijacking**: The prefix of a group of IP addresses is hijacked by corrupting IP routing tables in routing configuration. The hijacked group of addresses would experience reachability problems. This could lead to inaccessibility of services. **Example:** DDoS and Espionage.

Example 10.1 illustrates possibilities of a few of these attacks.

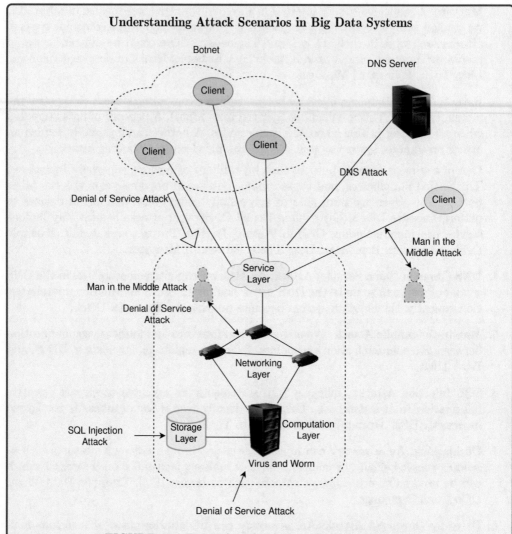

FIGURE 10.2 Examples of attacks in big data systems

Example 10.1 (Attack Scenarios in Big Data Systems). *Figure 10.2 illustrates different scenarios of security attacks in big data systems. Three clients are part of a botnet and launch a DDoS attack. Man-in-the-middle attacks is also shown in the figure. They can be initiated either by an insider or by an outsider. In the figure, the computation layer has been attacked through virus and worm. DDoS can be launched through various means including network flooding and DNS unavailability.*

10.4 ATTACK DETECTION AND PREVENTION

Detection [265] and attribution [321] of attacks and prevention from them is an important requirement for big data systems. In this section, we will study a few fundamental techniques for ensuring security in big data systems. Each of these techniques could either be used as a standalone measure or could be implemented as an integrated solution with few other techniques.

10.4.1   Encryption

A major challenge in ensuring security is that communication between two end points of a network can be sniffed by a third party. We studied man-in-the-middle attack in the previous section, which allows a third entity to sniff messages between two hosts. To maintain confidentiality, communication could be encrypted. Encryption allows a message to be encoded with a certain scheme such that it cannot be understood by any entity. A message encrypted by the sender is decrypted by the recipient at the receiver end. The encrypted text is also known as **ciphertext**.

Example 10.2 illustrates a scenario of encrypted communication between two end points. It can prevent the man-in-the-middle attack. Encryption is not necessarily incorporated for communication. It can also be used to encrypt stored data. In such a scenario, encryption can ensure data anonymity. Even in case of data theft, encrypted data will prevent leakage of data.

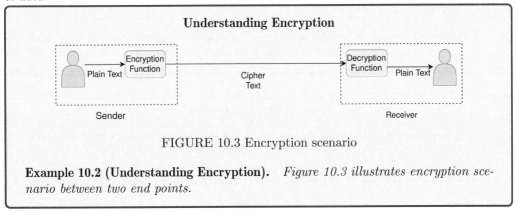

Understanding Encryption

FIGURE 10.3 Encryption scenario

Example 10.2 (Understanding Encryption). *Figure 10.3 illustrates encryption scenario between two end points.*

For encryption, two attributes are important, i.e., encryption function and encryption key. The former specifies the algorithm which is used to encrypt a message, whereas the latter determines the functional output of the encryption algorithm. Based on the type of encryption keys, there are two types of techniques for encryption:

1. **Symmetric Key**: In this type of cryptography, the same key is used for encryption as well as for decryption. Both the sender and the receiver must devise a mechanism to exchange the key. Secrecy of the key must be maintained between the two parties. Any entity with access to the secret key can either encrypt or decrypt the message.

2. **Public/Private Key**: In public/private key cryptography, a pair of public and private keys is used. Each entity must maintain its separate public, private key pair. If a message is encrypted with a public key it can only be decrypted with the corresponding private key and vice versa. For each entity, the public key is known to everyone, whereas, the private key has to be kept confidential to the entity alone.

Out of the two types of encryption techniques, Symmetric key encryption is lighter, i.e., it takes less computational resources. However, it is not scalable. This is because for point to point communication between "n" nodes, n * (n-1) keys are needed. In addition, exchanging keys between n nodes remains a challenge.

In comparison, public, private key pair-based cryptography takes higher computational resources. However, it is scalable. For communication between "n" nodes, "n" pairs of public, private keys are needed.

10.4.2 Digital Signatures

The main goal of encryption is to ensure message integrity as well as confidentiality. However, if only integrity of data is needed to be maintained then encryption is not needed. In such a scenario, digital signatures are implemented. Example 10.3 explains the operation of digital signatures.

Digital Signatures

Example 10.3 (Digital Signatures). *Digital Signature is a process of digitally signing the hash of the message (or data) with the private key of the sender. It ensures that any changes in the data (or the message) can be detected easily.*

Q. What is a hash function? *A hash function is used to compute a deterministic output. It can take variable size input but yields an output of fixed size. The function has following important characteristics:* $h = H(input)$

1. **Collision free**: *It is highly unlikely that two different inputs will yield the same output value of hash. That is, if $input_1$ is different from $input_2$ then $H(input_1)$ is different from $H(input_2)$.*

2. **Irreversible**: *It is irreversible, i.e., a hash function is a one-way function. Given h, it is computationally impossible to compute input.*

3. **Deterministic**: *For a given input, the hash function will always give the same output.*

4. **Fixed Size Output**: *The output of the hash function is always of the same size.*

Q. How hash of a message is used in digital signatures? *To ensure integrity, the hash of the message is signed with the private key of the sender and is sent to the recipient. Along with this, the message is also sent. Remember that the goal is to verify integrity i.e., to check if the message has been changed. At the receiver end, the receiver applied the corresponding public key of the sender and gets the unsigned hash. The receiver also computes the hash. If the computed hash equal to the signed hash then the message is considered as valid.*

Q. How digital signatures are less costly? *Since the output of the function is fixed, the process of digitally signing a message will be less costly as compared to encrypting the whole message.*

10.4.3 Firewall

A firewall is a combination of software and hardware, which is placed at the entry point of a network. Its purpose is to inspect all incoming and outgoing network packets in order to prevent attacks against networks. A firewall can either inspect packets against different rules or it can review packets against signatures of malware.

Example 10.4 illustrates that the firewall has a set of rules. For instance, DNS packets (UDP port 53) is prohibited from outside network.

Understanding Firewall Operations

Src IP	Src Port	Dest IP	Dest Port	Protocol	Action
Any	Any	Value 3	10.2.3.12	TCP	Allow
10.2.3.12	80	Any	Any	TCP	Allow
10.2.3.*	Any	Any	53	UDP	Allow
Any	Any	10.2.3.*	53	UDP	Deny

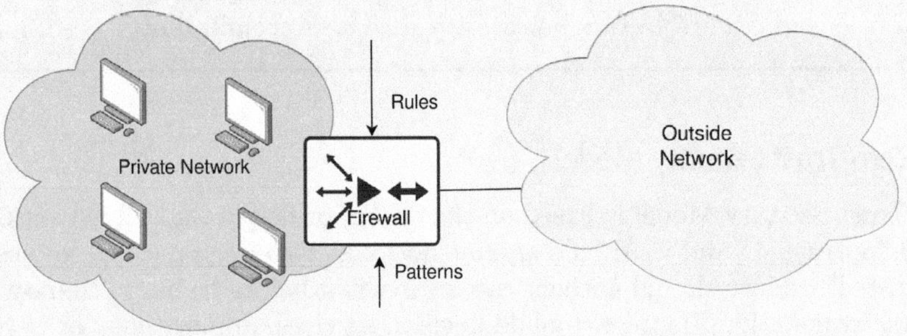

FIGURE 10.4 Firewall operation

Example 10.4 (Understanding Firewall Operations). *Figure 10.4 illustrates operation of Firewall. It can accept or reject packets based on two criteria, i.e., rules or patterns. In a rule-based firewall, a set of rules is configured by the administrator. The firewall accepts or rejects packets according to these set of rules. In a pattern-based firewall, incoming packets are matched against a database of malicious signatures. If the match is found then the packet is classified as malware and the packet is rejected.*

10.4.4   Access Control Systems

Access Control systems provide important services for controlling and limiting the access of sensitive information. These services are provided through different measures including authentication, authorization, and accountability:

1. **Authentication**: It is the process of authenticating a user based on some secret credentials such as Personal Identification Number (PIN) and passwords. OTP (one-time passwords) have also been used to strengthen the authentication mechanisms.

2. **Authorization**: It is the process of authorizing a user based on the credentials entered during the authentication process.

3. **Accountability**: It is the process of tracking and recording user activities.

Example 10.5 explains the concepts.

Access Control Mechanisms

Example 10.5 (Access Control Mechanisms). *Suppose Alice tries to access her bank account through her mobile application. She logs on the application using her credentials. Her banking application allows her to login after necessary verification from the bank. This process is considered as* **Authentication**. *After authentication, Alice's bank allows her to access all the relevant accounts. This process is called as* **Authorization**. *During the login session, all the activities of Alice are monitored and tracked to ensure security. This process is called as* **Accountability**.

10.4.5 Zero Trust Security Model

The Zero Trust Security Model is based on the design principle that all networks should be considered "untrusted" and we should assume nothing (zero-assumption). No user or device can be "trusted" and we should authenticate everything before trying to connect to the systems (users, workstations/laptops/mobile devices, services, applications, or network flow). Access will be granted just at the right time and only when the resource is required following the principle of least privilege, with strong authentication and authorization performed before granting them access.

Zero trust model is different from a traditional security model which assumes that every device inside a secure network can be trusted. Instead, in the zero trust architecture, the network is always assumed to be hostile. It focuses on protecting individual or narrowly defined groups of resources by adding smaller scoped controls and barriers. This approach avoids the need to allow broad-scoped trust zones and also eliminates the core concept of trusting network location as the primary component to the security posture of these resources. As a result, it increases the visibility of the security relationships between the system resources.

Zero trust security model has been evolved to include a variety of security controls and paradigms to drive trust in protecting systems and sensitive data from breaches. It allows us to create more dynamic and hardened security mechanisms when constructing new systems to protect against malicious threat.

Zero trust architecture has been used and implemented by many prominent organizations. Google has introduced BeyondCorp, which is a large-scale zero trust networking framework [17, 366]. Apart from Google, Microsoft and VMware have also developed their own security framework based on the zero trust model.

10.4.6 Virtual Private Network

A Virtual Private Network (VPN) is a virtual network which is established between a client and a server. Users can send and receive data as they are directly connected to the private networks. The network ensures end to end secure connection between the client and the server. Since VPN is a private network, the system can implement its own policies for network and user management. For instance, password-based authentication can be used to allow a user to enter the network. VPN can incorporate encryption to ensure end to end confidentiality. It can also prevent man-in-the-middle attack. Example 10.6 shows how VPN can enhance security.

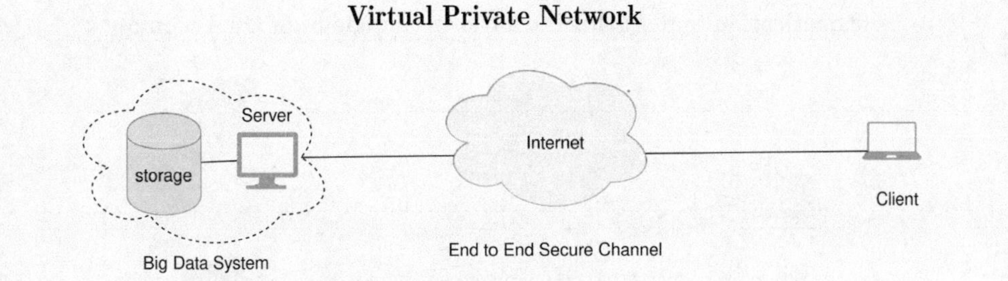

FIGURE 10.5 Virtual private network

Example 10.6 (Virtual Private Network). *Figure 10.5 illustrates functionality of VPN. A client accesses a big data system using the secure VPN channel.*

10.4.7 DNSSEC

A DNS server is used to resolve a host name to an IP address. If this resolution is altered then it can be a security threat to a big data system. For instance, DNS record of a big data system could be targeted – thereby making the big data system unavailable.

Traditional DNS servers are vulnerable to two kinds of attacks, i.e., man-in-the-middle attack and DNS cache poisoning attack. In the former case, an intruder can listen and alter the DNS communication between a DNS client and a DNS server. Whereas, in the latter case, local DNS client receives fake DNS receives a flood of bad DNS record entries making the DNS resolution targeted to a fake server.

The Domain Name System Security Extensions (DNSSEC) is a set of security protocols which can be used to ensure protection from these attacks. DNSSEC ensures integrity and security by sending digitally signed DNS records to the client. Signature ensures that messages cannot be altered by an attacker.

10.4.8 Single Sign on

A large number of attacks, which we have studied could occur due to insider attackers. That is, these attacks are launched mostly from within the network and thus cannot be protected from firewalls.

In order to protect from insider attacks, Single Sign On (SSO) techniques are effectively used. In an SSO system, a user authenticates herself with a dedicated authentication server. This could be achieved using any sign in technique such as password-based authentication. Once the authentication is completed, the user can access the desired services based on the authorization associated with the account [184,339]. Example 10.7 shows the functionality of SSO.

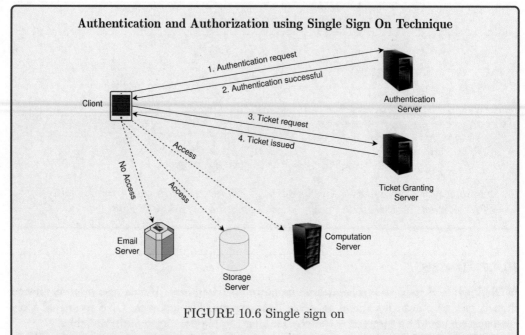

FIGURE 10.6 Single sign on

Example 10.7 (Single Sign On Technique). *Figure 10.6 illustrates authentication and authorization using SSO. In steps 1 and 2, a user authenticates herself. In steps 3 and 4, authorization is provided through a ticket. Once the user receives the authorization ticket, she can present the ticket to access desired servers. In the example, access to computation and storage servers is provided. However, the user does not have authorization to the Email server. Kerberos – a popular authentication and authorization system works on this principle [283].*

10.4.9   Blockchain

We have studied digital signatures, which ensures the integrity of data. However, when the integrity of a large number of transactions is needed to be maintained then blockchain is a useful solution.

Blockchain is a distributed ledger which is immutable [356]. This implies that data is stored in a distributed manner among many nodes and cannot be altered. Since data is distributed, there is no single point of failure. The major characteristic of a blockchain system is its integrity. Transactions are arranged in the form of blocks such that each block has many transactions. Blocks are arranged in the form of a chain. Each block's header has a hash which is computed from the hash of all the transactions in the block and the hash of the previous block in the chain. For the computation of hash, we should refer to the example 10.3.

Since each block has a hash of all the transactions in the block, if any transaction is modified then it will alter the hash of the block. Similarly, since each block is linked to its previous block through cryptographic hash, it will also alter its hash value.

Blockchain systems have been largely used to record transactions of crypto currencies. However, they can also be used for other systems such as supply chain [197]. Example 10.8 explains a blockchain system.

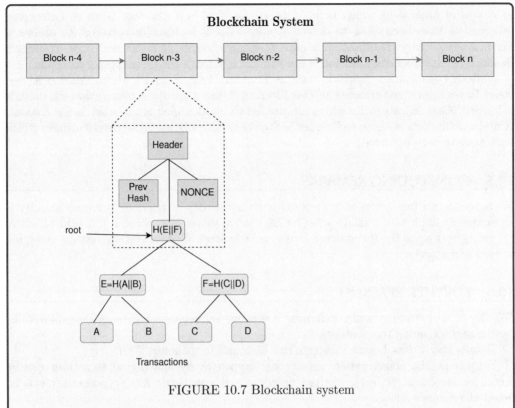

FIGURE 10.7 Blockchain system

Example 10.8 (Blockchain System). *Figure 10.7 illustrates the layout of a blockchain system. It is organized in the form of a chain of blocks. A tree-based system is used to store hash and data. Transactions (data) is stored at the leaf nodes, whereas subsequent levels of tree store hash values. In this manner, the root of the tree has the hash of all the data. Any changes of data at the leaf node will alter the hash values and thus integrity violations can be detected easily. Actual blocks has a header part, which contains a hash of the previous block, the root of the tree, and NONCE (number only used once) – a random number to introduce variation in the overall header of the block.*

10.4.10 SDN-based DDoS detection

SDN-based DDoS detection mechanisms have also been introduced. We should recall from our study in section 9.3 that SDN allows separation of control and data plane such that a network can be programmed through network switches. The same idea can also be used to detect DDoS attacks. If in a network, a large number of packets are sent to a target host, then the possibility of DDoS attack exists. The attack is detected at the SDN controller and the packets are prevented from being sent to the target host. In this manner, DDoS attack can be averted [93] and [94].

10.4.11 Machine Learning-based DDoS detection

Big data systems can also be used to detect security attacks [240, 265]. For this purpose, Machine Learning (ML)-based data classification models have been utilized. Classification is a type of process in which input data is classified into different types or categories. ML models have been used to detect attacks as well to identify patterns for malware. For instance, binary classification is used to classify events as either malicious or benign. Similarly, multi-label classification is used to identify more then one type of malware.

Various classification methods such as Decision Tree, Support Vector Machines, and Naive Bayes algorithms are used for classification. These algorithms require that the dataset is labeled. That is, categories which are needed to be identified are labeled in the dataset. A major limitation of these techniques is that they are only useful to detect attacks which have already been occurred.

10.5 CONCLUDING REMARKS

We have studied fundamental concepts about the security of big data systems. Security is an extremely important consideration for big data systems. New attacks and vulnerabilities are emerging frequently. It remains a challenge to protect big data systems against emerging threats and attacks.

10.6 FURTHER READING

Security is an extensive topic. Following are a few references which may be explored for further strengthening the concepts.

Details about data breach incidents can be found in reference [335].

Further details about public, private key cryptography and digital signatures can be found in references [88, 151], whereas details about symmetric key cryptography can be found at reference [269].

Details about firewall can be found in references [97, 248, 347]. SDN-based flooding attack detection is explained in references [106, 152].

More details about blockchain can be found in references [119, 162, 197, 355, 356].

Virtual Private Networks are explained in references [196, 357].

Access control systems are explained in references [244, 291].

Details about authentication mechanisms using single sign on techniques can be found in references [184, 283, 339].

DNSSec is explained in detail in references [143, 224]. Details about SQL injection attacks can be found in references [187, 217]. Details about clickjacking and it's prevention techniques can be found in references [120, 296].

10.7 EXERCISE QUESTIONS

1. Explain the security requirements for a big data system.

2. What are some types of security attacks for a big data system?

3. Explain the detection and prevention techniques of security attacks.

4. Explain the difference between Symmetric Key and Public/Private Key encryption.

5. How can we use digital signature to improve security?

6. Explain the use of access control mechanisms. How it helps to improve security?

7. Explain the difference between Denial of Service (DoS) and distributed DoS (DDoS) attack.

8. Explain the use of Virtual Private Network.

9. What is DNSsec and how it works?

10. How single sign on works and why it is important?

GLOSSARY

Access Control Systems: It is a kind of system with formalized set of rules or policies for granting or restricting user access to information, systems, and other resources.

Adversary: It refers to an entity who has malicious intent and aims to induce security attacks.

Attack Vector: It is a list of attacks that could happen in any system.

Botnet: It refers to an entire network of compromised devices (bots) without the knowledge of their owners.

Bots: The term is inspired from robots. It refers to a set of automated programs which are designated to perform tasks and respond to instructions. Auto registrations in online services are one example.

Clickjacking: It is a process of misleading a user to click on a hidden malicious link or button performing unintended actions without realizing it.

Denial of Service (DoS) attack: It is a kind of attack which disrupts the availability of applications, servers, and network resources to legitimate users.

Distributed Denial of Service (DDoS) attack: It refers to an attack which is launched from a distributed set of sources each of which is focused on launching a denial of service attack against the same target.

Espionage: It is a method to find out confidential information from non-disclosed sources.

Intrusion: It is a process of intruding into the system through some vulnerability.

Zero-Day Attack: It refers to an undiscovered or previously unknown attack.

Zero Trust Security Model: It is based on the design principle that all networks should be considered "untrusted" and we should assume nothing (zero-assumption).

Privacy for Big Data

CONTENTS

BIG DATA systems have been instrumental in solving many computational problems such as business intelligence and predictive analysis. They have opened new corridors of opportunities for predictive analysis. From social networks to financial transactions, a massive amount of data is being collected, analyzed, and used for prediction. While predictive analysis on big data has been useful in solving many data analysis problems, it has also highlighted privacy issues of users. This chapter provides an overview of privacy in the context of big data and also highlights the legitimate guidelines which can be used to strengthen privacy of the users.

11.1   INTRODUCTION

The term big data computing refers to massive amount of data – whereby storing, analyzing, and understanding such data can push the frontiers of technologies to the limit [317]. Massive data is being collected for big data systems by enterprises, organizations, and government agencies either with or without a user's knowledge. When a huge amount of data is collected from different sources, it brings the potential of solving many unanswered queries. Meticulous analysis and methodological prediction of big data have revealed useful results and solved unresolved queries for many applications.

While this meticulous analysis and methodological prediction has revealed useful results and solved unresolved answers, it has also raised privacy concerns of users. A user may be totally unaware that privacy is being violated in the collection of data. Ensuring that the privacy of a user does not violate and confidential information is not shared in big data systems is a massive challenge.

The purpose of this chapter is to provide an overview of privacy violations and concerns in the context of big data. This chapter explains the categorization of different privacy violations types which exist in big data systems and assesses the effectiveness and limitations of their protection techniques. The chapter also reviews legal propositions, laws, and social effects in privacy preservation and studies significant measures that can be implemented to strengthen privacy of the users in big data systems.

11.2 UNDERSTANDING BIG DATA AND PRIVACY

From social networks to financial transactions and shopping records, a large amount of data is being collected, integrated, and analyzed. Such analysis is extremely useful for forecasting and predictions in which different quantitative and qualitative methods can be used to solve relevant problems and predict the outcome. For predictive analysis, often data from several sources is integrated for improved analysis.

For instance, a departmental store can keep track of its customers' spending and determine relevancy between types of products purchased at the store and their relationship to customers age groups. The store can then focus on popular items to increase its sales. Similarly, in a smart city, movement of vehicles can be tracked [235] through sensors to determine volumes and patterns of traffic. This information can then be linked with information of vehicle owners in order to determine the relationship between age groups and their travel time and locations. The analysis can then be utilized for improved city planning.

The two examples mentioned above reflect the diversity and capabilities of big data applications in analyzing and solving many data science problems. Governments identify criminals, detect terrorist activities, and enhance citizen services. Similarly, corporate organizations improve user experience, generate revenues, and provide cost-effective solutions. This realization has not only increased the significance of big data, it has also enhanced the amount of data which is being collected for analysis.

While the impact of big data is massive, it has also led to increased concerns and violations of privacy. There are numerous instances happening where the information collected by government agencies and corporate organizations may lead to leakage of private and confidential information.

11.3 PRIVACY VIOLATIONS AND THEIR IMPACT

There could be two different types of methods in which data may be collected and confidential information may be inferred [280]. These include:
a) Direct Methods
b) Indirect Methods

11.3.1 Direct Methods

These methods directly collect user's confidential data with or without a user's knowledge. For instance, an email provider may auto-scan user's emails. The provider may pretend to use the scanned data for marketing and advertisement purpose. However, such information may also be used for building user profiles and to inquire confidential information related to a user's activities. The provider may legalize the data collection method and information inference technique through "terms of privacy" approved by the user at the time of registration. It is pertinent to note that legalization does not necessarily mean that a user's privacy is not violated. It only provides a legal cover to the organization that it is legally justified to collect the information.

Other techniques for inferring confidential information include collecting user search results, collecting credit card shopping trends, inferring electricity consumption through average monthly bills. All such methods may directly reveal specific information about a user.

11.3.2 Indirect Methods

Using indirect methods confidential information can be inferred through multiple sources. For instance, data from a user's credit card bill and medical bills can be integrated to generate health advice on the user's eating habits. Such types of information extraction methods are more difficult to detect and prevent.

11.4 TYPES OF PRIVACY VIOLATIONS

There are numerous possibilities of privacy violation in big data systems which could have variable impact on users. We have divided them into the following four categories [319] as illustrated in table 11.1.

a) Tracking by Governments
b) Utilization of confidential information by service providers
c) Re-identification attacks through external sources
d) Data breach

11.4.1 Tracking by Governments

Government is collecting an increasing amount of data as well as many different types of information about the individual. These records include data that contain personal information about individuals, from voter registrations, driver license records, property records, and death certificates. The government may well have important reasons for collecting this information and can use data to improve job, training, financial or evaluating equal opportunities policies.

However, the most significant reason for the increased collection of personal information is to improve security. They often store user's private data and information with the promise of improved security and enhanced services for their citizens. They execute monitoring and surveillance programs which include detecting traffic violations for implementing traffic laws or executing surveillance programs for enhancing national security and identifying anti-state elements.

While tracking by the government is operational in many countries as a good faith and to offer valuable citizen services, it also carries a potential of violating the privacy of citizens. According to the BBC, the UK government has access to people's phone and Internet records. The law has raised criticism and concerns about the availability of personal data. In the same way, the US government is collecting large amount of data from disparate sources in the interest of counter terrorism. The information collected can be used to determine confidential information of users [235]. A number of the anti-terrorism methods results with new laws that directly or indirectly affect personal privacy.

There is no doubt that increased levels of collecting information by the Government have raised privacy concerns.

TABLE 11.1 Categories of Privacy Violations

Possibilities for Privacy Violations	Description	Example
Tracking by Governments	Governments run surveillance programs to improve security. They can collect confidential information through multiple means.	**-PRISM** For intelligence purposes, the US government collects data from major service providers [153]. **-Monitoring** City governments collect data for improved citizen services such as traffic monitoring and speeding violations [235].
Information Collection by Service Providers	A Service Provider can collect and use a user's private data. This could be done for monetary purposes or financial gains. Note that in some cases privacy may be violated unintentionally, i.e., due to an error from the provider.	**-Auto scan** Email messages or posts from social network websites are scanned to reveal relevant advertisements. **-Accidental sharing of Google documents**. Google accidentally shared documents of users with other users.
Re-identification attacks through external sources	Individuals can be identified through correlation of big datasets.	**-Data Correlation** Confidential information about Governor William was identified by linking medical insurance records and voter registration database [91].
Data Breach	A data source can be hacked leading to exposure of private data to hackers.	**-Ashley Madison** (2015) Dating website was hacked and confidential information was made public Suspected insider attack. **-Talk Talk** (2015) Personal Details of almost 157,000 Customers of UK's major telecom provider were hacked Hacking and Unencrypted data.

11.4.2 Utilization of Confidential Information by Service Providers

A service provider often stores user's private data and utilizes confidential information to improve business models, marketing or advertisement purpose, and generate revenue. These providers, in various instances, provide free services in return to the user, for example, emails and social networking.

Consider an example of the service provider which uses big data techniques to process the high volume of data in order to create comprehensive user profiles from different sources.

These user profiles provide service providers with the ability to improve service to end users. For instance, Facebook and LinkedIn exploit this information for insights and recommend friends, jobs, groups, etc. Google, for instance, states that it scans users' emails for virus and spam protection, spell check, relevant search results, and features such as priority inbox and auto-detection of calendar events [247].

This utilization of information, however, raises a significant threat to user privacy. Service providers may utilize these confidential information without user approval and can result in disclosure of personal information. For instance, they can utilize these personal information in user profiles for targeted advertising. They can sell personal data to third parties for monetary purposes or financial gains without users' effective knowledge or consent. These information may then be used for commercial or even malicious purposes. In recent years, this increased utilization of information has shown the importance of taking privacy into consideration when contributing data in online services.

11.4.3   Re-identification Attacks Through External Sources

Re-identification attacks occur on public anonymous datasets when particular anonymous data is linked to multiple sources in order to reveal confidential information or the anonymity of data is compromised through the process of re-identification. Any information that distinguishes one person from another can be used for re-identifying anonymous data [281]. These datasets may have been published for social, personal, or research purposes. An attacker may have personal or financial aims for re-identification attacks. The number of publications has been developed on re-identification.

We explain few of the well-known case studies for re-identification attacks in example 11.1.

Re-identification attacks

Example 11.1 (Re-identification attacks). Netflix-IMDb attack: *An example of re-identification attack can be taken from the Netflix incident in 2007 where it published anonymous data from its customers with an aim to improve its movie recommendation system. In order to protect the privacy of its customers, all the personal information was obfuscated. However, using the date of the rating and utilizing the IMDb database, it was proved that confidential information from the Netflix dataset could be partially revealed [280].*

Re-identification of Massachusetts Governor William: *Another instance about re-identification is published from MIT in which confidential information about Governor William was identified by linking medical insurance records and voter registration database [91].*

AOL breach: *Similarly, in 2006, a re-identification attack was successful on the anonymized data from AOL such that identity of a user was exposed from the anonymous dataset published by the search engine organization [89].*

The Re-identification attacks [210] can be classified into three categories:

1. **Correlation attacks**: This type of attack requires an adversary to correlate two or more datasets to obtain a more clear and distinct record. In this attack, A distinguishing feature of the correlation attack is that it does not reveal information about any particular person. Instead sensitive information about a group of individuals is iden-

tified. The data breach caused in the Netflix dataset is an example of the correlation attack [280].

2. **Arbitrary Identification attacks**: In this type of re-identification attack, the objective is to relate at least one data entry in an accumulated dataset to the identity of a particular individual, with an adequate level of likelihood. This leads to learning all anonymously released information about that individual. Privacy breaches caused by AOL search data [89] is an example of this attack in which analyzing the anonymized dataset resulted in identification of specific members.

3. **Target Identification attacks**: This type of re-identification attack is considered most threatening which involves an intentional attack to a particular person's privacy. The objective of this type of attack is to target a given individual and succeed only if it can link some dataset records to the identity of an individual, with an adequate level of likelihood. The confidential information revealed about Governor William [91] is an example of such an attack.

Although we have described re-identification attacks on public anonymous datasets, the process of reidentification is also performed on information collected by government and service providers.

11.4.4 Data Breach

Data breach incidents are considered most disastrous among these types in which incidents generally involve theft of confidential information through hacking of large datasets. Data breach incidents are prime contributors to stealing private information. Confidential information such as credit cards, personal records, and social security numbers can be breached and exploited.

There could be various causes of data breach ranging from insider threats to malware and misconfigured networks [21]. For example, the Ashley Madison incident has been suspected to be an insider job; whereas, the Target breach occurred due to malware exploiting configuration issues in the network. Malware-based attacks and impersonation of the organization have been the biggest contributors to data breach incidents [320]. Other possibilities such as SQL injection attacks, physical thefts, and privilege escalation are also possible. Table 11.1 lists some of the known data theft incidents along with their root causes. These incidents have caused immeasurable loss to customers. For instance, in the case of Ashley Madison incident, some of the victims have claimed to commit suicide.

Financial systems and public datasets have been the biggest victim of data theft. This is understandable as data theft from such systems is likely to have the biggest impact [21]. Stolen data can be sold to black market and used for ID thefts as well.

Of the above-mentioned four types of privacy violations, the first two types, i.e., Tracking by the Government and Information Collection by Service Providers are often protected through laws and privacy policies. This provides rights of information collection and assessment to the two entities. However, as we elaborate in the next section, concerns exist about the limits, restrictions, and legality of data collection and information retrieval through these means.

11.5 PRIVACY PROTECTION SOLUTIONS AND THEIR LIMITATIONS

The foremost requirement of enhancing user privacy is the existence of laws, which can protect user privacy. This is followed by privacy preserving and data anonymity techniques. In addition, physical and security measures should also be employed to prevent data theft.

Note that these solutions are inter-related. For instance, strong laws can enforce providers to implement these measures against data breach.

11.5.1 Privacy Laws and Regulations

The impact of laws has been instrumental in preserving privacy. These laws can control government tracking and bind service providers to limit reading, analyzing, or publishing users' private data. Laws can also enforce service providers to implement proper mechanisms for ensuring data secrecy and prevent data theft. Further, laws can bind service providers to incorporate privacy by design – a requirement which ensures that privacy is incorporated during the process of system design and software development [147].

Tangible laws which can preserve and protect privacy are still in evolution. National security has always been given the highest precedence and is being rightly considered as the utmost priority. Governments collect private information with the promise of improved security [153] and enhanced services for their citizens [235]. This raises important privacy concerns related to the extent of private data collection and the intent of its usage.

PRISM [153] allows the US government to track and access customers' data directly from service providers. Similarly, under the Phone Metadata Program, telecommunication providers provide customers metadata to government agencies and Internet providers. In addition, governments can demand providers to bypass their privacy and security measures and provide access to confidential information. In the "United States against the Lavabit" case, the US government demanded Lavabit's private keys (SSL) to seek information about Edward Snowden. Handing over the private key to the government means compromising the security of every user. In this case, the government compromised the privacy of more than 400,000 Lavabit account holders in order to track Snowden's account.

While governments have been able to collect information from corporate organizations, there are a few instances where service providers have resisted sharing confidential information of their customers. For instance, Apple resisted sharing confidential information with the FBI about a shooter who was involved in a shooting incident in California.

Service providers publish their data usage and privacy policies, which grant rights to service providers for sharing user information with third parties and governments. Consequently, users have limited options available in selecting service providers which safeguard their privacy. Many users remain ignorant about privacy and data sharing policies. The European Union (EU) has regulated data control through General Data Protection Regulation (GDPR) which regulates the control and export of data originating from EU [147]. More laws and regulations are being passed to restrict and govern the use of personal data while giving consumers greater control over the use of their data.

Cyber laws also exist to prevent data theft incidents. These laws require service providers to be more accountable for storing and collecting confidential information. In case of data breach incidents, service providers are also fined by the governments and are asked to financially compensate users as well.

11.5.2 Techniques for Preventing Re-identification Attacks

Confidential information in public data can be hidden by introducing anonymity and diversity. A dataset has some identifiers called Quasi Identifier – Qid, which is used to identify individual data items. Qid attributes are released in public, whereas sensitive attributes are hidden and kept confidential. Sensitive information can be identified by integrating the publicly available dataset with some external sources. We explain a few of the important techniques for providing anonymity in public datasets along with their limitations:

1. **K-anonymity**: K-anonymity [257] is a privacy preserving technique which relies on introducing anonymity. The dataset has some identifiers called as Quasi Identifier - Qid, which are used to identify an individual data item. The dataset may also have some sensitive attributes which are desired to be kept secret from the public. In a normal scenario for publicly available dataset, sensitive attributes are hidden whereas QID attributes are released. However, sensitive information can be identified by integrating the publicly available dataset through some external source. The K-anonymity scheme suggests that there should be a k number of redundant QiDs in order to ensure anonymity. The minimum number of k is 2 however, larger numbers are also possible.

Example 11.2 illustrates how K-anonymity can be achieved.

An example of K-anonymity

Example 11.2 (K-anonymity). *Figure 11.1 illustrates a sample scenario. For the input data shown in figure 11.1 (a), k-anonymity has been introduced in figure 11.1(b). With k = 4, for each set of similar Qids, there are four rows with identical information about sensitive data (disease).*

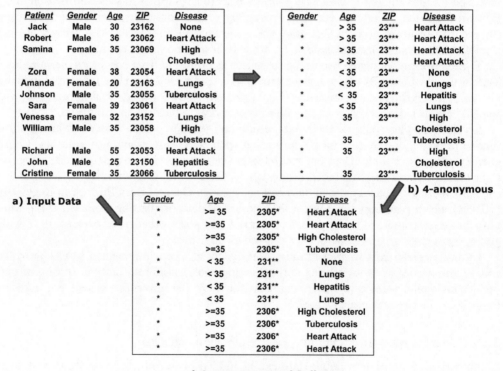

FIGURE 11.1 Re-identification attacks

The K-anonymity technique has suffered from the *homogeneity attack* and the *background attack*. Both homogeneity and background attacks are caused by the fact that there is not sufficient diversity in the set of sensitive values present in a QID group.

(a) **Homogeneity Attack**: The homogeneity attack occurs when each record, with the same value for the quasi-identifier, also assumes the same value for the sensitive attribute. Using homogeneity attack, an adversary can identify sensitive information related to an individual if there is not much diversity in the data as illustrated in example 11.3.

An example of Homogeneity Attack

Example 11.3 (Homogeneity Attack). *In figure 11.1(b), individuals can be identified since sensitive information is homogenous across multiple records for age above 35.*
Consider an example where suppose that Tom knows his friend Robert is a male age 36 living in 23062 area, Tom can therefore easily infer that Robert had a Heart Attack.

(b) **Background Knowledge Attack**: K-anonymity does not guarantee privacy against attackers which have background knowledge about the target respondent. An adversary with background knowledge about gender, zip, and physical condition of the victim can also identify sensitive information as illustrated in example 11.4.

An example of Background Knowledge Attack

Example 11.4 (Background Knowledge Attack). *Consider another scenario in which Clair knows that her friend Samina is a female 35 years old and living in the 23069 area. Observing the 4-anonymous table in figure 11.1(b), Clair can assume that Samina is suffering from either High Cholesterol or Tuberculosis. Assume that Clair knows Samina is overweight and has diabetes, she can conclude that Samina is not suffering from Tuberculosis and therefore suffering from High Cholesterol.*

---

2. **L-diversity**: The L-diversity anonymization technique has been motivated to solve the limitations of the K-anonymity. This technique proposes that there should be enough diversity in the sensitive attributes so that the QID attributes remain unidentifiable [257] as illustrated in example 11.5.

It is also easy to see that L-diversity prevents both homogeneity and background knowledge attacks. L-diversity counteracts homogeneity attack since each equivalence class includes at least l well-represented values for the sensitive attribute. It also reduces the effectiveness of background knowledge attack since the adversary requires more knowledge to associate a unique sensitive attribute value with a particular respondent.

An example of L-diversity

Example 11.5 (L-diversity). *With our example of 4-anonymous and 3-diverse table in figure 11.1(c), we can easily observe that there is enough diversity for the sensitive attribute for each set of similar QIDs such that determining exact value is not possible.*
Suppose that Clair knows that her friend Samina is a female 35 years old who currently lives in the 23069 area. Based on this information, Clair learns that Samina information is contained in record number 9, 10, 11 or 12 and she is suffering from either High Cholesterol, Heart Attack or Tuberculosis. Since Clair knows that Samina is overweight and diabetes, she can exclude the fact that Samina suffers from Tuberculosis, however, she still cannot precisely conclude whether Samina suffers from High Cholesterol or Heart Attack.

Datasets using L-diversity techniques can suffer from *skewness* and *similarity* attacks.

(a) **Skewness Attack**: The skewness attack occurs where the distribution of the sensitive attribute value within a given equivalence class is significantly different with respect to the frequency distribution of sensitive attribute values in the overall dataset.

(b) **Similarity Attack**: The similarity attack is possible where an adversary can determine likely possibilities of the disease when the values for the sensitive attribute for an equivalence class are although distinct but semantically similar. On this assumption, an adversary can infer important information as illustrated in example 11.6.

An example of Similarity Attack

Example 11.6 (Similarity Attack). *As another example, with reference to the table in figure 11.1(c), it is possible to infer that anyone less than 35 years old has 75% probability of suffering from lungs related diseases.*

3. **T-closeness**: To overcome the limitations of l-diversity, i.e., to prevent skewness and similarity attacks, t-closeness is proposed. This states that the frequency distribution of sensitive attributes within each equivalence class should be "close" (t-close, where "t" is a fixed threshold value) to their distribution of the sensitive attributes in the entire dataset [337].

Using this technique, the likelihood of both the skewness attack and the similarity attack is reduced. The t-closeness reduces the difference between the distribution of a sensitive attribute in each equivalence class with respect to the distribution of the attribute in the whole dataset and therefore, the skewness attack is not possible. It also reduces the effectiveness of the similarity attack, because the semantically similar values in each equivalence class do not provide additional information to the adversary with respect to the whole dataset information.

Although T-closeness protects against skewness and similarity attacks, it lacks computational procedures to reach t-closeness with minimum data utility loss. That is, data utility loss is likely when achieving for T-closeness.

4. **Differential Privacy**: Differential privacy [337] is a privacy model offers strong privacy guarantees. It aims to limit the disclosure of sensitive data by limiting the impact of each individual in the answered query. This is achieved by adding appropriately chosen noises, e.g. Laplace mechanism and geometric mechanism, to the aggregate results.

This technique protects the individual privacy by adding sufficient noise to the query result; however, the original data still resides at the server where it is vulnerable to data breaches. Improper disclosure of the original data can cause data privacy breaches.

11.6 CONCLUDING REMARKS

The rise of big data systems has resulted in a huge compromise of users' privacy. Users' information can be collected to infer lifestyle and assess income patterns. Citizens are being tracked by governments and service providers to enhance services and increase revenues. Private information can also be stolen through data breaches and hacking. A corporate organization can also sell users' data to generate revenue.

Big data systems have been instrumental in improving citizens' services and enhancing users experience. However, they have also been influential in leakage of private information. While the importance of big data systems has been established in analytics and prediction, it is imperative that means should be adopted to preserve confidential information and prevent leakage of privacy in big data systems. We have highlighted important factors which can be effective in improving users' privacy. Cohesive efforts are needed in order to achieve this important goal.

11.7 FURTHER READING

Verizon has published its annual Data Breach Investigations Report (DBIR) and can be obtained from reference [21].

Details about Re-identification attacks can be found in reference [210]. References [89, 91, 280] explain different examples and well-known case studies for Re-identification attacks, whereas references [257, 337] explain techniques for preventing re-identification attacks.

References [147, 153, 235] present a detailed discussion on privacy laws and regulations.

11.8 EXERCISE QUESTIONS

1. Explain Re-identification attacks. How it leads to re-identified data?

2. Explain K-anonymity with example.

3. Explain the difference between Homogeneity and Background Knowledge attack.

4. Explain L-diversity with example.

5. Explain how L-diversity can suffer from skewness and similarity attacks?

6. Explain T-closeness. How this technique can be used to reduce the likelihood of skewness and similarity attacks?

7. Describe how differential privacy can be useful?

8. Explain how data breach incidents can cause privacy issues?

9. Elaborate how information collected by service providers can yield to privacy violations?

10. Describe the significance of laws in protecting privacy of individuals.

GLOSSARY

Arbitrary Identification Attack: This type of attack attempts to relate with high probability at least one entry in an accumulated dataset to the identity of a particular individual.

Correlation Attack: This attack involves correlating different datasets to obtain a more distinct and cohesive set of database records.

Cyber Security: This refers to technologies, processes, and measures that are designed to protect systems, networks and data from cybercrimes.

Data Breach: It refers to the act of security breach that leads to the accidental or unlawful destruction, loss, alteration, unauthorized disclosure of, or access to protected data transmitted, stored or otherwise processed.

Differential Privacy: This technique aims to limit the disclosure of sensitive data by limiting the impact of each individual in the answered query.

K-anonymity: It is a technique of providing anonymity to data by adding at least k number of redundant quasi-identifiers (QIDs) in the dataset; provides anonymity for k1 individuals.

L-diversity: It is a technique, which relies on distribution of a sensitive attribute such that each equivalence class has at least 1 well-represented value.

PRISM: It is a program which allows the US government to collect data from major service providers for intelligence purposes.

Re-identification Attacks: It is an attack which utilizes anonymized data to find individuals in public datasets.

Service Provider: It refers to an organization that provides a service to a normal user, e.g. The Internet Service Provider.

Surveillance: It refers to an act of closely observing a person or a group, especially one under suspicion.

Target Identification Attack: It refers to initiating an intentional attack in order to target a specific identity.

T-closeness: It refers to an anonymity technique in which the frequency distribution of sensitive attributes within each equivalence class should be close (t-close, where t is a fixed threshold value) to their distribution of the sensitive attributes in the entire dataset.

IV

Computation for Big Data

CHAPTER 12

High-Performance Computing for Big Data

CONTENTS

B IG DATA systems require massive amount of computational and storage resources for their proper execution. The notion of High-Performance Computing (HPC) is often utilized to meet the large scalability demands of big data systems.

The purpose of this chapter is to explain the usage of HPC systems for Big Data.

12.1 INTRODUCTION

A fundamental requirement of big data systems is that they require large computational resources for storage and processing massive volume of data. High-Performance Computing (HPC) is a type of computing in which large computational resources (computational power or storage) are utilized to achieve higher performance. HPC involves integration using hardware and software. In the context of big data, HPC systems are intrinsic as they provide necessary computational and storage resources for execution.

In chapter 2, we discussed organization of big data systems into clusters. We also studied distributed and shared memory paradigms in section 2.3. These concepts are necessary to understand organization of HPC systems.

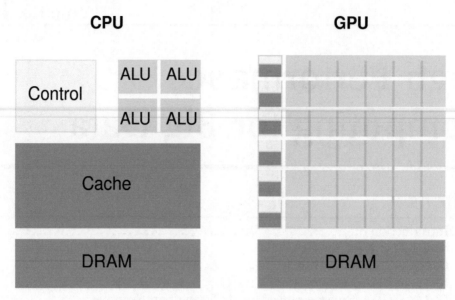

FIGURE 12.1 Support for parallelism – Difference between GPU and CPU

12.2 SCALABILITY: NEED FOR HPC

Scalability is the driving factor for implementing HPC systems. It refers to the ability of the system to adapt to increasing needs of processing or storing data. In general, there are two possibilities of scaling systems [329]:

1. **Horizontal Scaling**: This involves adding more computational resources such as independent workstations or adding more processors. This type of scaling often requires adding more resources without replacing existing resources. Therefore, commodity hardware and workstations can also be deployed. Horizontal scaling employs distributed memory model for communication among the workstations. Google's MapReduce system has been based on horizontal scaling.

2. **Vertical Scaling**: Vertical scaling involves upgrading or replacing hardware with a more powerful unit. This type of scaling often involves a single server with a more capable execution unit. Vertical scaling often relies on a shared memory model.

As discussed, horizontal scaling systems employ a distributed memory model. These systems are based on shared nothing architecture such that workstations (or processing units) works independently. A middleware (or a software) is used to unleash the parallelism in the shared nothing architecture. In comparison, vertical scaling systems are tightly bound such that processors may share memory, cache, and disk system. HPC systems are tightly coupled systems, which are interconnected via high-speed interconnects.

To enhance scalability, big data systems often incorporate **accelerated computing**. It refers to the use of special hardware to enhance the capability of computation and increase scalability of the system. We will now discuss GPUs and TPUs – the two widely known platforms for accelerated computing.

12.3   GRAPHIC PROCESSING UNIT

Figure 12.1 highlights major differences between GPU and CPU. GPUs are capable to compute at high FLOPS (Floating Point Operations), which is a unit of measuring the capability of a processor in performing computations involving floating point operations.

A GPU achieves high FLOPs through a specific architecture in which less space is devoted to caching and comparably more space is allocated to ALU (Arithmetic Logic Units). The dense ALU architecture allows a GPU to perform arithmetic operations with a higher speed. This is because more transistors are available, which can be utilized for processing data.

The difference in architecture also makes GPUs highly suitable for data parallelism or SIMT (Single Instruction Multiple Thread) architecture (section 2.2.5). In that, the same code (but different data) is executed at each thread of the GPU. The code is executed in parallel on each thread of the GPU. As a GPU could consist of hundreds of threads, it is highly suitable for data-intensive tasks. Example 12.1 explains the concept of data parallelism through matrix addition.

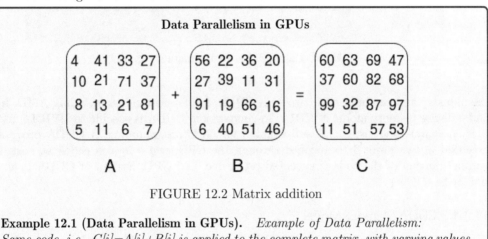

Data Parallelism in GPUs

FIGURE 12.2 Matrix addition

Example 12.1 (Data Parallelism in GPUs).   *Example of Data Parallelism: Same code, i.e., C[i]=A[i]+B[i] is applied to the complete matrix, with varying values of i.*

$$C[i] = A[i] + B[i] \qquad (12.1)$$

A GPU program (also called as a kernel) is organized into blocks of threads. Architecturally, a GPU consists of scores of Streaming Multiprocessors (SMs). Each SM consists of a number of Streaming Processors (SPs). An SP is an execution mapping of a thread.

A GPU program is divided into execution units called threads and is executed on SPs. These threads are organized into thread blocks which are mapped on SMs. Each thread has access to a small and fast cache memory as well as larger and slower global memory. Threads within the same block can be synchronized for execution. This implies that check points can be inserted for execution. They also share a memory block called shared memory. This is smaller and faster than global memory. Thread-communication across blocks is restrictive. That is, threads in one block are not allowed to communicate with the threads in the other block. This is because it is not guaranteed that all thread blocks will be executed at the same time.

OpenCL (Open Computing Language) and **CUDA** (Compute Unified Device Architecture) are two major programming platforms for GPUs. OpenCL is an open standard of

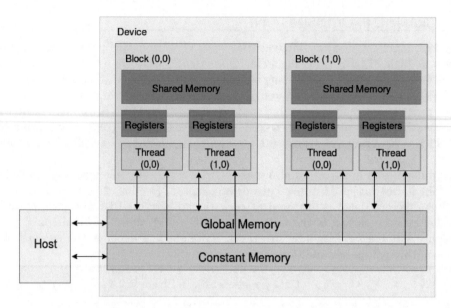

FIGURE 12.3 GPU – device memory model

the industry and can be used to program GPUs of different vendors including AMD, Intel, and – device memory model NVIDIA. In comparison, CUDA is specific to NVIDIA GPUs. It is comparatively, easier and well-adapted for GPU programming. A CUDA program is executed in two parts. It is invoked through the CPU, which is also called as host. The parallel portion of the code is executed on device, i.e., GPU. Syntax of CUDA is almost similar to C/C++.

12.3.1 CUDA Memory Model

Figure 12.3 shows memory model of GPU for CUDA. Global Memory is used to transfer data between host and device. It is much slower then constant memory; however, contents of constant memory cannot be changed. A CUDA kernel consists of many blocks, each block may contain many threads. The figure shows two blocks with dimension (0,0) and (1,0). This can be interpreted as there are two blocks which are identified as "0" and "1" along the x-axis, whereas the identifier is the same along the y-axis. In general, dimensions of a CUDA kernel are represented as blocks in x,y, and z directions. Similarly, blocks can have dimensions along x, y, and z axis as well.

Registers are local to each thread. They are used to store automatic variables, whereas shared memory is used to share data within a block. Global memory can be assessed by threads within a kernel.

12.3.2 CUDA Programming Model Through an Example

Let us understand parallel programming in GPU using CUDA through a code example. In example 12.1, we observed that two matrices can be added and the result can be stored in a third matrix. A matrix can be extended as a one-dimensional array. We will now see CUDA code to add two arrays. But before seeing the code, it is important to understand some preliminaries.

As we discussed earlier, code in CUDA is divided into two parts, i.e., host (CPU) code and device (GPU) code. Below are the sequence of steps for addition:

1. Creating input arrays A and B and the resultant array C on the host.

2. Creating arrays on the device using **cudaMalloc**.

3. Copying data from host to device using **cudaMemcpy**.

4. Calling the Kernel function, which performs the required task in parallel on the device.

5. Copying result from the device to the host.

6. Printing the result.

Example 12.2 shows CUDA code addition of two arrays A and B into the third array C. Addition is performed in the kernel function "add". The function takes three parameters, i.e., pointers to three memory locations a, b, and c. The function simply adds the values of a and b and stores them in c. Since the function is called separately for each thread of the GPU and each thread only adds one index element from arrays A and B, the program is capable to add the total number of elements as declared by the variable arraySize.

The main function declares the two input arrays and the resultant array c. The function **cudaMalloc** is responsible for allocating memory on CUDA device. It takes two parameters. The first parameter is the pointer while the second parameter is the desired number of bytes to allocate.

We should observe that cudaMalloc only allocates memory in the global memory, it does not copy the contents. In order to load the memory with input values, we use the **cudaMemcpy** function. The function is used to copy data from CPU (host) to GPU (device) and vice versa. It has four options for data copying. These are **cudaMemcpyHostToHost**, **cudaMemcpyHostToDevice**, **cudaMemcpyDeviceToHost**, and **cudaMemcpyDeviceToDevice**. These options specify the direction of the copy from host to host, host to device, device to host, and device to device, respectively. Subsequently, there are two calls to cudaMemcpy, one before calling the kernel function for copying host to device, and the second after the kernel function for copying data from device to host.

Addition of Two Arrays – CUDA Example [368]

Example 12.2 (Addition of Two Arrays – CUDA Example).
```
    #include <stdio.h>
/* Kernel Function */
__global__ void add(int *c, const int *a, const
    int *b)
{int i = threadIdx.x;
c[i] = a[i] + b[i];}
/* Main Program */
int main()
{
const int arraySize = 4;
const int a[arraySize] = { 10, 9, 8, 7};
const int b[arraySize] = { 1, 2, 3, 4};
int c[arraySize] = { 0 };
// declare three pointers for A,B,and C
int *dev_a = 0;
int *dev_b = 0;
int *dev_c = 0;
// Create buffers to store i/o
cudaMalloc((void**)&dev_c, size * sizeof(int));
cudaMalloc((void**)&dev_a, size * sizeof(int));
cudaMalloc((void**)&dev_b, size * sizeof(int));
// Copy input vectors from host memory to GPU
    buffers.
cudaMemcpy(dev_a, a, size * sizeof(int),
    cudaMemcpyHostToDevice);
cudaMemcpy(dev_b, b, size * sizeof(int),
    cudaMemcpyHostToDevice);
// Launch a kernel on the GPU with one thread for
    each element.
add<<<1, size>>>(dev_c, dev_a, dev_b);
// Copy output vector from GPU buffer to host
    memory.
cudaMemcpy(c, dev_c, size * sizeof(int),
    cudaMemcpyDeviceToHost);
printf("result is = %d,%d,%d,%d,%d \n",
c[0], c[1], c[2], c[3]);}//end of Main
```

More details about CUDA programming can be obtained from references [223, 308].

12.3.3 Usage and Advancements for Big Data

GPUs provide increased parallelism for handling and managing big data. This capability has enabled many efficient solutions. We can understand the details of a few efficient GPU-enabled solutions for big data through following examples:

1. **MapReduce**: It is a popular big data platform, which has been explained in chapter 4. MapReduce has been ported to GPUs [137, 194, 345, 346]. In that, each thread of a

GPU can act either as a mapper or a reducer. Remember that during the map phase of MapReduce, SIMD (Single Instruction Multiple Data) architecture is followed. This makes GPUs ideal to solve MapReduce tasks.

For GPU-compliant MapReduce, execution can follow two steps. During the first step, map phase is executed and each GPU thread can individually execute mapper. Alternatively, threads within a block can collaborate to combine map tasks operating within a block. The resultant data from the map phase can be written back to the CPU, where values are aggregated according to keys. A second kernel can be launched for reduce task.

A core advantage for GPU-based MapReduce is that the Map phase can utilize the inherent parallelism of GPUs. Further, communication bottleneck between mapper and reducer can be reduced as CPU to GPU bandwidth is higher than the network bandwidth.

2. **Spark**: It is another popular big data platform and has been discussed in chapter 6. Spark has been ported on GPUs [243, 380]. We should recall that Spark utilized in memory computation to overcome shortcomings of MapReduce for iterative tasks and streaming. GPUs can meet this requirement through availability of shared memory per block. Further, stream-processing and pipelining in GPUs can be utilized to develop efficient Spark solutions. However, memory in graphic cards is smaller as compared to CPU memory; therefore, capabilities of GPU-enabled Spark remain limited unless multiple GPUs are connected together.

3. **Machine Learning and Deep Learning**: These are two important applications of big data. Deep Learning will be discussed in chapter 13. GPUs can be greatly helpful for both these applications. Machine learning requires iterative computing based solutions, where interim results are needed to be stored in memory instead of writing to hard disk. In a related context, deep learning requires layers of computation for feature extraction and testing. Both techniques require extensive parallelism for faster execution. GPUs can be greatly useful in proving an efficient parallel solution.

12.4 TENSOR PROCESSING UNIT

Tensor Processing Unit (TPU) has been developed and designed by Google to expedite Neural Network-based predictive analysis on big data systems [4, 211].

TPU is an ASIC (Application Specific Integrated Circuit), which exist as a co-host to the existing cloud. The need for TPUs emerged when load on Google data centers surged due to a rise in speech recognition usage at Google Cloud. This anticipated Google that it needs to build specific hardware for neural networks.

The design of TPU has been motivated by several important needs and considerations. Figure 12.4, which is re-drawn from the official Google blog shows software stack for TPU. API calls from TensorFlow graphs are translated to TPU instructions. The TPU includes the following computational resources:

1. **Matrix Multiplier Unit (MXU)**: For matrix multiplication, there are 65,536 8-bit multiply-and-add units.

2. **Unified Buffer (UB)**: 24MB of dedicated SRAM. The RAM includes registers.

3. **Activation Unit (AU)**: Hardwired activation functions.

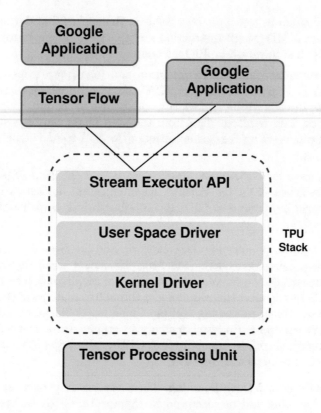

FIGURE 12.4 TPU stack [4]

The process of running a trained model and classifying data or estimating missing labels in the data is called **inference**. The process of inference using a Neural Network takes the following steps:

1. Multiply input value (X) with input weights to produce the input signal.

2. The resultant values (i.e., input of all the features and their weights) are aggregated to produce a single value.

3. An activation function (such as RELU, Sigmoid, tanh) is applied to assess the activity of neuron.

We can assess that this is multiplication and addition intensive work, which is required for the process of inference. The process can also be termed as **Matrix Multiplication** as this represents a series of steps, which are involved in matrix multiplication.

For instance, given three inputs (with weights) and three neurons for a fully connected neural network, there will be nine multiplications and six additions in total. In general, a big data application could have hundreds to thousands of features. Therefore, the task of inference is matrix multiplication intensive.

Google observed that many of the applications that are being executed on Google data centers have considerable load of matrix multiplication. So if the process of matrix multiplication could be made efficient with respect to energy and time, it could have a considerable impact on Google cloud.

TABLE 12.1 TPU Instructions

Instruction	Purpose
Read_Host_Memory	Read data from memory
Read_Weights	Read weights from memory
MatrixMultiply/Convolve	Multiply or convolve with the data and weights, accumulate the results
Activate	Apply activation functions
Write_Host_Memory	Write result to memory

TPU is an ASIC which has been built with two major modifications:

1. **Quantization**: It has been observed that neural network-based predictions often do not require precision of floating point operations. Without compromising much on the accuracy, these applications can use quantization, which is an approximation technique that uses a preset minimum and maximum value. Quantization uses 8-bit integer approximation instead of 16-bit or 32-bit floating point approximations. This greatly reduces the hardware footprint and energy consumption of TPUs. In this manner, up to 65,536 8-bit multipliers can be incorporated in a TPU as compared to a few thousand 32-bit or 16-bit floating point units in a GPU. Without compromising much on accuracy up to 25 x times more multipliers can be added.

2. **Complex Instruction Set**: Many CPUs implement RISC (Reduced Instruction Set Computer). This allows them to incorporate simpler instructions (such as load, store, add, and multiply), which are common in the majority of the applications. By adapting the RISC architecture set, computers focus more on speed. However, for the design of TPU, Google adopted CISC (Complex Instruction Set Computer), which allows it to provide programming support for complex tasks such as matrix multiplication.

Figure 12.5 shows a simplified architecture of TPU. The core of TPU is Matrix Multiplier Unit (MXU), which has 65,536 8-bit multiply-and-add units for matrix operations. MXU receives input from two sources. These include the FIFO weight scheduler and systolic data setup. The former is used for input features and weights, while the latter is used to input activation function.

TPU has special instructions to support operations: Table 12.1 shows a few sample instructions mentioned by Google official blog [309].

12.5 HIGH SPEED INTERCONNECTS

High speed interconnects are useful in building supercomputers. The prime purpose of interconnects is to provide high speed data transfer. They are useful in achieving scalability and enhancing parallelism. In chapter 9, we discussed IB architecture to promote high speed data transfer. In this chapter, we explain NVLink, another very popular interconnect. NVLink is a high-speed interconnect from NVIDIA. It can be used for GPU to GPU connectivity as well as for the GPU to CPU connection. For GPU to GPU connectivity, NVLink offers high speed pair to pair communication, whereas for GPU to CPU connectivity, it can be used to establish a high-speed hybrid computing model.

As compared to a normal PCI BUS, NVLink can be used to communicate up to 80 Gbps. Figure 12.6 shows different types of connectivity using NVLink.

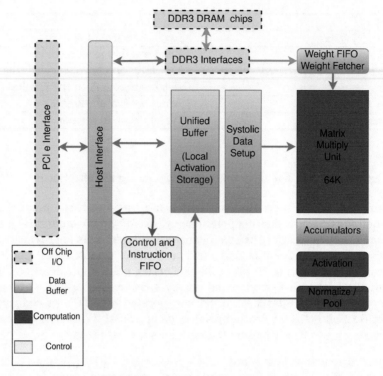

FIGURE 12.5 TPU block diagram
[211]

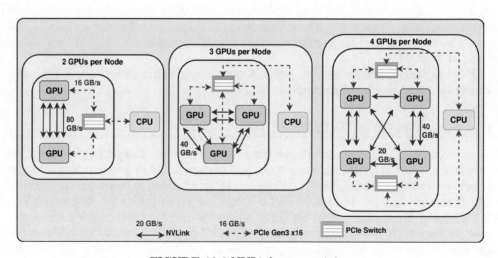

FIGURE 12.6 NVLink connectivity

12.6   MESSAGE PASSING INTERFACE

Message Passing Interface (MPI) is a programming interface which is built upon a distributed memory model. An MPI code is executed on a cluster consisting of n nodes (also called as processors). Each processor has a unique identifier which is known as a rank. Processors communicate with each other using send and receive commands.

We can understand the basic functionality of MPI using example 12.3. A WordCount problem is solved through one head node and four worker nodes. We should recall from section 2.3.2 that a head node is the node which distributes tasks to worker nodes. With a little modification, the head node can act as a worker node as well.

An MPI cluster is an example of Beowulf cluster as mentioned in section 2.3.2.

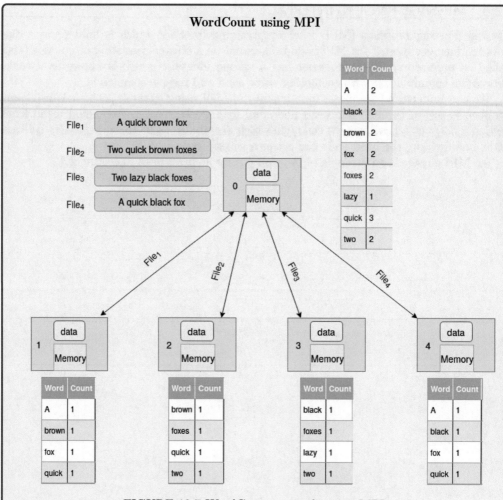

FIGURE 12.7 WordCount example using MPI

Example 12.3 (WordCount using MPI). *Figure 12.7 illustrates execution of Word-Count problem using MPI. Five nodes are shown with separate storage for data and memory. Ranks (IDs) of the nodes are marked from 0 to 4. The head node (rank 0) has four files. It sends one file to each node to perform the WordCount operation. This communication is done using the* MPI_Send *function. At the receiving end, nodes 1 to 4 have corresponding* MPI_Recv *functions. Each node (1 to 4) receives the file, performs the WordCount operation, and sends the result of local computation back to the head node. The head node aggregates the result.*

An MPI code needs to include <mpi.*h* > file. This provides an interface for MPI commands. In MPI, processors can communicate with each other if they share a communicator. A communicator can be considered as a group of processes which can communicate with each other. MPI_Comm_World is a standard communicator.

Table 12.2 lists standard MPI functions along with their description. "*" and "&" symbols in the table denote the pointer and address notions in the C language.

Example 12.4 illustrates functionality of four MPI collaborative functions.

TABLE 12.2 MPI Commands

Functions	Description
MPI_Init(argc,&argv)	This function must be called only once in every MPI program. It initializes the MPI execution environment. Other MPI functions follow this function. It also marks the beginning of a parallel section of code.
MPI_Comm_size (comm,&size)	It returns the total number of MPI processes in the specified communicator. The number of processes are stored in the size parameter.
MPI_Comm_rank (comm,&rank)	It returns the rank of the current process. The rank is stored in the "rank" argument. The total number of each process will vary from 0 to n-1, where n is the total number of processes.
MPI_Send (*buf, count, datatype, dest, tag,comm)	It sends "count" no. of bytes, which are stored at location "buf" and of "datatype" to the process with rank "dest". "comm" specifies the communicator, and "tag" can be used to distinguish different messages.
MPI_Recv (*buf, count, datatype, source, tag, comm,*status)	It is a blocking call. It receives "count" no. of bytes of datatype from the process "source", and stores them. "comm" is the communicator and "tag" is used to distinguish messages. "status" specifies the success or error status.
MPI_Abort (comm,errorcode)	It terminates all processes associated with the communicator.
MPI_Barrier(comm)	It is a synchronization operation. It creates a barrier synchronization in the group. When a process reaches MPI_Barrier call it blocks until all the processes reach the synchronization point.
MPI_Bcast (&buffer,count, datatype,root ,comm)	This function is used to broadcast (sends) a message of "datatype" to all the processes. "comm" specifies the communicator, "root" is the rank of the sending process, "buffer" is the storage location of the message, and "count" denotes the no. of bytes.
MPI_Scatter (&sendbuf,sendcnt, sendtype,&recvbuf, recvcnt,recvtype, root,comm)	This function is used to distribute chunk of messages to all the processes in the group. However, unlike the broadcast function which distributes the same message to all the processes, this function sends individual chunk to each process.
MPI_Gather (&sendbuf,sendcnt, sendtype,&recvbuf, recvcount,recvtype, root,comm)	This function gathers distinct messages from each process in the group and sends to a single destination process specified by "root". It is the reverse of MPI_Scatter.
MPI_Reduce (&sendbuf,&recvbuf,count, datatype,op,root,comm)	This process is a collective computation operation. It applies a reduction operation on all processes in the group and places the result in one process.
MPI_Finalize	It terminates the MPI execution environment. It is the last MPI function in the program.

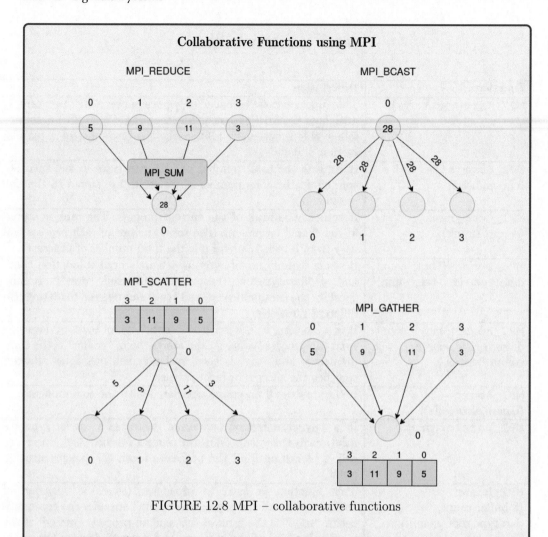

FIGURE 12.8 MPI – collaborative functions

Example 12.4 (Collaborative Functions using MPI). *Figure 12.8 illustrates functionality of four collaborative functions of MPI. In* MPI_Reduce *a reduce operation (such as sum) is applied. The result is stored at the "root" process. In* MPI_Bcast, *the intended value is sent to all the processes in the group. In* MPI_Scatter *a chunk of values are passed to processes such that each process receives its corresponding value. In* MPI_Gather, *individual values from each process are gathered at the root process.*

We can learn MPI programming from example 12.5 [47]. Each process in the program prints a Hello world message.

MPI Hello World

Example 12.5 (MPI Hello World).

```
1.  #include <mpi.h>
2.  #include <stdio.h>
3.  int main(int argc, char** argv) {
4.  MPI_Init(NULL, NULL);
5.  int worldsize;
6.  MPI_Comm_size(MPI_COMM_WORLD, &worldsize);
7.  int worldrank;
8.  MPI_Comm_rank(MPI_COMM_WORLD, &worldrank);
9.  char name_of_processor[MPI_MAX_PROCESSOR_NAME];
10. int length_name;
11. MPI_Get_processor_name(name_of_processor, &
    length_name);
12. printf("Hello world message: processor %s,
    rank %d out of %d processors\n",
processor_name, worldrank, worldsize);
13. MPI_Finalize();
}
```

Lines 1-3 are standard files for inclusion of library and declaration of main function. Line 4 is the initialization code for MPI. Line 6 gets the total number of processors in the MPI cluster. Line 8 gets the rank of the processor. This function gets the individual rank of each of the processor. Line 11 gets the name of the processor. Line 12 prints a hello world message, whereas line 13 concludes the MPI code.

In chapter 4, we studied MapReduce and solved the WordCount problem with it. A major difference between MPI and MapReduce is that the former provides more flexibility to a developer. On the contrary, MapReduce has stronger abstraction at the cost of lesser flexibility.

12.7 OPENMP

OpenMP is a shared memory programming platform. It is based on a thread-based programming model, where a cluster of processors share memory among themselves. Since memory is shared between the processors, there is no need to send and receive messages. The major primitives will be to ensure that critical section remains protected.

We will now learn OpenMP from an example 12.6 [48].

OpenMP Hello World

Example 12.6 (OpenMP Hello World).

```c
#include <omp.h>
#include <stdio.h>
#include <stdlib.h>
int main (int argc, char *argv[])
{
int nthreads, tid;
printf("Hello this is a serial part");
/* Forking threads */
#pragma omp parallel private(nthreads,tid)
{/* Get the Id of the thread */
tid = omp_get_thread_num();
/* Printing Greetings for the thread */
printf("Greetings from thread= %d\n",tid);
/* For the master thread only */
if (tid == 0)
{/* Get the total number of threads */
nthreads = omp_get_num_threads();
/* Printing total number of threads */
printf("Number of threads = %d\n", nthreads);
}}  /* All threads join master thread */
printf("End of Parallel region");
}
```

Initially, header files are included and variables are declared. pragma omp is the declaration of the OpenMP directive where the two variables, number of threads and thread id, are considered as private to each thread. The function omp_get_thread_num returns the id of the thread. The condition "if (tid==0)" ensures that the code is executed in the master thread only.

The function omp_get_num_threads() returns the total number of threads. Figure 12.9 illustrates the execution with serial and parallel regions. Messages, which are printed by the program, are shown in italics.

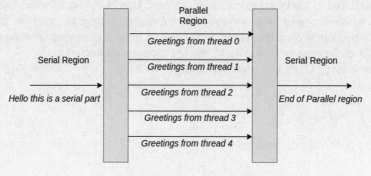

FIGURE 12.9 OpenMP

12.8   OTHER FRAMEWORKS

We will now briefly describe the two other significant frameworks that are used for the large-scale big data processing.

12.8.1   Volunteer Computing

Volunteer computing (VC) is a form of distributed computing, which allows public participants to share their idle computing resources and helps run computationally expensive projects [160]. VC incorporates a middleware to coherently utilize a large number of resources at volunteers in order to solve a computationally expensive task. Nodes in VC can be distributed around the Internet and are susceptible to different kinds of failures such as communication, processor, and storage. In VC, a master node sends tasks to all the worker nodes and receives consistent updates about task completion. Volunteer computing platforms have largely been focused on specific computing problems such as protein folding [95], astronomy [295], bioinformatics [85], and hydrology [78]. Since nodes in VC are distributed across the Internet, they are not connected through high-speed links. Therefore, such systems are not useful for high-speed inter-node communication.

12.8.2   Supercomputing

Supercomputing is a form of computing which involves computation through extensive computational power to solve computationally expensive problems. Supercomputing is generally referred as the integration of hardware, software, networking, and algorithms to solve an expensive problem. Some of the applications of supercomputing include weather analysis, astronomy, predictive analysis on items, sales, stocks, protein, and other experiments involving large amount of data. Supercomputing can be considered as a type of HPC with enormously high computational power. Table 12.3 shows a list of top 10 supercomputers along with their speed and architecture.

12.9   CONCLUDING REMARKS

In this chapter, we studied HPC systems and assessed their requirements and capabilities for solving big data problems. HPC systems have been intrinsic in solving computationally expensive problems. They can utilize big data for improved and enhanced solutions. Similarly, big data systems can gain the potential power of HPC systems in achieving timely completion of results. This chapter will serve as a baseline for understanding related topics. A reader can explore the further reading section for enhanced learning.

12.10   FURTHER READING

Details about volunteer computing are included in reference [160]. Details about Super computing can be found at reference [338].

Details about CUDA programming can be obtained from references [223, 308].

Different variants of GPU-based spark have been proposed. References [104, 243, 380] explain their methodologies and differences in detail.

Mars [194] is a single GPU-based variation of MapReduce. The work has been extended to multiple GPUs by many researchers [137, 345, 346].

GPUs have been actively used for many Machine Learning [133, 252] and Deep Learning [144, 270, 344] solutions. Machine Learning algorithms such as K-means [164, 198],

TABLE 12.3 Top Ten Supercomputers [67]

S. No	Name	Location	Peta FLOPs	Configuration
1	Summit	US Department of Energy Oak Ridge National Laboratory	148.6	2282544 IBM Power9 cores and 2090880 NVIDIA volta GV100 cores
2	Sierra	Lawrence Livermore National Laboratory, California	94.6	1572480 Cores of IBM power 9 processors and 1382400 cores of NVIDIA volta GV100
3	Sunway Tai-huLight	China National Supercomputing Center Wuxi	93	40,960 Sunway 26010 each 260 cores
4	Tianhe-2A	National Supercomputer Centre, Guangzhou, China	61.4	Intel Xeon E5-2692v2 and Matrix 2000 5 million cores
5	Frontera	Texas Advanced Computing Center, University of Texas Austin	23.5	Intel Xeon Platinum 8280 Processors
6	Piz Daint	Swiss National Supercomputing Centre	21.2	Intel Xeon and NVIDIA Tesla P100
7	Trinity	Los Alamos National Laboratory	20.2	Intel Xeon and Xeon Phi Processors
8	AIBC	National Institute of Advanced Industrial Science and Technology (Japan)	19.9	CX2550 Servers with Xeon Gold Processors and NVIDIA Tesla V100 GPUs
9	SuperMUC-Ng	Leibniz Supercomputing center Germany	19.5	Xeon Processors and Omni-Path Interconnect
10	Lassen	Lawrence Livermore National Laboratory	15.4	IBM Power 9/NVIDIA V100 GPU

KNN [172], and Decision Trees [251, 322] have been effectively implemented on GPUs. Similarly, TensorFlow [75] and Theano [92] are popular deep learning-based solutions.

12.11 EXERCISE QUESTIONS

1. What is the primary requirement for implementing parallelism?

2. Differentiate between horizontal and vertical scaling.

3. Highlight major differences between OpenCL and CUDA.

4. Write a CUDA program to multiple two large matrices.

5. Highlight major differences between GPU and CPU.

6. Highlight the significance of Hardware-Assisted Virtualization.

7. Explain the architecture of TPU.

8. Write an MPI program to search for a string in a sequence of files.

9. Write an OpenMP program to search for a string in a sequence of files.

10. Explain the significance of high speed interconnects in achieving parallelism.

GLOSSARY

CUDA: It is a programming language, which is specific to NVIDIA GPUs. It allows the CPU for performing general tasks and the GPU for data parallel tasks.

GPU: It is a processor designed for processing graphics. It has hundreds of cores, which makes it efficient for data parallel processes.

Horizontal Scaling: It is a method of scaling, which involves increasing overall application capacity by adding more computational resources.

NVLink: It is a high speed interconnect from NVIDIA that can be used for GPU to GPU connectivity as well as for GPU to CPU connection.

OpenCL: It is a framework suited for parallel programming of heterogeneous systems.

Supercomputing: It is a form of computing which involves computation through extensive computational power to solve computationally expensive problems.

Tensor Processing Unit (TPU): It is a custom application-specific integrated circuit (ASIC) built by Google to expedite Neural Network based predictive analysis on big data systems.

Vertical Scaling: It is a method of scaling, which involves increasing the capacity by upgrading or replacing hardware with a more powerful unit.

Deep Learning with Big Data

CONTENTS

DEEP Learning is a popular research area. It refers to the class of machine learning which involves deep neural networks such that several layers of a neural network are utilized for feature extraction, training, and transformation. With the availability of big data, machine learning [206] and deep learning have been popular in providing new dimensions for prediction, classification, recognition, and analysis [179]. There are many applications of big data and deep learning [279]. These include computer vision [135], speech recognition, image and video analysis, and network flow analysis [256]. The purpose of this chapter is to elucidate readers about the emerging topic of deep learning. We will only be covering initial concepts about the topic.

13.1 INTRODUCTION

Deep learning is an emerging and active area of data analytics. It is a class of machine learning which allows a machine to be fed with raw data and to automatically discover the representations needed for detection or classification. Deep learning achieves this representation through multiple layers in which each layer transforms the underlying layer to provide a better abstraction than the preceding layer.

Deep learning models follow deep neural networks, a class of neural networks in which there are more than one hidden layers. Hidden layers allow improved learning and promote deeper understanding. We shall revert to a more deeper understanding of deep neural network in later sections. For now, let's explore the impact of deep learning on big data.

13.1.1   Big Data and Deep Learning

Big data provides enormous potential for information extraction and knowledge discovery. However, harvesting useful information from such a huge amount of data is unprecedentedly challenging. Deep learning provides ways and methods to extract this information through classification.

Big data analytics can greatly benefit from deep learning. A large amount of available data being generated is unlabeled. In this context, deep learning can help in understanding patterns of data. Domains such as speech recognition, image classification, collaborative filtering, computer vision, disease diagnosis, and medical image analysis can greatly benefit by utilizing deep learning patterns for information learning and analysis.

In comparison to classical machine learning algorithms where only a few parameters are selected for learning, deep learning algorithms provide a more powerful model where numerous parameters can be considered for learning. This is achieved through a large number of hidden layers and a number of neurons at the input layer. Deep learning can be helpful in learning from large volumes using large models of data.

In deep neural networks, there are consecutive layers of processing such that the output of a layer is applied as an input to the following layer. In a Deep Neural Network (DNN), each layer applies a nonlinear transformation on its input and provides representation in its output. The goal of this transformation is to learn and collect abstract representation of data through a hierarchy of layers. The transformation is nonlinear in order to utilize the true potential of a deep architecture – consisting of a number of layers.

Deep learning is beneficial for high volume and high variety of data. For instance, deep learning can be utilized to learn useful features from different components of a dataset – thereby enabling utilization of a large amount of existing data. Even if data is uncategorized or unlabeled, deep learning can be used to discover intermediate patterns and extract useful information [135, 256, 279]. Deep learning can be applied to a number of big data problems including image classification, face recognition, speech recognition, and semantic text analysis.

13.2   FUNDAMENTALS

Having identified the usefulness of deep learning in extracting useful information from big data, it is important to study a few fundamentals of deep learning.

Deep learning is inspired by the neural network (NN) – a computational model which is modeled after the human brain. An NN consists of many simple, connected processors called neurons, which is a specialized cell that is used to stimulate electrical impulses. Each neuron produces a sequence of real-valued activations. Neurons at the input layer get activated through sensors perceiving the environment. Neurons at other layers are activated through weighted connections from previously active neurons [313].

In this chapter, we will mainly consider two types of neurons, a perceptron, and sigmoid neuron.

A **perceptron** is a neuron which inputs several binary values, x_1, x_2, x_n, and produces a single binary output value. Here binary means that the value could either be 0 or 1. Normally a weight w_i is assigned to each input x_i such that the output depends upon the product of inputs and their corresponding weights.

Further, a constant value, called as bias, is added to the product sum. We can define bias as a constant which is used to best fit the model according to the given data. The value

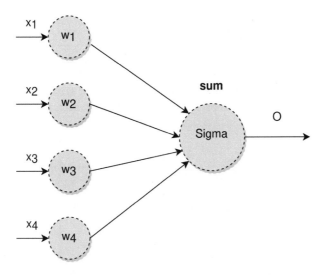

FIGURE 13.1 Perceptron – sum of weights and inputs

of the bias is changed along with the weights to fit the model with the input. However, bias differs from weights as its value is independent of the output from previous layers.

$$z = \sum_{i=0}^{n} w_i x^i + bias \qquad (13.1)$$

The above equation denotes the output of a neuron, as depicted in figure 13.1. However, the equation 13.1 does not denote a trigger value, i.e., the output could vary from $-\infty$ to $+\infty$, without us having any knowledge if the output will be triggered.

Therefore, often an activation function (also called as transfer function) is associated with the neuron. The purpose of the activation function is to decide whether the neuron should be considered as triggered (or activated). The activation function is actually a non-linear function. Example 13.1 explains the reasons of non-linearity for an activation function. Figure 13.3 shows the impact of an activation function on triggering a neuron.

Equation 13.1 can be re-written as follows:

$$output = activation\ function(\sum_{i=0}^{n} w_i x^i + bias) \qquad (13.2)$$

A key point to consider is that both input and output are binary values in perceptrons, i.e., they are either zero or one. This is considered a major limitation because continuous values cannot be predicted or classified.

For continuous values, sigmoid neuron is used. A **sigmoid neuron** is a special type of neuron in which input can be a fraction value. Similarly, the output could also be a fraction value. Note that a sigmoid neuron is similar to perceptron as it can take multiple inputs with distinct weights.

The sigmoid neuron has a specific type of activation function called sigmoid function. This is governed by the following equation.

$$output = \frac{1}{1 + e^{-z}} \qquad (13.3)$$

$$output = \frac{1}{1 + e^{-(\sum_{i=0}^{n} w_i x^i + bias)}} \qquad (13.4)$$

or

$$output = \frac{1}{1 + exp-(\sum_{i=0}^{n} w_i x^i + bias)} \quad (13.5)$$

In equation 13.3, if z is large, then e^{-z} tends to zero and the value of sigmoid is equivalent to the value of perceptron function. Figure 13.2 illustrates the output of the sigmoid activation function.

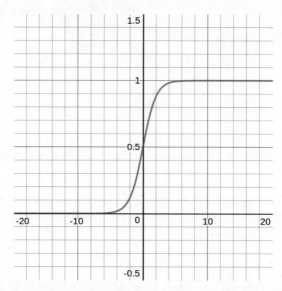

FIGURE 13.2 The sigmoid activation function

Can we have a linear Activation Function in a DNN?

Example 13.1 (Can we have a linear Activation Function in a DNN?). *A linear activation function would have following two issues:*
a) Gradient Problem *The gradient will be constant and has no relationship with the input. It means that if there is an error in prediction, that error would continue throughout the deep architecture of DNN.*
b) Impact of Deep layers *In case of linear transformation the output of every layer is linear. That is, the final output will also be linear so there is no point of applying a number of hidden layers.*

Accuracy of a DNN is measured as a **cost function** which is the difference between the actual value – estimated value. Equation 13.6 shows how the cost function can be computed.

The objective is to select the values of weights (w's) and bias (b) to minimize the cost function.

$$J(w, b) = \frac{1}{n} \sum_{i=0}^{n} \frac{1}{2}(actualvalue - predictedvalue)^2 \quad (13.6)$$

There are two known algorithms which are used to minimize the cost function and improve the accuracy.

1. **Gradient Descent**: The gradient descent technique utilizes the gradient, i.e., the slope of the cost function. The slope is computed with respect to the input parameters

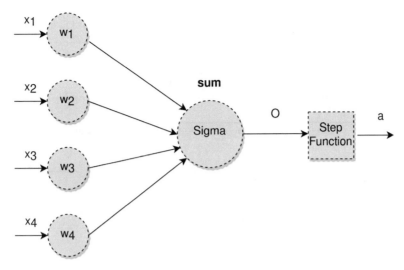

FIGURE 13.3 Neuron with activation function

activation function i.e., w and b. The rationale is that the shortest path to the minimal cost is through the steepest slope. The slope could be positive, negative, or zero. A negative value of the slope implies that the direction is opposite and should be changed. Based on the slope, the values of weights and bias should be adjusted. The amount of adjustment is important as it is desired to compute an optimal value and the convergence point.

2. **Back Propagation**: The back propagation technique is used in conjunction with the gradient descent algorithm to find an optimal point. To understand the idea, let us reconsider figure 13.6. The cost function is not directly related to the input parameters w and b. In order to adjust the values, back propagation technique is used such that the values are traced back from the output layer to the input layer in order to minimize the error. Back propagation is based on the fact that in order to find the gradient of the cost function with respect to both w and b, we need to find the partial derivative of the cost with all the variables in the preceding layers. Using back propagation, the error is back propagated in the network using derivatives. An iterative process is followed such that the loss function reaches to a minimum value and the derivative becomes zero.

13.3 NEURAL NETWORK

Having covered the fundamentals, we are now ready to see our first neural network.

Figure 13.4 shows a simple Neural Network (NN). The figure shows three layers: an input layer, a hidden layer, and an output layer. A Deep Neural Network (DNN) is distinguished from an NN with respect to the number of hidden layers such that a DNN could have many hidden layers.

Number of nodes (also called as neurons) could also vary in an NN and its variant DNN. At the input layer, the number of nodes is equivalent to the number of input features. Similarly, the number of output nodes is equivalent to the number of classes. Number of nodes in the hidden layer could vary between the nodes at the input layer and the output layer. Figure 13.5 shows a sample DNN.

TABLE 13.1 Types of Deep Neural Networks and Their Mapping with Big Data Applications

Type of DNN	Usage for Big Data Applications
Feed Forward Neural Network	Object Recognition, General Classification problems
Convolution Neural Network (CNN)	Image recognition, video analysis, natural language processing
Recurrent Neural Network (RNN)	Speech Recognition, Handwriting recognition

13.3.1 Why NN or DNN

In big data analytics, there are many features or variables that differentiate an object from another object. For instance, a fruit can be differentiated with its color, shape, and size. Similarly, a car may have unique features of color, shape, position, brightness, and size. The factors that capture the sense of variability in data are called as **factors of variation**. These factors are useful in classifying a particular object. When looking for an object, we tend to utilize the related features and tend to ignore the features that are irrelevant.

An NN (or a DNN) could be helpful in this context. It can be used to discover the representation and map the output from the representation. The class of machine learning which discovers the representation of features and maps them to an output is known as **representation learning**. A DNN simplifies the complex problem of identifying representations by introducing layers, each of which is responsible to extract meaningful information. Example 13.2 illustrates the process of object identification and classification through a DNN.

This powerful usage of DNN in representation learning has assisted in finding intelligent solutions for many big data problems such as natural language processing, image recognition, handwriting recognition, and speech recognition.

13.4 TYPES OF DEEP NEURAL NETWORK

Having studied the significance of DNN, we are now ready to discuss different types of deep neural networks:

13.4.1 Feed Forward Neural Network

Feed forward model is an architecture of a neural network in which the input flows into a single direction from input layer to the output layer without any loops. This implies that output of a layer does not affect the neurons within the same layer but to the neurons in the following layer.

A cost function is used to compute the difference between estimated and predicted values. Backward pass is performed to adjust the weights in the network to get the accurate or near to accurate prediction score.

Figure 13.5 shows an example for feed forward deep neural network, whereas example 13.2 shows an example of object recognition through feed forward neural network [179].

Deep Neural Networks suffer with difficulty in training the model. Remember that gradient-based learning methods when utilizing back propagation adjust weights and bias

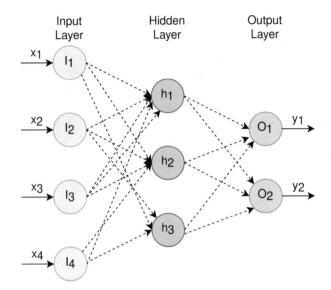

FIGURE 13.4 A neural network

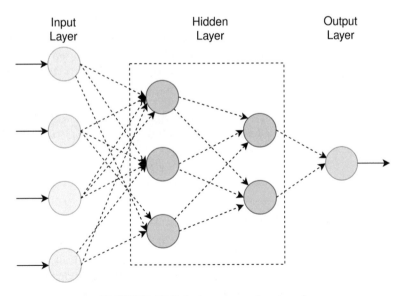

FIGURE 13.5 A deep neural network

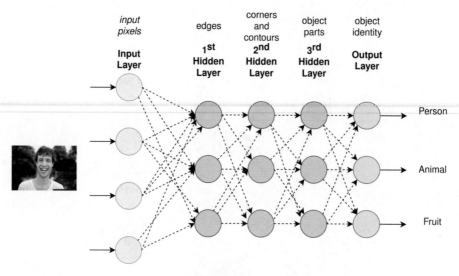

FIGURE 13.6 Object recognition through a feed forward neural network

based on the gradient of the cost function. This adjustment is made in each iteration during the training phase. In some cases, when the gradient is small, the training process nearly stalls because weights can't be changed much (due to low value of the gradient) to reduce the cost function. This problem is referred as the **Vanishing Gradient Problem**. It is a known problem in DNN. We shall study how the problem is tackled in the other variants of DNN.

Object Recognition through a Feed Forward Neural Network

Example 13.2 (Object Recognition through a Feed Forward Neural Network). *Figure 13.6 shows the process of object recognition. The input layer is responsible to read input pixels from an image. The layer is also called as the visible layer because all the information provided to it is visible or observable. In contrast, the next three layers are hidden layers, as the information presented to these layers is not visible and the DNN model is expected to determine the related concepts with the assistance of the preceding layers.*
For instance, the output of the input layer (i.e., pixels) is presented to the first hidden layer to determine edges. These are identified by comparing the brightness of neighboring pixels. The second hidden layer computes corners and contours through collection of edges. The third hidden layer detects object parts through contours and corners. Finally, the output is classified by the output layer.

13.4.2 Recurrent Neural Network

A Recurrent Neural Network or an RNN is a class of artificial neural network which maintains a sequence of directed nodes to produce a directed graph. In that, the output of the current sequence depends on the input and the output of the previous occurrence in the sequence. In other words, an RNN maintains a memory for producing the output. In an RNN, the previous state is maintained through a loop, which takes the input from the previous time stamp and produces the output using the current sequence. In other words, it uses memory for producing the desired output.

RNN retains information from previous input using a simple loop. Using this loop, information from the previous time stamp is added to the input of the current time stamp.

Figure 13.7 shows a neuron for RNN. X_t is the input to the network and y_t is the output of the network at time "t", whereas "h" is an RNN cell. In principle, the self loop allows the neuron to recall the output at y_{t-1} to produce y_t.

An RNN can be considered as a sequence of RNN cells, each of which is connected with its successor to produce a desired output. Figure 13.8 expands the idea from figure 13.7 to develop a full RNN.

This characteristic of RNN has enabled their usage in a number of big data applications including machine translation, speech recognition, and text summarization.

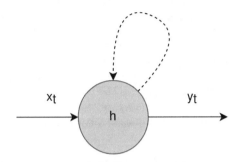

FIGURE 13.7 Recurrent neural network (RNN) neuron with a loop

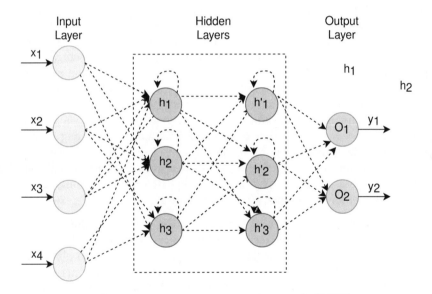

FIGURE 13.8 Recurrent neural network (RNN)

Figure 13.8 illustrates the most fundamental architecture of RNN. Long Short-Term Memory (LSTM) and Gated Recurrent Units (GRU) are the two popular variations of RNN. They differ upon how much memory is maintained by RNNs. A detailed explanation of these networks is beyond the scope of this book. Readers are advised to refer to references [43] and [142] for a detailed understanding.

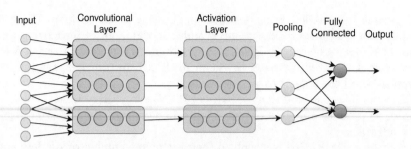

FIGURE 13.9 A convolutional neural network

13.4.3   Convolutional Neural Network

Convolutional Neural Networks (CNN) are a class of NN which relies on applying convolution (or filter) on input data. CNNs are extremely useful for applications such as Optical Character Recognition (OCR), image recognition, and facial recognition.

A convolution is an integral that expresses the amount of overlap of one function "g" as it is shifted over another function "f". It therefore "blends" one function with another [367].

Figure 13.9 depicts a sample convolutional neural network. A CNN consists of any combination of three layers:

1. **Convolution**: The first layer in CNN is convolution. The purpose of the convolution is to apply filter on the input value in order to transform the input. Conv. layer applies filter or computes the output of neurons that are connected to local regions of the input only. For instance, if the input volume has 16x16x3 size, that is, if a 16 x16 image is represented with RGB values, then given a 4x4 filter, each neuron in the conv layer will have weights to 4x4x3 size. The purpose of this transformation is to detect separation of information. In the context of image processing, this separation could denote edges of objects or boundaries of color. The filtration process also sums up the values along each unit in order to produce a single cohesive value. The process of convolution can be considered as a sliding window, where values in the window are multiplied by the filter. The values are then aggregated to produce a single coherent value. The process of activation is also called as **feature mapping** as it allows the filter to be trained and recognize many features of an object. Figure 13.10 explains the process of convolution. Example 13.3 illustrates that the process of convolution is applied through a 3x3 filter. The process is repeated for the remaining values of the input layer in order to produce a 3x3 hidden layer.

2. **Activation Layer**: The output of the convolution layer is applied to an activation function. The purpose of the activation function is to decide which cells or neurons are considered activated. The activation function is basically a non-linear function for the reasons explained in example 13.1. One of the most popular activation functions for CNN is RELU (Rectified Linear Unit), which is equivalent to the value of input if x is +ve, otherwise the output of the function is zero.

3. **Pooling**: The purpose of the pooling layer is to down sample the data without losing much of the information. This is achieved by reducing the number of dimensions. The output of the activation layer is applied to the pooling layer to reduce the dimensions of the data and ease out the computations. The pooling layer could apply a number of pooling functions such as max pooling or average pooling. Example 13.5 explains the concept of max pooling.

The fourth layer is called the **fully connected (FC) layer**. The purpose of the FC layer is to aggregate the output from the above layers using weights and produce a classification.

Filter in CNN

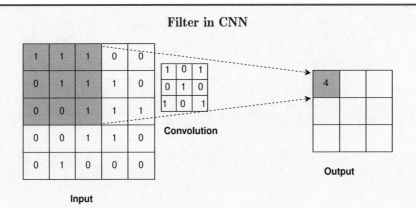

FIGURE 13.10 Filter in CNN

Example 13.3 (Filter in CNN). *Filter of size 3x3 is applied to the input. The process is repeated for the remaining values of the input layer in order to produce a 3x3 hidden layer.*

The RELU Activation Function

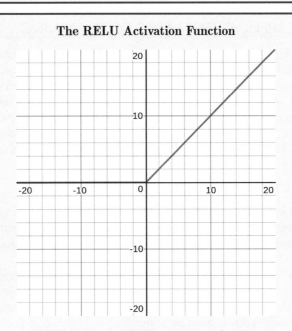

FIGURE 13.11 RELU activation function

$$f(x) = max(0, x) \tag{13.7}$$

Example 13.4 (The RELU Activation Function). *The RELU activation function is zero, when the value of x<0, otherwise the output of the function is equivalent to the input. The function is resistant to the vanishing gradient problem, when the value of X>0. RELU is computationally very efficient because it is implemented using simple thresholding.*

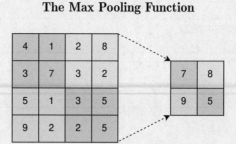

The Max Pooling Function

FIGURE 13.12 Max pooling function

Example 13.5 (The Max Pooling Function). *The max pooling function is applied to the above figure, having a matrix size of 2x2. The maximum value from each matrix is selected.*

We have studied a few fundamental types of DNNs. The next section is focused on explaining the use of different types of DNNs for big data applications.

13.5 BIG DATA APPLICATIONS USING DEEP LEARNING

Deep learning and big data together can solve many extensive problems. In that, deep learning can be useful for developing and testing computational models, whereas big data can provide necessary datasets for testing, evaluation, and improvement of these models. The purpose of this section is to elaborate on the use of deep learning for many big data applications. Our approach will be explaining the methodology and design of DNNs for big data applications [44]. We will not be explaining code for our examples. However, libraries such as TensorFlow [63, 75] and Theano [66, 92] can be explored for this purpose.

13.5.1 Machine Translation

Machine translation is an important application involving linguistics and natural language processing. Empowering computers to understand and comprehend what has been written, extract the useful contents, and translate the context into another language is a significant and complex process.

A simple approach to translate from one language to another language is to replace each word to its corresponding translated word. However, this does not provide a viable solution as the context of each language is different and word to word translation does not provide context and holds poorly with respect to grammar.

A possible solution to this problem is to add rules of language such as placement of verbs and nouns and combination of words. The addition of rules may improve the efficiency of translation; however, it does not provide a generic and universally acceptable solution [253]. This is because rules for grammar and context vary for each language. Further, grammatical rules may also vary for each variation of the language.

To cater this problem, statistical machine translation techniques are used. Using this technique, instead of generating one exact translation, the possibilities of translated text are generated. Each of this text is then statistically ranked in order to find the best possible answer. For ranking, a large training dataset is used. Such a dataset is obtained from existing translated documents such as newspapers, books, articles, and blogs. The larger the training dataset, higher the accuracy of the translated text.

While statistical translation systems work better than rule-based systems, they require extensive analysis and complicated computations.

Alternatively, encoding[1]-based systems are gaining popularity. For sentences, encoding can differentiate one sentence from another using set of features which are distinct to each sentence. Example 13.6 explains the process of machine translation using deep learning.

Machine Translation using Sentence Encoding

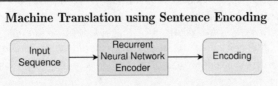

FIGURE 13.13 Encoding of sentence

Example 13.6 (Machine Translation using Sentence Encoding). *In machine translation using encoding, an RNN can be used to generate sentence encoding. Each word can be sent to the RNN separately. Remember that an RNN represents a sequence, in which output at each instant depends upon sequence. Therefore, output of the final word represents the encoding of the whole sentence. The above figure explains the process of encoding for a sentence.*

FIGURE 13.14 Machine translation using sentence encodings and decodings

The process of encoding is followed by the process of decoding; however, decoding is performed in the intended language of translation. Both encoding and decoding require extensive data and immense computational power for training.

The idea of sequence to sequence learning can be extended to many other applications. For instance, sequence to sequence learning can be used to develop a chatbot. In this, queries from users are considered as input text, whereas response from the chatbot is considered as the translated text. Automated responses from chatbot can be very useful in managing customer flows and enhancing support.

Sequence to sequence learning has also been used to build an image search engine. For this, the first RNN in figure 13.14 is replaced with a CNN for image identification. An image can be encoded through a CNN and then decoded into text through an RNN. Once trained, the model can be used to generate description of images.

Sequence to sequence learning can also be used for generating summaries of articles [327]. Similarly, textual encodings can be used to find related images. This is useful for an image search engine.

13.5.2   Image Recognition

Image recognition is another very popular application for DNNs. As explained in section 13.4.3, CNNs can be utilized to identify objects. Filtration is used to detect edges of an object; this is followed by an activation function, which can trigger the detection. Finally, pooling can be applied to reduce dimensions.

---

[1]Encoding is a process of coding an object, i.e., a data item, such as an image or a document in order to uniquely identify a set of features which are distinct to an object.

Example 13.7 explains the process of object identification in an image. The accuracy of the DNN model depends upon the amount of training data used for classification of objects.

Detecting Objects in an Image

Example 13.7 (Detecting Objects in an Image). *Suppose we want to develop a framework to detect, whether a given image contains a cat or a dog. However, we are not aware that where is the position of the object in an image. That is, the object could either be in the center of an image or it could be at any of the corners. For simplicity, we divide the process of object identification in following steps:*

1. *Instead of feeding the whole image directly to our neural network, we tiled the image into many smaller images of equal size. Tiling allows us to detect an object irrespective of its placement in an image.*

2. *Tiled images are fed into the Conv layer. This is used to detect edges of objects.*

3. *The output of the conv layer is fed into the activation layer, which decides which of these tiny and tiled images contain our desired object (or components of an object).*

4. *The next step is downsampling using any of the appropriate techniques (such as max pooling). The idea is to keep the most appropriate component of the object.*

5. *Final output is made through a fully connected neural network which can classify if an image contains a cat or a dog or both.*

The idea of detecting objects can be extended to detect handwritten objects as well.

13.5.3 Speech Recognition

Speech Recognition is another very useful application which could benefit from DNN. Recognizing spoken words is challenging because speaking patterns such as accent and speed of variation vary from person to person.

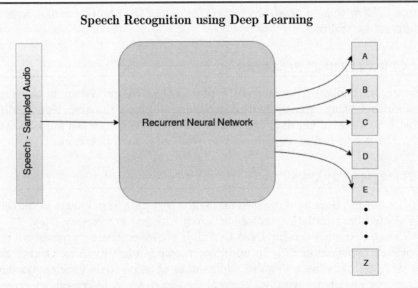

Speech Recognition using Deep Learning

FIGURE 13.15 Speech recognition using RNN

Example 13.8 (Speech Recognition using Deep Learning). *1. The first step in speech recognition is to sample the sound waves without losing data. Sampling implies that readings of sound waves are taken at a rate which appropriately retains enough information for recognizing human words. As per literature, sampling at least twice the rate of desired frequency can lead to reconstruction of the original input.*

2. The next step is to group the samples which can help recognizing words. This grouping is useful in recognizing words as duration of the voice signal can vary.

3. These chunks of audio are then fed to an RNN for recognizing characters. Big dataset is needed for training and testing. Remember that an RNN can remember previous output. Therefore, each character can either initiate a new word or can be a part of an existing word.

The three steps outlined here are the most basic and fundamental steps. However, in reality, a voice signal can contain several background noises or can contain signals of different variations. Fourier transform can be applied to separate signals of different pitch.

13.5.4 Recognizing Handwritten Digits

Another very important application for DNN is to recognize digits in an image. This can be further extended to recognize characters and develop OCR. For the purpose of this example, we will focus on recognizing digits only. Our understanding is that given an application for recognizing digits, extension of the application to recognize characters is trivial. We need to utilize large data for training. MNIST dataset is one of a very popular dataset [376].

The idea is similar to section 13.5.2. However, instead of building a classifier for cat and dog, we build a classifier for recognizing digits from 0 to 9. As explained earlier that a digit could be anywhere in an image, tiling is performed for improved detection. Each tiled image is fed to a CNN with an activation function, to detect the occurrence of a digit. We need a large data set for training.

13.6 CONCLUDING REMARKS

This chapter has explained fundamental topics on Deep Neural Networks. DNN is an emerging area which is being extensively used in computer science research. New models of DNNs are being built to solve big data applications. Readers can take the fundamental concepts from this chapter to further explore and develop big data applications.

13.7 FURTHER READING

MNIST dataset has been used released for digit recognition from images [372]. Details about Statistical Machine translation techniques are mentioned in reference [253].

For Speech Recognition using Deep Learning, course on coursera provides a more deeper and thorough explanation [22]. In addition, research work by Alex Graves and his colleagues [181, 182] provides a detailed explanation of using RNN for classification and segmentation and speech recognition. Recently, researchers at Microsoft have developed an efficient DNN for speech recognition [373].

Use of Fourier transform speech signal analysis has been explained in reference [316]. In [390], deep CNNs have been used for speech recognition. Use of RNNs for sequence to sequence machine learning has been explained in reference [389].

References [27,388] provide a more deeper explanation and understanding for using CNN for text analysis and comprehension.

13.8 EXERCISE QUESTIONS

1. Highlight the significance of DNN for big data systems.

2. Is it possible to have a linear activation function in DNN? Explain.

3. Describe how cost function is minimized to improve the accuracy in DNN?

4. Explain the vanishing gradient problem.

5. Describe how objects can be recognized through a feed forward network?

6. Explain the benefits of RNN. Which big data applications can be solved using RNN?

7. Describe the architecture of CNN and explain how it can be useful for big data?

8. Identify how the accuracy of speech recognition can be improved using DNN?

9. Describe and explain the process of machine translation using sentence encoding.

10. In section 13.5, we have studied three big data applications, which can benefit from DNN. Identify another application, which can utilize deep learning for improved accuracy.

GLOSSARY

Activation Function: It is a non-linear function whose purpose is to decide whether the neuron should be considered as triggered (activated) or deactivated. It is also called as transfer function.

Back Propagation: It is a technique to efficiently calculate the gradients in a Neural Network.

Conv Neural Network: It is a type of DNN, which involves a filter and (one or more) convolution layers.

Cost function: It is a function, which denotes the difference between estimated value and the actual value.

Factors of Variation: These are considered as factors that determine the sense of variability in data.

Feature Mapping: In a CNN, the process of applying convolution is also called as feature mapping. The process of feature mapping allows to map and extract features from the input.

Sampling: It is a process to collect a sample of data from a large dataset.

Sigmoid Function: It is a function used in feed forward neural networks because of its nonlinearity and computational simplicity of its derivative.

Vanishing Gradient Problem: This problem occurs when gradient descents to zero. The problem may occur if either weights are not smartly initialized or if the network is too deep.

V

Case Studies and Future Trends

CHAPTER 14

Big Data: Case Studies and Future Trends

CONTENTS

B IG DATA is already being used to solve problems that were previously impossible due to their massive computational requirements. This chapter will provide detailed case studies selected from different industry domains to demonstrate the practical implementation of big data. It will also highlight a few approaches which tend to deviate from normal trends.

14.1 GOOGLE EARTH ENGINE

Google Earth Engine [180, 328] is a cloud-based platform for large-scale geospatial analysis. It utilizes Google's large-scale computational capabilities to study a wide variety of societal issues including disease, deforestation, disaster, food security, drought, water management, climate monitoring, and environmental protection. Google Earth Engine is a unique integrated platform, which incorporates massive data with useful API. It is useful for scientists as well as for common users. Figure 14.1 shows the layered architecture of Google Earth Engine.

It consists of following technologies, which are available within the Google data center:

1. Borg: For cluster Management (section 3.6.1)

2. Bigtable and Spanner: For Distributed database storage (section 8.4.3)

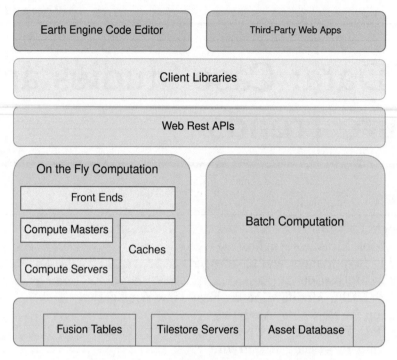

FIGURE 14.1 Google Earth Engine
[180]

3. Colossus: For file system storage.

4. FlumeJava framework: For Parallel pipeline execution (section 5.8).

Google Earth Engine Programs are written in client libraries such as Python and JavaScript. The code editor and third-party applications are written using these client libraries. Either interactive or batch processing modes can be used for execution.

Earth Engine Code Editor and third-party applications use client libraries to send interactive or batch queries to the system through a REST API. Batch queries are handled through FlumeJava. Front End servers handle on the fly computation requests. These are sent to compute masters, which manage compute servers for workload distribution. Borg is used for cluster management. Data services are provided to both batch computation and on the fly computation.

A variety of satellite and aerial imaging systems, environmental variables, and climate forecasts are available as data services. The asset database stores metadata.

Users can utilize Google Earth Engine without the need to having expertise in programming languages.

14.2 FACEBOOK MESSAGES APPLICATION

Facebook has developed an application called Facebook Messages, which is the foundation of a social inbox. This application provides each user a facebook.com email address and also provides strong controls over from which user messages can be received from. It integrates all emails, chat messages, and SMS between a pair or group of users to display.

14.2.1   Requirement and Challenges

Facebook Messages application is a high write throughput application. This implies that the application has low overhead in performing write operations. The application not only requires cheap and elastic storage but also requires low-latency and disk efficient read performance for sequential and random reads.

The application expects more than 500 million users immediately after release to production with billions of instant messages is expected to create each day. The application also requires to scale to many petabytes of data and, therefore, requires high aggregate write throughput.

The high volume of data is another requirement in which the application is required to provide each user a mailbox, which is expected to grow indefinitely. Although old messages are expected to read rarely by user, it is still required that all the messages must be available at all times and with low-latency. As a result, the archiving of data has become challenging.

Another problem is that application is required to store each user ever-growing list of new messages with heavy write workload, which will lead to high volume of random IO operations for the system.

14.2.2   Motivation

Hadoop is an efficient framework for large-scale batch processing of data. To use Hadoop for real-time system, there are many challenges.

First, HDFS was originally designed for batch processing rather than interactive use by its users. It is optimized for high-throughput of data access. Second, Hadoop has a single point of failure which is another reason it cannot be used for real-time application. When the master goes down, the entire HDFS cluster is unusable unless the NameNode is back up.

Third, real-time application often requires failover to be performed within seconds. However, with using existing BackupNode strategy, failover times could be high which is not acceptable for such an application.

And last, since every update from NameNode to BackupNode is synchronously transferred, entire system is dependent upon the reliability of the NameNode.

14.2.3   HDFS Modification for Real-Time Application

HDFS was originally designed for offline batch processing systems where scalability and streaming performance are considered most critical. For using HDFS in real-time and in an online system, following modifications have been made by the Facebook team:

1. **New Nodes for High Availability**: There are two new nodes introduced in existing HDFS Cluster called the *Active* and *Standby* Avatar Node. These nodes are simply wrapper around a normal NameNode.

   The *Active* AvatarNode writes transaction logs to an NFS filesystem. whereas the *Standby* Node keeps its namespace as close as possible to primary by reading and applying transaction at the same time in its own namespace. The secondary NameNode is not needed because the *Standby* AvatarNode can take care of the backup when needed.

   The DataNodes communicate with both the *Active* AvatarNode and the *Standby* AvatarNode and sends updates and heartbeat messages to both the nodes. The *Standby* AvatarNode is synchronous with the *Active* AvatarNode. In case of failure, it can take up the desired role.

2. **Improving Transaction Logging**: In the modified system, AvatarNode continuously writes new block-id as allocated in the transaction log. It is in contrast with the conventional HDFS system, where new blocks are written to transaction log only when the file is either closed or it is flushed. This allows *Standby* Node to remain continuously synchronous and have information about all the block allocation before the failover event occurs.

3. **Transparent Application Failover**: The Facebook team desired that in case of fault, the recovery process should be completely transparent to an application. To achieve this, Facebook developed a Distributed Avatar FileSystem (DAFS), a layered file system on client integrated with Zookeeper.

   Zookeeper contains information about the physical address of the primary AvatarNode for a given cluster. When the client tries to connect with HDFS cluster, DAFS looks up the actual address of the primary AvatarNode and directs all the succeeding calls to that address.

   In the event that failover in progress, the DAFS will block the incoming requests until the failover event completes. After failover event successfully completes, the DAFS directs the client requests to new Primary AvatarNode.

4. **Multiple Hadoop Cluster Interoperability**: Real-time applications like Facebook Messages need to run multiple Hadoop clusters. In order to avoid interoperability issues of Hadoop client talking to servers running different version of Hadoop, Facebook implemented an active approach in which the version of software running on the server first is determined, and then the appropriate protocol is selected.

5. **HDFS Configuration Tuning for Improving Performance**: Response time for real-time application is critical even in error situations; however, HDFS is originally designed for high-throughput systems where throughput is considered more important than the system response time. To support real-time applications, offering reasonable response time is a major requirement.

6. **Fail-fast Strategy**: The Facebook team implemented a timeout mechanism in Remote Procedure Call (RPC) between client and server. This timeout reduces delays in case of failures between client and server.

7. **Improving Latency**: For a real-time application, latency of reading and writing data to a file is an important factor. Since the latency of reading and writing to an HDFS file is quite high, Facebook implemented enhancements to read data from local replica nodes.

The above features allow enhancements through which Facebook was able to achieve real-time behavior for its messaging application.

14.3   HADOOP FOR REAL-TIME ANALYTICS

A large number of data analytics jobs are less than 100 GB. For instance, Microsoft and Yahoo have median jobs of sizes under 14 GB, and for Facebook, 90% of jobs have less than 100 GB size [304].

Motivated by this observation, researchers from Microsoft Cambridge have argued the need of scaling up instead of scaling out. That is, instead of increasing the number of servers for large data analytics, it may be feasible to have one computationally powerful server with enough memory and computational resources. We should understand that this research hypothesis has been driven by the fact that prices of memory are continuously decreasing such that it is cheaper to have one server with 192 GB of RAM instead of 24 servers with 8 GB RAM. Further, the research hypothesis has been strengthened by the fact that many analytical problems such as K-means and clustering are iterative. They require iterative execution with many rounds such that input to the next round is prior to the next round. In such a scenario, shared memory systems are feasible to limit network-based communication. Instead in-memory communication is much faster and feasible.

Researchers from Microsoft Cambridge have performed experimental analysis to evaluate this hypothesis. The researchers used two algorithms, namely Adpredictor and Frequent Itemset Mining (FIM) [304]. The former algorithm utilizes machine learning to predict click-through rate (CTR). This is used by the Bing search engine to accommodate for sponsored search on Bing. Whereas, the latter algorithm is used to determine frequently used items. For both the algorithms, MR++, a modified version of MapReduce, which effectively retains states for iterative algorithms, was used. The authors observed that for both the algorithms, performance on a single server with large memory was substantially better than a distributed cluster. However, we must understand that this observation is only valid for iterative algorithms which require retention of states and which become too complex for distributed processing. Further, as the size of data is relatively smaller, analytics can be performed on a single machine with high processing power and memory. However, as the size would increase more computational power may be needed.

14.4   BIG DATA PROCESSING AT UBER

We can understand the challenges and developments of big data by studying development of big data platforms at Uber [18]. Uber initially employed Hadoop-based system for data storage and analytics. However, with increasing usage and popularity, Uber started facing some challenges:

1. **HDFS Scalability Limitation**: There were a large number of small files. This increases load on namenode and limited scalability of the big data infrastructure. At Uber's end, the organization limited the number of small files and distributed them across the cluster in order to solve this problem.

2. **Faster Data in Hadoop**: Uber requires access to fresh data. The Hadoop infrastructure was able to provide them analytical data with 24-hour access latency. But as the operations expanded, it was realized that access to fresh data is more desirable. To speed up data delivery, Uber redesigned data ingestion pipeline for providing access to incremental data.

3. **Updates and Deletes**: Hadoop does not cater for updates and deletes. However, it was a requirement because incremental updates were needed to be processed.

4. **Faster ETL and Modeling**: ETL and modeling jobs were snapshot-based. This requires the platform to be rebuild in every run. However, incremental processing was required which could only pull the changed data.

Uber team built Hadoop Upserts anD Incremental (Hudi) to cater their big data system needs. It is an open-source Spark library that utilizes HDFS and provides scalable support for deletes as well as updates. Using Hudi, Uber was able to adapt to an incremental ingestion model. Users (or applications) can retrieve all the records that have been updated or added since a specified time. Users can also pass checkpoint as a reference to retrieve records. Example 14.1 illustrates the big data model at Uber.

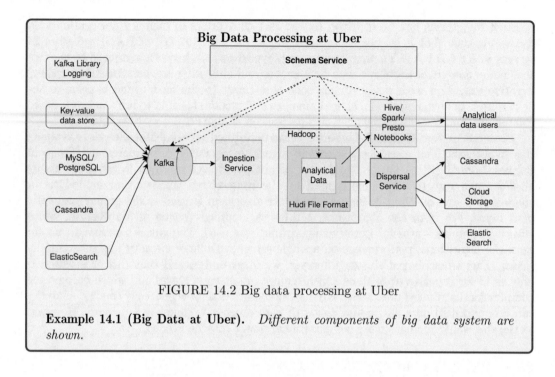

FIGURE 14.2 Big data processing at Uber

Example 14.1 (Big Data at Uber). *Different components of big data system are shown.*

14.5   BIG DATA PROCESSING AT LINKEDIN

LinkedIn team has developed Venice Hybrid, a big data solution to cater for batch as well as stream processing.

This development is based on the fact that at LinkedIn, data is organized into primary data and derived data:

1. **Primary Data**: This is a type of data which is obtained directly from source. For instance, a LinkedIn user may update her education profile.

2. **Derived Data**: This is a type of data, which is derived from the primary data source. For instance, the People You May Know (PYMK) feature is derived from a user's existing connections and profile.

LinkedIn team observes that both these data types have different requirements. For instance, the PYMK feature doesn't need to be optimized for writes. Since this is derived data, it does not involve write operations. However, the derived data requires low-latency reads and high-speed bulk ingestion of complete datasets.

LinkedIn team initially incorporated Voldermort read-only to ingest bulk data on Hadoop. However, the latency of data ingestion was quite high, which restricted the data ingestion operation to once per day.

14.5.1   The Lambda Architecture

The solution adopted by the LinkedIn team was motivated from the lambda architecture. We should recall from section 2.1.1 that the lambda architecture has a batch processing layer as well as a speed layer. The LinkedIn team observed that their architecture is similar to the lambda architecture. They have a need for bulk data ingestion and batch processing using Hadoop, and a stream processing layer, catering writes for the primary data. At LinkedIn, streaming data is handled through Kafka.

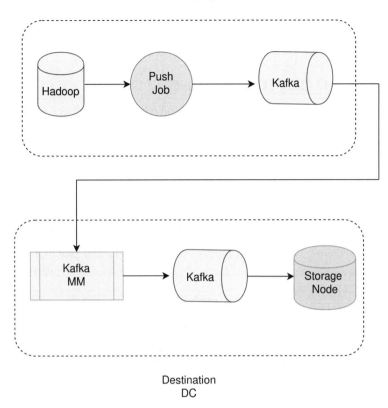

FIGURE 14.3 Venice data flow

The LinkedIn team observes that while the lambda architecture is operational; however, it has a few drawbacks [41].

1. Data is required to be read from two different data sources, streaming layer as well as batch layer. This implies that the speed will be restricted to the slower of the two.

2. Availability of the application is restricted to the availability of both the data sources.

3. Integration from both of the systems is required to get the computed results.

The LinkedIn team modified the lambda architecture to cater these limitations. The team introduced Venice, a distributed <key,value> storage.

Venice solves the problem of keeping two different data storage. It does so by providing a single database that accepts both batch and streaming ingestions. It reconciles them both at the time of writing. Thus it avoids a complex, multi-system lambda architecture by using one system to manage.

Venice data flow is shown in figure 14.3. The push job is responsible to read data off the Hadoop cluster. It will run as a MapReduce job and produce a Venice data message to the source Kafka cluster.

The Kafka Mirror Maker (MM), deployed in the destination cluster, will replicate all the messages from the Kafka cluster in the source data center to the Kafka cluster in the destination data center. Venice Storage Node will consume the Venice data message from the local Kafka cluster and persist data in a local database.

The core resource in Venice is a store. A store has schemas, owners, and is isolated from other stores. A store represents a single use case for a team using Venice. When a team pushes a dataset into their Venice store, they create a new version of that store. Every bulk push of data into Venice is a complete snapshot of the dataset.

14.6 DISTRIBUTED GRAPH PROCESSING AT GOOGLE

Google has needs to process billions of web pages and compute their page rank. Google Team has developed a PageRank algorithm and an optimized graph processing framework [340]. Following are a few optimizations:

1. Reduce the communication, by only exchanging message payloads between different partitions.

2. For targets that received frequent messages, messages are partially aggregated from the source. This conserves network bandwidth.

These modifications allow Google to compute ranks for up to 100 billion web pages.

14.7 FUTURE TRENDS

Data is being generated and collected at a massive rate. New systems are being built to cater emerging issues from big data. In this section, we will study a few emerging challenges and open issues which are likely to derive development of these systems.

1. **Availability**: With large data, there are increasing expectations of replication and availability such that faults can be isolated.

2. **Parallelism**: As data is being generated at an immensely higher rate, there are growing needs for enhancing data parallelism such that speed of computation can be enhanced.

3. **Scalability**: As data is growing, scalable solutions for processing and storage are needed.

4. **Transaction Processing**: OLTP solutions are needed which can process big data. We have studied that there is a trade-off between scalability and capability to process transactions. This trade-off is likely to exist in the coming years. However, a balance is needed to be explored.

5. **Stream Processing**: Real-time processing of data is an ongoing challenge. With the increase data arrival rate, new techniques and solutions are needed which can process data in real-time.

6. **Power Efficiency**: Big data systems employ massive computational power, which consumes high electricity. Power efficient solutions are needed to conserve electrical power. In this scenario, alternate energy solutions are also needed.

7. **Heterogeneous Environment**: Big data systems utilize heterogeneous computing environments. Often they include commodity hardware solutions. Efficient solutions are needed which can cater the needs of heterogeneity while enhancing efficiency.

8. **Efficient Network Processing**: Network is an important requirement for big data processing and storage. High-speed efficient network solutions are also needed for implementing parallel computing framework.

14.8 CONCLUDING REMARKS

Big data systems have been increasingly used in many organizations. In several cases, existing systems have been modified to cater specific needs of the organization. These case studies present a diverse set of enhancements which have been incorporated. The case studies also explain different needs of these organizations.

14.9 FURTHER READING

Various challenges about big data are explained in research papers [238, 331]. Case studies using different big data systems have been published in many papers [101, 249, 262, 354, 361].

14.10 EXERCISE QUESTIONS

1. Describe what are the issues of processing big data at Uber?

2. How Uber team addressed these issues?

3. Describe how Venice solves big data processing at LinkedIn?

4. Describe different open issues and challenges which exist in big data.

5. Explain why HDFS is unstable for real-time applications?

6. How Facebook achieves real-time behavior for its messaging application?

7. Describe how Scaling up would be useful as compared to scaling out?

8. Highlight open issues in big data systems.

9. What modifications were performed by Google for enhancing scalability in graph processing?

10. Out of the eight issues presented in section 14.7, which issues are more challenging to address? Explain.

GLOSSARY

Avatar Node: It is a node used to create as a backup for a namenode in Hadoop.

Bigtable: It is a distributed storage system which is designed to scale into the petabyte range. It is used as Google's internal database system that runs on top of the Google File System (GFS). It scales across thousands of commodity servers and is used extensively to support many of its core services, such as Gmail, YouTube, and Google Maps. In May 2015, Google released a public version of Bigtable as a managed NoSQL database service in the Google Cloud Platform (GCP).

Click Through Rate: It is a ratio of users who clicked on a specified link as compared to the total number of users who view the page.

DAFS: It refers to the Distributed Avatar File System, which is a modified HDFS with an Avatar node.

ETL: The term refers to Extract, Transform, and Load – the three fundamental functions of a database.

Frequent Item Mining: It is an algorithm to determine frequent items from a dataset.

Graph Processing: It refers to the process utilizing graphs to solve distributed system problems.

Google Earth Engine: It is a big data system for providing geospatial data. It has been developed by Google.

Incremental Data: The term refers to the changed data. That is, data which has been changed from previous reference.

Bibliography

[1] Accumulo. https://accumulo.apache.org/.

[2] Amazon Hybrid Cloud. http://aws.amazon.com/directconnect/.

[3] Ambari. https://ambari.apache.org.

[4] An in-depth look at Googles first Tensor Processing Unit (TPU). https://cloud.google.com/blog/big-data/2017/05/an-in-depth-look-at-googles-first-tensor-processing-unit-tpu.

[5] Apache Drill – Schema-free SQL for Hadoop, NoSQL and Cloud Storage. https://drill.apache.org/.

[6] Apache Flink: Stateful Computations over Data Streams. https://flink.apache.org/.

[7] Apache Flume. https://flume.apache.org/.

[8] Apache Hadoop Distributed Copy – Distcp Guide. https://hadoop.apache.org/docs/r1.2.1/distcp.html.

[9] Apache Hadoop YARN. https://hadoop.apache.org/docs/current/hadoop-yarn/hadoop-yarn-site/YARN.html.

[10] Apache HBase. http://hbase.apache.org/acid-semantics.html.

[11] Apache HBase Docs. http://hbase.apache.org/poweredbyhbase.html.

[12] Apache Kafka for Beginners. https://blog.cloudera.com/blog/2014/09/apache-kafka-for-beginners/.

[13] Apache Nifi. https://nifi.apache.org/.

[14] Apache Samza: A Distributed Stream Processing Framework. https://samza.apache.org/.

[15] Apache Spark Cluster Managers Yarn, Mesos and Standalone. https://data-flair.training/blogs/apache-spark-cluster-managers-tutorial/.

[16] Apache Storm. https://storm.apache.org/.

[17] BeyondCorp - Enterprise Security. https://cloud.google.com/beyondcorp/.

[18] Big Data at Uber. https://eng.uber.com/.

[19] Bigquery: Cloud Data Warehouse – Google Cloud. https://cloud.google.com/bigquery/.

[20] Boto Library for AWS. `https://boto3.amazonaws.com/v1/documentation/api/latest/index.html`.

[21] Data Breach Investigations Report 2016. `http://www.verizonenterprise.com/resources/reports/rp_DBIR_2016_Report_en_xg.pdf`.

[22] Deep Learning with Speech Recognition. `https://www.coursera.org`.

[23] Docker Documentation. `https://www.docker.com`.

[24] Graph Databases Comparison: AllegroGraph, ArangoDB, InfiniteGraph, Neo4j.

[25] Graphx Programming Guide. `https://spark.apache.org/docs/latest/graphx-programming-guide.html`.

[26] Handling Five Billion Sessions a Day. `https://blog.twitter.com/engineering/en_us/a/2015/handling-five-billion-sessions-a-day-in-real-time.html`.

[27] How to Read: Character Level Deep Learning. `https://offbit.github.io/how-to-read/`.

[28] Impala. `https://impala.apache.org`.

[29] Internet Small Computer System Interface. Technical report.

[30] Kafka. `https://yahooeng.tumblr.com/post/109994930921/kafka-yahoo`.

[31] Kafka Access. `https://cwiki.apache.org/confluence/display/KAFKA/`.

[32] Kafka Documentation. `https://kafka.apache.org/documentation.html`.

[33] Kafka Ecosystem at LinkedIn. `https://engineering.linkedin.com/blog/2016/04/kafka-ecosystem-at-linkedin`.

[34] Kafka Inside Keystone Pipeline. `https://netflixtechblog.com/kafka-inside-keystone-pipeline-dd5aeabaf6bb`.

[35] Kubernetes API. `https://kubernetes.io/docs/reference/using-api/`.

[36] Kubernetes Deployments. `https://kubernetes.io/docs/concepts/workloads/controllers/deployment/`.

[37] Kubernetes Ingress. `https://kubernetes.io/docs/concepts/services-networking/ingress/`.

[38] Kubernetes Objects. `https://kubernetes.io/docs/concepts/overview/working-with-objects/`.

[39] Kubernetes Pods. `https://kubernetes.io/docs/concepts/workloads/pods/`.

[40] Kubernetes Service. `https://kubernetes.io/docs/concepts/services-networking/service/`.

[41] LinkedIn Engineering. `https://engineering.linkedin.com/`.

[42] Linux Containers. `https://linuxcontainers.org/`.

[43] Long Short-Term Memory Recurrent Neural Network Architectures for Large Scale Acoustic Modeling.

[44] Machine learning is fun. https://medium.com/.

[45] Machine Learning Library MLlib Guide. https://spark.apache.org/docs/latest/ml-guide.html.

[46] MLlib: RDD-based API. https://spark.apache.org/docs/latest/mllib-guide.html.

[47] MPI Hello World Tutorial. https://mpitutorial.com/tutorials/.

[48] OpenMP Hello World Tutorial. https://www.dartmouth.edu.

[49] Pig Guide. https://pig.apache.org/docs/r0.17.0/func.html.

[50] Pig Optimizations. https://cwiki.apache.org/confluence/display/PIG/.

[51] Powered By Spark. http://spark.apache.org/powered-by.html.

[52] Presto – Distributed SQL Query Engine for Big Data. https://prestosql.io.

[53] Spark Documentation. https://spark.apache.org/docs.

[54] Spark ML online documentation. https://spark.apache.org/docs/latest/ml-pipeline.html.

[55] Spark Programming Guide. https://spark.apache.org/docs/latest/rdd-programming-guide.html.

[56] Spark SQL. https://spark.apache.org/docs/latest/sql-programming-guide.html.

[57] Spark Streaming. https://spark.apache.org/docs/latest/streaming-kafka-integration.html.

[58] Spark Streaming Example. http://spark.apache.org/.

[59] Spark Streaming Guide. https://spark.apache.org/docs/latest/structured-streaming-programming-guide.html.

[60] Spark Structured Streaming Guide. https://spark.apache.org/docs/latest/structured-streaming-programming-guide.html.

[61] Sqoop. https://sqoop.apache.org.

[62] Sqoop Docs. https://sqoop.apache.org/docs/.

[63] TensorFlow. https://www.tensorflow.org/.

[64] The Official Kubernetes Documentation. https://kubernetes.io/docs/home/.

[65] The Official SPARK Graphx Documentation. https://spark.apache.org/docs/latest/graphx programming guidc.html.

[66] Theano Documentation. http://deeplearning.net/.

[67] Top Ten Supercomputers. https://www.networkworld.com/article/3236875/embargo-10-of-the-worlds-fastest-supercomputers.html.

[68] The Trouble with Kappa Architecture. https://www.linkedin.com/pulse/trouble-kappa-architecture-michael-segel.

[69] VMware Hybrid Cloud. http://www.vmware.com/products/vcloud-hybrid-service.

[70] VMware Private Cloud. http://www.vmware.com/cloud-computing/private-cloud.html.

[71] Xen Cloud Platform. http://www-archive.xenproject.org/products/cloudxen.html.

[72] Jans Aasman. Allegro Graph: RDF Triple Database. *Cidade: Oakland Franz Incorporated*, 17, 2006.

[73] Mohammad Aazam and Eui-Nam Huh. Fog Computing and Smart Gateway Based Communication for Cloud of Things. In *Future Internet of Things and Cloud (Fi-Cloud), 2014 International Conference on*, page 464–470. IEEE, 2014.

[74] Abadi. Problems with Cap and Yahoos Little Known NOSQL System. 2010. http://dbmsmusings.blogspot.com/2010/04/problems-with-cap-andyahoos-little.html.

[75] Martjn Abadi, Paul Barham, Jianmin Chen, Zhifeng Chen, Andy Davis, Jeffrey Dean, Matthieu Devin, Sanjay Ghemawat, Geoffrey Irving, Michael Isard, et al. TensorFlow: A System for Large-scale Machine Learning. In *OSDI*, volume 16, page 265–283, 2016.

[76] Tim Abels, Puneet Dhawan, and Balasubramanian Chandrasekaran. An Overview of Xen Virtualization. *Dell Power Solutions*, (8):109–111, 2005.

[77] Keith Adams and Ole Agesen. A Comparison of Software and Hardware Techniques for x86 Virtualization. *ACM SIGARCH Computer Architecture News*, 34(5):2–13, 2006.

[78] Ramil Agliamzanov, Muhammed Sit, and Ibrahim Demir. Hydrology@ Home: A Distributed Volunteer Computing Framework for Hydrological Research and Applications. *Journal of Hydroinformatics*, 22(2):235–248, 2020.

[79] Mohammad Alizadeh, Albert Greenberg, David A Maltz, Jitendra Padhye, Parveen Patel, Balaji Prabhakar, Sudipta Sengupta, and Murari Sridharan. Data Center TCP DCTCP. In *Proceedings of the ACM SIGCOMM 2010 Conference*, page 63–74, 2010.

[80] Mohammad Alizadeh, Adel Javanmard, and Balaji Prabhakar. Analysis of DCTCP: Stability, Convergence, and Fairness. *ACM SIGMETRICS Performance Evaluation Review*, 39(1):73–84, 2011.

[81] EC Amazon. Amazon Elastic Compute Cloud (Amazon EC2). *Amazon Elastic Compute Cloud (Amazon EC2)*, 2010.

[82] J Chris Anderson, Jan Lehnardt, and Noah Slater. *CouchDB: The Definitive Guide: Time to Relax*. "O'Reilly Media, Inc.", 2010.

[83] Michael Armbrust, Reynold S Xin, Cheng Lian, Yin Huai, Davies Liu, Joseph K Bradley, Xiangrui Meng, Tomer Kaftan, Michael J Franklin, Ali Ghodsi, et al. Spark SQL: Relational Data Processing in Spark. In *Proceedings of the 2015 ACM SIGMOD International Conference on Management of Data*, page 1383–1394. ACM, 2015.

[84] Jason Arnold, Boris Glavic, and Ioan Raicu. Hrdbms: Combining the Best of Modern and Traditional Relational Databases. *arXiv preprint arXiv:1901.08666*, 2019.

[85] Francesco Asnicar, Nadir Sella, Luca Masera, Paolo Morettin, Thomas Tolio, Stanislau Semeniuta, Claudio Moser, Enrico Blanzieri, and Valter Cavecchia. TN-Grid and Gene@ Home Project: Volunteer Computing for Bioinformatics. In *BOINC: FAST 2015 International Conference BOINC: FAST 2015Second International Conference BOINC-based High Performance Computing: Fundamental Research and Development*. Russian Academy of Sciences, 2015.

[86] Kyle Banker. *MongoDB in Action*. Manning Publications Co., 2011.

[87] Narsimha Banothu, ShankarNayak Bhukya, and K Venkatesh Sharma. Big-data: Acid Versus Base for Database Transactions. In *Electrical, Electronics, and Optimization Techniques (ICEEOT), International Conference on*, page 3704–3709. IEEE, 2016.

[88] Feng Bao and Robert H Deng. A Signcryption Scheme with Signature Directly Verifiable by Public Key. In *International Workshop on Public Key Cryptography*, page 55–59. Springer, 1998.

[89] Michael Barbaro, Tom Zeller, and Saul Hansell. A Face is Exposed for AOL Searcher no. 4417749. *New York Times*, 9(2008):8For, 2006.

[90] Cristian Andrei Baron et al. NoSQL Key-Value DBs Riak and Redis. *Database Systems Journal*, 4:3–10, 2016.

[91] Daniel C Barth-Jones. The 'Re-identification' of Governor William Weld's Medical Information: A Critical Re-examination of Health Data Identification Risks and Privacy Protections, Then and Now. *Then and Now (July 2012)*, 2012.

[92] Frederic Bastien, Pascal Lamblin, Razvan Pascanu, James Bergstra, Ian Goodfellow, Arnaud Bergeron, Nicolas Bouchard, David Warde-Farley, and Yoshua Bengio. Theano: new features and speed improvements. *arXiv preprint arXiv:1211.5590*, 2012.

[93] Narmeen Zakaria Bawany and Jawwad A Shamsi. SEAL: SDN Based Secure and Agile Framework for Protecting Smart City Applications from DDoS Attacks. *Journal of Network and Computer Applications*, 145:102381, 2019.

[94] Narmeen Zakaria Bawany, Jawwad A Shamsi, and Khaled Salah. DDoS Attack Detection and Mitigation Using SDN: Methods, Practices, and Solutions. *Arabian Journal for Science and Engineering*, 42(2):425–441, 2017.

[95] Adam L Beberg, Daniel L Ensign, Guha Jayachandran, Siraj Khaliq, and Vijay S Pande. Folding@ home: Lessons from Eight Years of Volunteer Distributed Computing. In *2009 IEEE International Symposium on Parallel & Distributed Processing*, page 1–8. IEEE, 2009.

[96] Andras Beleczki and Balint Molnar. Modeling Framework for Designing and Analyzing Document-Centric Information Systems based on HyperGraphDB. In *CEUR Workshop Proceedings (ISSN: 1613-0073)*, volume 2046, page 17–22, 2016.

[97] Andrew John Bernoth. Identifying Additional Firewall Rules that may be needed, July 3 2018. US Patent 10,015,140.

[98] Janki Bhimani, Zhengyu Yang, Miriam Leeser, and Ningfang Mi. Accelerating Big Data Applications Using Lightweight Virtualization Framework on Enterprise Cloud. In *High Performance Extreme Computing Conference (HPEC), 2017 IEEE*, page 1–7. IEEE, 2017.

[99] Carsten Binnig, Andrew Crotty, Alex Galakatos, Tim Kraska, and Erfan Zamanian. The End of Slow Networks: It's Time for a Redesign. *Proceedings of the VLDB Endowment*, 9(7):528–539, 2016.

[100] MKABV Bittorf, Taras Bobrovytsky, CCACJ Erickson, Martin Grund Daniel Hecht, MJIJL Kuff, Dileep Kumar Alex Leblang, NLIPH Robinson, David Rorke Silvius Rus, John Russell Dimitris Tsirogiannis Skye Wanderman, and Milne Michael Yoder. Impala: A Modern, Open-Source SQL Engine for Hadoop. In *Proceedings of the 7th Biennial Conference on Innovative Data Systems Research*, 2015.

[101] Linda Camilla Boldt, Vinothan Vinayagamoorthy, Florian Winder, Melanie Schnittger, Mats Ekran, Raghava Rao Mukkamala, Niels Buus Lassen, Benjamin Flesch, Abid Hussain, and Ravi Vatrapu. Forecasting Nike's Sales using Facebook Data. In *2016 IEEE International Conference on Big Data (Big Data)*, page 2447–2456. IEEE, 2016.

[102] Flavio Bonomi, Rodolfo Milito, Jiang Zhu, and Sateesh Addepalli. Fog Computing and its Role in the Internet of Things. In *Proceedings of the First Edition of the MCC Workshop on Mobile Cloud Computing*, page 13–16. ACM, 2012.

[103] Dhruba Borthakur, Jonathan Gray, Joydeep Sen Sarma, Kannan Muthukkaruppan, Nicolas Spiegelberg, Hairong Kuang, Karthik Ranganathan, Dmytro Molkov, Aravind Menon, Samuel Rash, et al. Apache Hadoop goes Realtime at Facebook. In *Proceedings of the 2011 ACM SIGMOD International Conference on Management of Data*, page 1071–1080. ACM, 2011.

[104] Roland N Boubela, Klaudius Kalcher, Wolfgang Huf, Christian Nasel, and Ewald Moser. Big Data Approaches for the Analysis of Large-Scale fMRI Data using Apache Spark and GPU Processing: A Demonstration on Resting-State fMRI Data from the Human Connectome Project. *Frontiers in Neuroscience*, 9:492, 2016.

[105] David Bradley, Richard Harper, and Steven Hunter. Power-Aware Workload Balancing using Virtual Machines, March 17 2005. US Patent App. 10/663,285.

[106] Rodrigo Braga, Edjard Mota, and Alexandre Passito. Lightweight DDoS Flooding Attack Detection Using NOX/OpenFlow. In *IEEE Local Computer Network Conference*, page 408–415. IEEE, 2010.

[107] Eric Brewer. A Certain Freedom: Thoughts on the Cap Theorem. In *Proceedings of the 29th ACM SIGACT-SIGOPS Symposium on Principles of Distributed Computing*, page 335–335. ACM, 2010.

[108] Eric Brewer. Cap Twelve Years Later: How the "Rules" Have Changed. *Computer*, 45(2):23–29, 2012.

[109] Eric Brewer. Pushing the cap: Strategies for Consistency and Availability. *Computer*, 45(2):23–29, 2012.

[110] Eric Brewer. Spanner, Truetime and the CAP Theorem. 2017.

[111] Eric A Brewer. Towards Robust Distributed Systems. In *PODC*, volume 7, 2000.

[112] Martin C Brown. *Getting Started with Couchbase Server: Extreme Scalability at Your Fingertips.* "O'Reilly Media, Inc.", 2012.

[113] Barbara Brynko. NuoDB: Reinventing the Database. *Information Today*, 29(9):9–9, 2012.

[114] Yingyi Bu, Bill Howe, Magdalena Balazinska, and Michael D Ernst. Haloop: Efficient Iterative Data Processing on Large Clusters. *Proceedings of the VLDB Endowment*, 3(1-2):285–296, 2010.

[115] Yingyi Bu, Bill Howe, Magdalena Balazinska, and Michael D Ernst. The Haloop Approach to Large-Scale Iterative Data Analysis. *The VLDB Journal The International Journal on Very Large Data Bases*, 21(2):169–190, 2012.

[116] Brendan Burns, Brian Grant, David Oppenheimer, Eric Brewer, and John Wilkes. Borg, omega, and kubernetes. *Queue*, 14(1):70–93, 2016.

[117] Rajkumar Buyya et al. High Performance Cluster Computing: Architectures and Systems (volume 1). *Prentice Hall, Upper Saddle River, NJ, USA*, 1:999, 1999.

[118] Rajkumar Buyya, Chee Shin Yeo, Srikumar Venugopal, James Broberg, and Ivona Brandic. Cloud Computing and Emerging it Platforms: Vision, Hype, and Reality for Delivering Computing as the 5th utility. *Future Generation Computer Systems*, 25(6):599–616, 2009.

[119] Christian Cachin et al. Architecture of the Hyperledger Blockchain Fabric. In *Workshop on Distributed Cryptocurrencies and Consensus Ledgers*, volume 310, page 4, 2016.

[120] Stefano Calzavara, Sebastian Roth, Alvise Rabitti, Michael Backes, and Ben Stock. A Tale of Two Headers: A Formal Analysis of Inconsistent Click-jacking Protection on the Web. 2020.

[121] Josiah L Carlson. *Redis in Action.* Manning Shelter Island, 2013.

[122] Rick Cattell. Scalable SQL and NoSQL Data Stores. *Acm Sigmod Record*, 39(4):12–27, 2011.

[123] Ugur Cetintemel, Nesime Tatbul, Kristin Tufte, Hao Wang, Stanley Zdonik, Jiang Du, Tim Kraska, Samuel Madden, David Maier, John Meehan, et al. S-store: A Streaming NewSQL System for Big Velocity Applications. 2014.

[124] Mallikarjun Chadalapaka, Hemal Shah, Uri Elzur, Patricia Thaler, and Michael Ko. A Study of iSCSI extensions for RDMA (iSER). In *Proceedings of the ACM SIGCOMM Workshop on Network-I/O Convergence: Experience, Lessons, Implications*, page 209–219, 2003.

[125] Prabhakar Chaganti and Rich Helms. *Amazon SimpleDB Developer Guide.* Packt Publishing Ltd, 2010.

[126] Swetha Prabha Chaganti. Voldemort NoSQL Database. 2016.

[127] Bill Chambers and Matei Zaharia. *Spark: The Definitive Guide: Big Data Processing Made Simple.* "O'Reilly Media, Inc.", 2018.

[128] Fay Chang, Jeffrey Dean, Sanjay Ghemawat, Wilson C Hsieh, Deborah A Wallach, Mike Burrows, Tushar Chandra, Andrew Fikes, and Robert E Gruber. Bigtable: A distributed Storage System for Structured Data. *ACM Transactions on Computer Systems (TOCS)*, 26(2):1–26, 2008.

[129] Rocky KC Chang. Defending Against Flooding-Based Distributed Denial-of-Service Attacks: A Tutorial. *IEEE Communications Magazine*, 40(10):42–51, 2002.

[130] Jack Chen, Samir Jindel, Robert Walzer, Rajkumar Sen, Nika Jimsheleishvilli, and Michael Andrews. The MemSQL Query Optimizer: A Modern Optimizer for Real-Time Analytics in a Distributed Database. *Proceedings of the VLDB Endowment*, 9(13):1401–1412, 2016.

[131] Kai Chen, Ankit Singla, Atul Singh, Kishore Ramachandran, Lei Xu, Yueping Zhang, Xitao Wen, and Yan Chen. Osa: An optical switching architecture for data center networks with unprecedented flexibility. *IEEE/ACM Transactions on Networking (TON)*, 22(2):498–511, 2014.

[132] Qun Chen, Song Bai, Zhanhuai Li, Zhiying Gou, Bo Suo, and Wei Pan. GraphHP: A Hybrid Platform for Iterative Graph Processing. *arXiv preprint arXiv:1706.07221*, 2017.

[133] Tianqi Chen, Mu Li, Yutian Li, Min Lin, Naiyan Wang, Minjie Wang, Tianjun Xiao, Bing Xu, Chiyuan Zhang, and Zheng Zhang. Mxnet: A Flexible and Efficient Machine Learning Library for Heterogeneous Distributed Systems. *arXiv preprint arXiv:1512.01274*, 2015.

[134] Wen Chen, Peng Cheng, Fengyuan Ren, Ran Shu, and Chuang Lin. Ease the Queue Oscillation: Analysis and Enhancement of DCTCP. In *2013 IEEE 33rd International Conference on Distributed Computing Systems*, page 450–459. IEEE, 2013.

[135] Xue-Wen Chen and Xiaotong Lin. Big Data Deep Learning: Challenges and Perspectives. *IEEE access*, 2:514–525, 2014.

[136] Yanpei Chen, Rean Griffit, David Zats, and Randy H Katz. Understanding TCP incast and its implications for Big Data Workloads. *University of California at Berkeley, Tech. Rep*, 2012.

[137] Yi Chen, Zhi Qiao, Hai Jiang, Kuan-Ching Li, and Won Woo Ro. MGMR: Multi-GPU based MapReduce. In *International Conference on Grid and Pervasive Computing*, page 433–442. Springer, 2013.

[138] Avery Ching, Sergey Edunov, Maja Kabiljo, Dionysios Logothetis, and Sambavi Muthukrishnan. One trillion edges: Graph Processing at Facebook-Scale. *Proceedings of the VLDB Endowment*, 8(12):1804–1815, 2015.

[139] Kristina Chodorow. *Scaling MongoDB: Sharding, Cluster Setup, and Administration.* "O'Reilly Media, Inc.", 2011.

[140] Kristina Chodorow. *MongoDB: The Definitive Guide: Powerful and Scalable Data Storage.* "O'Reilly Media, Inc.", 2013.

[141] Mrs Rupali M Chopade and Nikhil S Dhavase. MongoDB, Couchbase: Performance Comparison for Image Dataset. In *2017 2nd International Conference for Convergence in Technology (I2CT)*, page 255–258. IEEE, 2017.

[142] Junyoung Chung, Caglar Gulcehre, Kyunghyun Cho, and Yoshua Bengio. Gated Feedback Recurrent Neural Networks. In *International Conference on Machine Learning*, page 2067–2075, 2015.

[143] Taejoong Chung, Roland van Rijswijk-Deij, Balakrishnan Chandrasekaran, David Choffnes, Dave Levin, Bruce M Maggs, Alan Mislove, and Christo Wilson. An End-to-End View of DNSSEC Ecosystem Management. *; login:*, 42(4), 2017.

[144] Dan Ciresan, Ueli Meier, Jonathan Masci, and Jurgen Schmidhuber. Multi-Column Deep Neural Network for Traffic Sign Classification. *Neural Networks*, 32:333–338, 2012.

[145] Cisco. Data Center: Load Balancing Data Center Services.

[146] Christopher Clark, Keir Fraser, Steven Hand, Jacob Gorm Hansen, Eric Jul, Christian Limpach, Ian Pratt, and Andrew Warfield. Live Migration of Virtual Machines. In *Proceedings of the 2nd conference on Symposium on Networked Systems Design & Implementation-Volume 2*, page 273–286. USENIX Association, 2005.

[147] Michael Colesky, Jaap-Henk Hoepman, and Christiaan Hillen. A Critical Analysis of Privacy Design Strategies. In *Security and Privacy Workshops (SPW), 2016 IEEE*, page 33–40. IEEE, 2016.

[148] James C Corbett, Jeffrey Dean, Michael Epstein, Andrew Fikes, Christopher Frost, Jeffrey John Furman, Sanjay Ghemawat, Andrey Gubarev, Christopher Heiser, Peter Hochschild, et al. Spanner: Googles Globally Distributed Database. *ACM Transactions on Computer Systems (TOCS)*, 31(3):1–22, 2013.

[149] Antonio Corradi, Mario Fanelli, and Luca Foschini. Vm consolidation: A Real Case Based on Openstack Cloud. *Future Generation Computer Systems*, 32:118–127, 2014.

[150] Laizhong Cui, F Richard Yu, and Qiao Yan. When Big Data Meets Software-Defined Networking: SDN for Big Data and Big Data for SDN. *IEEE Network*, 30(1):58–65, 2016.

[151] Ian Curry. An Introduction to Cryptography and Digital Signatures. *Entrust Securing Digital Identities and Information*, 2001.

[152] Nhu-Ngoc Dao, Junho Park, Minho Park, and Sungrae Cho. A Feasible Method to Combat Against DDoS Attack in SDN Network. In *2015 International Conference on Information Networking (ICOIN)*, page 309–311. IEEE, 2015.

[153] Marieke De Goede. The politics of Privacy in the Age of Preemptive Security. *International Political Sociology*, 8(1):100–104, 2014.

[154] Jeffrey Dean and Sanjay Ghemawat. MapReduce: Simplified Data Processing on Large Clusters. *Communications of the ACM*, 51(1):107–113, 2008.

[155] Jeffrey Dean and Sanjay Ghemawat. MapReduce: A Flexible Data Processing Tool. *Communications of the ACM*, 53(1):72–77, 2010.

[156] Casimer DeCusatis. Optical Interconnect Networks for Data Communications. *Journal of Lightwave Technology*, 32(4):544–552, 2014.

[157] Kevin Deierling. Ethernet Just Got a Big Performance Boost with Release of Soft RoCE, 2015.

[158] OrientDB Developers. OrientDB. *Hybrid Document-Store and Graph NoSQL Database [online]*, 2012.

[159] David HC Du, Tai-Sheng Chang, Jenwei Hsieh, Sangyup Shim, and Yuewei Wang. Two Emerging Serial Storage Interfaces for Supporting Digital Libraries: Serial Storage Architecture (SSA) and Fiber Channel-Arbitrated Loop (FC-AL). *Multimedia Tools and Applications*, 10(2):179–203, 2000.

[160] Muhammad Nouman Durrani and Jawwad A Shamsi. Volunteer Computing: Requirements, Challenges, and Solutions. *Journal of Network and Computer Applications*, 39:369–380, 2014.

[161] Michael Erbschloe. *Trojans, Worms, and Spyware: A Computer Security Professional's Guide to Malicious Code*. Elsevier, 2004.

[162] Hamza Es-Samaali, Aissam Outchakoucht, and Jean Philippe Leroy. A Blockchain-Based Access Control for Big Data. *International Journal of Computer Networks and Communications Security*, 5(7):137, 2017.

[163] Christian Esposito, Aniello Castiglione, and Kim-Kwang Raymond Choo. Challenges in Delivering Software in the Cloud as Microservices. *IEEE Cloud Computing*, (5):10–14, 2016.

[164] Reza Farivar, Daniel Rebolledo, Ellick Chan, and Roy H Campbell. A Parallel Implementation of K-means Clustering on GPUs. In *PDPTA*, volume 13, page 212–312, 2008.

[165] Nathan Farrington, George Porter, Sivasankar Radhakrishnan, Hamid Hajabdolali Bazzaz, Vikram Subramanya, Yeshaiahu Fainman, George Papen, and Amin Vahdat. Helios: A Hybrid Electrical/Optical Switch Architecture for Modular Data Centers. *ACM SIGCOMM Computer Communication Review*, 40(4):339–350, 2010.

[166] Maria Fazio, Antonio Celesti, Rajiv Ranjan, Chang Liu, Lydia Chen, and Massimo Villari. Open Issues in Scheduling Microservices in the Cloud. *IEEE Cloud Computing*, 3(5):81–88, 2016.

[167] M Fenn, MA Murphy, J Martin, and S Goasguen. An Evaluation of KVM for use in Cloud Computing. In *Proceedings of the 2nd International Conference on the Virtual Computing Initiative, RTP, NC, USA*, 2008.

[168] Michael J Flynn. Very High-Speed Computing Systems. *Proceedings of the IEEE*, 54(12):1901–1909, 1966.

[169] Julien Forgeat. Data Processing Architectures-Lambda and Kappa. *Ericsson Research Blog*, 2015.

[170] Ian Foster, Yong Zhao, Ioan Raicu, and Shiyong Lu. Cloud Computing and Grid Computing 360-Degree Compared. In *Grid Computing Environments Workshop, 2008. GCE'08*, page 1–10. IEEE, 2008.

[171] Michael Frampton. *Big Data Made Easy: A Working Guide to the Complete Hadoop Toolset*. Apress, 2014.

[172] Vincent Garcia, Eric Debreuve, and Michel Barlaud. Fast K Nearest Neighbor Search using GPU. *arXiv preprint arXiv:0804.1448*, 2008.

[173] Alan Gates and Daniel Dai. *Programming Pig: Dataflow Scripting with Hadoop.* "O'Reilly Media, Inc.", 2016.

[174] Alan Gates, Jianyong Dai, and Thejas Nair. Apache Pig's Optimizer. *IEEE Data Engineering Bulletin*, 36(1):34–45, 2013.

[175] Alan F Gates, Olga Natkovich, Shubham Chopra, Pradeep Kamath, Shravan M Narayanamurthy, Christopher Olston, Benjamin Reed, Santhosh Srinivasan, and Utkarsh Srivastava. Building A High-Level Dataflow System on Top of Map-Reduce: The Pig Experience. *Proceedings of the VLDB Endowment*, 2(2):1414–1425, 2009.

[176] Lars George. *HBase: The Definitive Guide: Random Access to your Planet-Size Data.* "O'Reilly Media, Inc.", 2011.

[177] Sanjay Ghemawat, Howard Gobioff, and Shun-Tak Leung. The Google File System. In *ACM SIGOPS Operating Systems Review*, volume 37, page 29–43. ACM, 2003.

[178] Seth Gilbert and Nancy A Lynch. Perspectives on the Cap Theorem. *Computer*, 45(2):30–36, 2012.

[179] Ian Goodfellow, Yoshua Bengio, and Aaron Courville. *Deep Learning.* MIT Press, 2016.

[180] Noel Gorelick, Matt Hancher, Mike Dixon, Simon Ilyushchenko, David Thau, and Rebecca Moore. Google earth engine: Planetary-scale geospatial analysis for everyone. *Remote sensing of Environment*, 202:18–27, 2017.

[181] Alex Graves, Santiago Fernandez, Faustino Gomez, and Jürgen Schmidhuber. Connectionist Temporal Classification: Labelling Unsegmented Sequence Data with Recurrent Neural Networks. In *Proceedings of the 23rd International Conference on Machine learning*, page 369–376. ACM, 2006.

[182] Alex Graves, Abdel-rahman Mohamed, and Geoffrey Hinton. Speech Recognition with Deep Recurrent Neural Networks. In *Acoustics, Speech and Signal Processing (ICASSP), 2013 IEEE International Conference on*, page 6645–6649. IEEE, 2013.

[183] Albert Greenberg, James R Hamilton, Navendu Jain, Srikanth Kandula, Changhoon Kim, Parantap Lahiri, David A Maltz, Parveen Patel, and Sudipta Sengupta. Vl2: A Scalable and Flexible Data Center Network. In *ACM SIGCOMM Computer Communication Review*, volume 39, page 51–62. ACM, 2009.

[184] Steven L Grobman. Server Pool Kerberos Authentication Scheme, March 21 2017. US Patent 9,602,275.

[185] Katarina Grolinger, Wilson A Higashino, Abhinav Tiwari, and Miriam AM Capretz. Data Management in Cloud Environments: NoSQL and NewSQL Data Stores. *Journal of Cloud Computing: Advances, Systems and Applications*, 2(1):22, 2013.

[186] Chuanxiong Guo, Guohan Lu, Dan Li, Haitao Wu, Xuan Zhang, Yunfeng Shi, Chen Tian, Yongguang Zhang, and Songwu Lu. Bcube: A High Performance, Server-Centric Network Architecture for Modular Data Centers. In *Proceedings of the ACM SIGCOMM 2009 Conference on Data Communication*, page 63–74, 2009.

[187] Himanshu Gupta, Subhash Mondal, Srayan Ray, Biswajit Giri, Rana Majumdar, and Ved P Mishra. Impact of SQL Injection in Database Security. In *2019 International Conference on Computational Intelligence and Knowledge Economy (ICCIKE)*, page 296–299. IEEE, 2019.

[188] Irfan Habib. Virtualization with KVM. *Linux Journal*, 2008(166):8, 2008.

[189] William G Halfond, Jeremy Viegas, Alessandro Orso, et al. A Classification of SQL-Injection Attacks and Countermeasures. In *Proceedings of the IEEE International Symposium on Secure Software Engineering*, volume 1, page 13–15. IEEE, 2006.

[190] Jing Han, E Haihong, Guan Le, and Jian Du. Survey on NoSQL Database. In *2011 6th International Conference on Pervasive Computing and Applications*, page 363–366. IEEE, 2011.

[191] T Harford. Big Data: Are We Making a Big Mistake? [internet]. London: Ft magazine; c2014 [cited at 2015 sep 28].

[192] Ibrahim Abaker Targio Hashem, Ibrar Yaqoob, Nor Badrul Anuar, Salimah Mokhtar, Abdullah Gani, and Samee Ullah Khan. The Rise of "Big Data on Cloud Computing: Review and Open Research Issues. *Information Systems*, 47:98–115, 2015.

[193] Michael Hausenblas and Jacques Nadeau. Apache Drill: Interactive Ad-hoc Analysis at Scale. *Big Data*, 1(2):100–104, 2013.

[194] Bingsheng He, Wenbin Fang, Qiong Luo, Naga K Govindaraju, and Tuyong Wang. Mars: A MapReduce Framework on Graphics Processors. In *Parallel Architectures and Compilation Techniques (PACT), 2008 International Conference on*, page 260–269. IEEE, 2008.

[195] Ying He, F Richard Yu, Nan Zhao, Victor CM Leung, and Hongxi Yin. Software-Defined Networks with Mobile Edge Computing and Caching for Smart Cities: A Big Data Deep Reinforcement Learning Approach. *IEEE Communications Magazine*, 55(12):31–37, 2017.

[196] Thomas A Hengeveld. Multi-Tunnel Virtual Private Network, March 29 2016. US Patent 9,300,570.

[197] Maurice Herlihy. Blockchains From a Distributed Computing Perspective. *Communications of the ACM*, 62(2):78–85, 2019.

[198] Bai Hong-Tao, He Li-li, Ouyang Dan-tong, Li Zhan-shan, and Li He. K-Means on Commodity GPUs with CUDA. In *2009 World Congress on Computer Science and Information Engineering*, page 651–655. IEEE, 2009.

[199] Weisheng Hu, Weiqiang Sun, Yaohui Jin, Wei Guo, and Shilin Xiao. An Efficient Transportation Architecture for Big Data Movement. In *Information, Communications and Signal Processing (ICICS) 2013 9th International Conference on*, page 1–5. IEEE, 2013.

[200] Yin Huai, Ashutosh Chauhan, Alan Gates, Gunther Hagleitner, Eric N Hanson, Owen O'Malley, Jitendra Pandey, Yuan Yuan, Rubao Lee, and Xiaodong Zhang. Major Technical Advancements in Apache Hive. In *Proceedings of the 2014 ACM SIGMOD International Conference on Management of Data*, page 1235–1246. ACM, 2014.

[201] Patrick Hunt, Mahadev Konar, Flavio Paiva Junqueira, and Benjamin Reed. Zookeeper: Wait-Free Coordination for Internet-Scale Systems. In *USENIX Annual Technical Conference*, volume 8. Boston, MA, USA, 2010.

[202] Jalal B Hur and Jawwad A Shamsi. A Survey on Security Issues, Vulnerabilities and Attacks in Android Based Smartphone. In *2017 International Conference on Information and Communication Technologies (ICICT)*, page 40–46. IEEE, 2017.

[203] Intel. Understanding iWARP: Delivering Low Latency to Ethernet.

[204] Borislav Iordanov. HyperGraphDB: A Generalized Graph Database. In *International Conference on Web-Age Information Management*, page 25–36. Springer, 2010.

[205] Waheed Iqbal. Service Level Agreement Driven Adaptive Resource Management for Web Applications on Heterogeneous Compute Clouds. Master's thesis, 2009.

[206] Tania Iram, Jawwad Shamsi, Usama Alvi, Saif ur Rahman, and Muhammad Maaz. Controlling Smart-city Traffic using Machine Learning. In *2019 International Conference on Frontiers of Information Technology (FIT)*, page 203–2035. IEEE, 2019.

[207] Sasha Issenberg. How President Obamas Campaign used Big Data to Rally Individual Voters, 2012.

[208] HV Jagadish, Johannes Gehrke, Alexandros Labrinidis, Yannis Papakonstantinou, Jignesh M Patel, Raghu Ramakrishnan, and Cyrus Shahabi. Big Data and its Technical Challenges. *Communications of the ACM*, 57(7):86–94, 2014.

[209] Raj Jain and Subharthi Paul. Network Virtualization and Software Defined Networking for Cloud Computing: A Survey. *IEEE Communications Magazine*, 51(11):24–31, 2013.

[210] Meiko Jensen. Challenges of Privacy Protection in Big Data Analytics. In *Big Data (BigData Congress), 2013 IEEE International Congress on*, page 235–238. IEEE, 2013.

[211] Norman P Jouppi, Cliff Young, Nishant Patil, David Patterson, Gaurav Agrawal, Raminder Bajwa, Sarah Bates, Suresh Bhatia, Nan Boden, Al Borchers, et al. In-datacenter Performance Analysis of a Tensor Processing Unit. *arXiv preprint arXiv:1704.04760*, 2017.

[212] Flavio P Junqueira and Benjamin C Reed. The Life and Times of a Zookeeper. In *Proceedings of the Twenty-First Annual Symposium on Parallelism in Algorithms and Architectures*, page 46–46. ACM, 2009.

[213] Dharmesh Kakadia. *Apache Mesos Essentials*. Packt Publishing Ltd, 2015.

[214] Robert Kallman, Hideaki Kimura, Jonathan Natkins, Andrew Pavlo, Alexander Rasin, Stanley Zdonik, Evan PC Jones, Samuel Madden, Michael Stonebraker, Yang Zhang, et al. H-store: A High-Performance, Distributed Main Memory Transaction Processing System. *Proceedings of the VLDB Endowment*, 1(2):1496–1499, 2008.

[215] Seny Kamara and Kristin Lauter. Cryptographic Cloud Storage. In *International Conference on Financial Cryptography and Data Security*, page 136–149. Springer, 2010.

[216] Karthik Kambatla, Giorgos Kollias, Vipin Kumar, and Ananth Grama. Trends in Big Data Analytics. *Journal of Parallel and Distributed Computing*, 74(7):2561–2573, 2014.

[217] Debabrata Kar, Suvasini Panigrahi, and Srikanth Sundararajan. SQLiGoT: Detecting SQL Injection Attacks Using Graph of Tokens and SVM. *Computers & Security*, 60:206–225, 2016.

[218] Holden Karau, Andy Konwinski, Patrick Wendell, and Matei Zaharia. *Learning Spark: Lightning-Fast Big Data Analysis*. "O'Reilly Media, Inc.", 2015.

[219] Wayne Karpoff and Brian Lake. Storage Virtualization System and Methods, August 18 2009. US Patent 7,577,817.

[220] Karambir Kaur and Monika Sachdeva. Performance Evaluation of NewSQL Databases. In *2017 International Conference on Inventive Systems and Control (ICISC)*, page 1–5. IEEE, 2017.

[221] Sawinder Kaur and Karamjit Guide Kaur. *Visualizing Class Diagram using OrientDB NoSQL Data-Store*. PhD thesis, 2016.

[222] Robert W Kembel and Horst L Truestedt. Fibre Channel Arbitrated Loop. 1996.

[223] David B Kirk and W Hwu Wen-Mei. *Programming Massively Parallel Processors: A Hands-on Approach*. Morgan Kaufmann, 2016.

[224] O Kolkman and R Gieben. DNSSEC Operational Practices. Technical report, RFC 4641, September, 2006.

[225] Richard T Kouzes, Gordon A Anderson, Stephen T Elbert, Ian Gorton, and Deborah K Gracio. The Changing Paradigm of Data-Intensive Computing. *Computer*, (1):26–34, 2009.

[226] Jay Kreps. Parallel Hardware Architecture. *Oracle, Dec.*

[227] Jay Kreps. The Log: What Every Software Engineer Should Know About Real-Time Datas Unifying Abstraction. *Linkedin. com, Dec*, 16, 2013.

[228] Jay Kreps. Questioning the Lambda Architecture. *Online Article, July*, page 205, 2014.

[229] Jay Kreps, Neha Narkhede, Jun Rao, et al. Kafka: A Distributed Messaging System for Log Processing. In *Proceedings of the NetDB*, page 1–7, 2011.

[230] Diego Kreutz, Fernando MV Ramos, Paulo Esteves Verissimo, Christian Esteve Rothenberg, Siamak Azodolmolky, and Steve Uhlig. Software-Defined Networking: A Comprehensive Survey. *Proceedings of the IEEE*, 103(1):14–76, 2015.

[231] Alexandros Labrinidis and Hosagrahar V Jagadish. Challenges and Opportunities with Big Data. *Proceedings of the VLDB Endowment*, 5(12):2032–2033, 2012.

[232] Kashif Laeeq and Jawwad A Shamsi. A Study of Security Issues, Vulnerabilities and Challenges in Internet of Things. *Securing Cyber-Physical Systems*, 10, 2015.

[233] Daniel Guimaraes do Lago, Edmundo RM Madeira, and Luiz Fernando Bittencourt. Power-Aware Virtual Machine Scheduling on Clouds using Active Cooling Control and DVFS. In *Proceedings of the 9th International Workshop on Middleware for Grids, Clouds and e-Science*, page 2. ACM, 2011.

[234] Avinash Lakshman and Prashant Malik. Cassandra: A Decentralized Structured Storage System. *ACM SIGOPS Operating Systems Review*, 44(2):35–40, 2010.

[235] Phillip A Laplante. Who's Afraid of Big Data? *IT Professional*, 15(5):6–7, 2013.

[236] David Lazer, Ryan Kennedy, Gary King, and Alessandro Vespignani. The Parable of Google Flu: Traps in Big Data Analysis. *Science*, 343(14 March), 2014.

[237] Brian Lebiednik, Aman Mangal, and Niharika Tiwari. A Survey and Evaluation of Data Center Network Topologies. *arXiv preprint arXiv:1605.01701*, 2016.

[238] Jae-Gil Lee and Minseo Kang. Geospatial Big Data: Challenges and Opportunities. *Big Data Research*, 2(2):74–81, 2015.

[239] Ken Ka-Yin Lee, Wai-Choi Tang, and Kup-Sze Choi. Alternatives to Relational Database: Comparison of NoSQL and XML Approaches for Clinical Data Storage. *Computer Methods and Programs in Biomedicine*, 110(1):99–109, 2013.

[240] Sangdo Lee and Jun-Ho Huh. An Effective Security Measures for Nuclear Power Plant Using Big Data Analysis Approach. *The Journal of Supercomputing*, 75(8):4267–4294, 2019.

[241] Joe Lennon. *Beginning CouchDB*. Apress, 2010.

[242] Hu Li, Tianjia Chen, and Wei Xu. Improving Spark Performance with Zero-Copy Buffer Management and RDMA. In *Computer Communications Workshops (INFOCOM WKSHPS), 2016 IEEE Conference on*, page 33–38. IEEE, 2016.

[243] Peilong Li, Yan Luo, Ning Zhang, and Yu Cao. Heterospark: A Heterogeneous CPU/GPU Spark Platform for Machine Learning Algorithms. In *Networking, Architecture and Storage (NAS), 2015 IEEE International Conference on*, page 347–348. IEEE, 2015.

[244] Qi Li, Jianfeng Ma, Rui Li, Ximeng Liu, Jinbo Xiong, and Danwei Chen. Secure, Efficient and Revocable Multi-Authority Access Control System in Cloud Storage. *Computers & Security*, 59:45–59, 2016.

[245] Jimmy Lin and Chris Dyer. *Data Intensive Text processing with MapReduce*. Morgan Claypool Publishers, 2010.

[246] Xuan-Yi Lin, Yeh-Ching Chung, and Tai-Yi Huang. A Multiple LID Routing Scheme for Fat-Tree-Based infiniband Networks. In *Parallel and Distributed Processing Symposium, 2004. Proceedings. 18th International*, page 11. IEEE, 2004.

[247] Maria Lindh and Jan Nolin. Information We Collect: Surveillance and Privacy in the Implementation of Google Apps for Education. *European Educational Research Journal*, 15(6):644–663, 2016.

[248] Alex X Liu and Mohamed G Gouda. Diverse Firewall Design. *IEEE Transactions on Parallel and Distributed Systems*, 19(9):1237–1251, 2008.

[249] Stephanie Q Liu and Anna S Mattila. Airbnb: Online Targeted Advertising, Sense of Power, and Consumer Decisions. *International Journal of Hospitality Management*, 60:33–41, 2017.

[250] Yimeng Liu, Yizhi Wang, and Yi Jin. Research on the Improvement of MongoDB Auto-Sharding in Cloud Environment. In *Computer Science & Education (ICCSE), 2012 7th International Conference on*, page 851–854. IEEE, 2012.

[251] Win-Tsung Lo, Yue-Shan Chang, Ruey-Kai Sheu, Chun-Chieh Chiu, and Shyan-Ming Yuan. Cudt: A CUDA Based Decision Tree Algorithm. *The Scientific World Journal*, 2014, 2014.

[252] Noel Lopes and Bernardete Ribeiro. Gpumlib: An Efficient Open-Source GPU Machine Learning Library. *International Journal of Computer Information Systems and Industrial Management Applications*, 3:355–362, 2011.

[253] Adam Lopez. Statistical Machine Translation. *ACM Computing Surveys (CSUR)*, 40(3):8, 2008.

[254] Yingping Lu and David HC Du. Performance Study of iSCSI-Based Storage Subsystems. *IEEE Communications Magazine*, 41(8):76–82, 2003.

[255] Marko Luksa. *Kubernetes in action*. Manning Publications Shelter Island, 2018.

[256] Yisheng Lv, Yanjie Duan, Wenwen Kang, Zhengxi Li, and Fei-Yue Wang. Traffic Flow Prediction with Big Data: A Deep Learning Approach. *IEEE Transactions on Intelligent Transportation Systems*, 16(2):865–873, 2015.

[257] Ashwin Machanavajjhala, Daniel Kifer, Johannes Gehrke, and Muthuramakrishnan Venkitasubramaniam. l-diversity: Privacy Beyond K-anonymity. *ACM Transactions on Knowledge Discovery from Data (TKDD)*, 1(1):3, 2007.

[258] Grzegorz Malewicz, Matthew H Austern, Aart JC Bik, James C Dehnert, Ilan Horn, Naty Leiser, and Grzegorz Czajkowski. Pregel: A System for Large-Scale Graph Processing. In *Proceedings of the 2010 ACM SIGMOD International Conference on Management of Data*, page 135–146, 2010.

[259] Claudio Martella, Roman Shaposhnik, Dionysios Logothetis, and Steve Harenberg. *Practical Graph Analytics with Apache Giraph*, volume 1. Springer, 2015.

[260] Nathan Marz. How to Beat the Cap Theorem. *Thoughts from the Red Planet*, 2011.

[261] Matthew L Massie, Brent N Chun, and David E Culler. The Ganglia Distributed Monitoring System: Design, Implementation, and Experience. *Parallel Computing*, 30(7):817–840, 2004.

[262] Yuan Mei, Luwei Cheng, Vanish Talwar, Michael Y Levin, Gabriela Jacques-Silva, Nikhil Simha, Anirban Banerjee, Brian Smith, Tim Williamson, Serhat Yilmaz, et al. Turbine: Facebooks Service Management Platform for Stream Processing. In *2020 IEEE 36th International Conference on Data Engineering (ICDE)*, page 1591–1602. IEEE, 2020.

[263] Peter Mell and Timothy Grance. The NIST Definition of Cloud Computing (draft). *NIST Special Publication*, 800(145):7, 2011.

[264] Sergey Melnik, Andrey Gubarev, Jing Jing Long, Geoffrey Romer, Shiva Shivakumar, Matt Tolton, and Theo Vassilakis. Dremel: Interactive Analysis of Web-Scale Datasets. *Proceedings of the VLDB Endowment*, 3(1–2):330–339, 2010.

[265] Laraib U Memon, Narmeen Z Bawany, and Jawwad A Shamsi. A Comparison of Machine Learning Techniques for Android Malware Detection using Apache Spark. *Journal of Engineering Science and Technology*, 14(3):1572–1586, 2019.

[266] Xiangrui Meng, Joseph Bradley, Burak Yavuz, Evan Sparks, Shivaram Venkataraman, Davies Liu, Jeremy Freeman, DB Tsai, Manish Amde, Sean Owen, et al. Mllib: Machine Learning in Apache Spark. *The Journal of Machine Learning Research*, 17(1):1235–1241, 2016.

[267] Dirk Merkel. Docker: Lightweight Linux Containers for Consistent Development and Deployment. *Linux Journal*, 2014(239):2, 2014.

[268] Ahmed Metwally and Christos Faloutsos. V-smart-join: A Scalable MapReduce Framework for All-Pair Similarity Joins of Multisets and Vectors. *Proceedings of the VLDB Endowment*, 5(8):704–715, 2012.

[269] Shivlal Mewada, Pradeep Sharma, and SS Gautam. Classification of Efficient Symmetric Key Cryptography Algorithms. *International Journal of Computer Science and Information Security*, 14(2):105, 2016.

[270] Yajie Miao, Hao Zhang, and Florian Metze. Distributed Learning of Multilingual DNN Feature Extractors using GPUs. 2014.

[271] Microsft. Data Center Bridging (DCB) Overview.

[272] Justin J Miller. Graph Database Applications and Concepts with Neo4j. In *Proceedings of the Southern Association for Information Systems Conference, Atlanta, GA, USA*, volume 2324, 2013.

[273] Christopher Mitchell, Yifeng Geng, and Jinyang Li. Using One-Sided RDMA Reads to Build a Fast, CPU-Efficient Key-Value Store. In *USENIX Annual Technical Conference*, page 103–114, 2013.

[274] Radhika Mittal, Alex Shpiner, Aurojit Panda, Eitan Zahavi, Arvind Krishnamurthy, Sylvia Ratnasamy, and Scott Shenker. Revisiting Network Support for RDMA.

[275] Inder Monga, Eric Pouyoul, and Chin Guok. Software-Defined Networking for Big-Data Science-Architectural Models from Campus to the Wan. In *2012 SC Companion: High Performance Computing, Networking Storage and Analysis*, page 1629–1635. IEEE, 2012.

[276] Roberto Morabito, Jimmy Kjällman, and Miika Komu. Hypervisors vs. Lightweight Virtualization: A Performance Comparison. In *Cloud Engineering (IC2E), 2015 IEEE International Conference on*, page 386–393. IEEE, 2015.

[277] Ruchika Muddinagiri, Shubham Ambavane, and Simran Bayas. Self-hosted kubernetes: Deploying docker containers locally with minikube. In *2019 International Conference on Innovative Trends and Advances in Engineering and Technology (ICITAET)*, pages 239–243. IEEE, 2019.

[278] Nitin Naik. Building a virtual system of systems using docker swarm in multiple clouds. In *2016 IEEE International Symposium on Systems Engineering (ISSE)*, pages 1–3. IEEE, 2016.

[279] Maryam M Najafabadi, Flavio Villanustre, Taghi M Khoshgoftaar, Naeem Seliya, Randall Wald, and Edin Muharemagic. Deep Learning Applications and Challenges in Big Data Analytics. *Journal of Big Data*, 2(1):1, 2015.

[280] Arvind Narayanan and Vitaly Shmatikov. Robust De-Anonymization of Large Sparse Datasets. In *Security and Privacy, 2008. SP 2008. IEEE Symposium on*, page 111–125. IEEE, 2008.

[281] Arvind Narayanan and Vitaly Shmatikov. Myths and Fallacies of Personally Identifiable Information. *Communications of the ACM*, 53(6):24–26, 2010.

[282] Rimma Nehme and Nicolas Bruno. Automated Partitioning Design in Parallel Database Systems. In *Proceedings of the 2011 ACM SIGMOD International Conference on Management of Data*, page 1137–1148. ACM, 2011.

[283] B Clifford Neuman and Theodore Ts'o. Kerberos: An Authentication Service for Computer Networks. *IEEE Communications Magazine*, 32(9):33–38, 1994.

[284] Krishna Nibhanupudi and Rimmi Devgan. Data Center Ethernet.

[285] Muhammad Nouman Durrani and Jawwad A Shamsi. Volunteer Computing: Requirements, Challenges, and Solutions. *Journal of Network and Computer Applications*, 2013.

[286] Daniel Nurmi, Richard Wolski, Chris Grzegorczyk, Graziano Obertelli, Sunil Soman, Lamia Youseff, and Dmitrii Zagorodnov. The Eucalyptus Open-Source Cloud-Computing System. In *Cluster Computing and the Grid, 2009. CCGRID'09. 9th IEEE/ACM International Symposium on*, page 124–131. IEEE, 2009.

[287] Christopher Olston, Benjamin Reed, Utkarsh Srivastava, Ravi Kumar, and Andrew Tomkins. Pig Latin: A Not-so-Foreign Language for Data Processing. In *Proceedings of the 2008 ACM SIGMOD International Conference on Management of Data*, page 1099–1110. ACM, 2008.

[288] Oyindamola Oluwatimi, Daniele Midi, and Elisa Bertino. Overview of Mobile Containerization Approaches and Open Research Directions. *IEEE Security & Privacy*, 15(1):22–31, 2017.

[289] Claus Pahl. Containerization and the Paas Cloud. *IEEE Cloud Computing*, 2(3):24–31, 2015.

[290] Claus Pahl, Antonio Brogi, Jacopo Soldani, and Pooyan Jamshidi. Cloud Container Technologies: A State-of-the-Art Review. *IEEE Transactions on Cloud Computing*, 2017.

[291] Rakesh Patel, Mara Nicholl, and Lindsey Harju. Access Control System for Implementing Access Restrictions of Regulated Database Records while Identifying and Providing Indicators of Regulated Database Records Matching Validation Criteria, September 19 2017. US Patent 9,767,309.

[292] Andrew Pavlo and Matthew Aslett. What's Really New with newSQL? *ACM Sigmod Record*, 45(2):45–55, 2016.

[293] Gregory F Pfister. An Introduction to the Infiniband Architecture. *High Performance Mass Storage and Parallel I/O*, 42:617–632, 2001.

[294] Jaroslav Pokorny. NoSQL Databases: A Step to Database Scalability in Web Environment. *International Journal of Web Information Systems*, 9(1):69–82, 2013.

[295] Lesandro Ponciano, Francisco Brasileiro, Robert Simpson, and Arfon Smith. Volunteers' Engagement in Human Computation for Astronomy Projects. *Computing in Science & Engineering*, 16(6):52–59, 2014.

[296] Andrea Possemato, Andrea Lanzi, Simon Pak Ho Chung, Wenke Lee, and Yanick Fratantonio. Clickshield: Are You Hiding Something? Towards Eradicating Clickjacking on Android. In *Proceedings of the 2018 ACM SIGSAC Conference on Computer and Communications Security*, page 1120–1136, 2018.

[297] Steve Pousty and Katie Miller. *Getting Started with OpenShift: A Guide for Impatient Beginners.* " O'Reilly Media, Inc.", 2014.

[298] Gil Press. A Very Short History of Big Data. *FORBES. Recuperado May*, 12:2014, 2013.

[299] Dan Pritchett. Base: An Acid Alternative. *Queue*, 6(3):48–55, 2008.

[300] Peng Qin, Bin Dai, Benxiong Huang, and Guan Xu. Bandwidth-Aware Scheduling with SDN in Hadoop: A New Trend for Big Data. *IEEE Systems Journal*, 2015.

[301] US Rackspace. Inc.,The Rackspace Cloud, 2010.

[302] Peter Rausch, Alaa F Sheta, and Aladdin Ayesh. *Business Intelligence and Performance Management: Theory, Systems and Industrial Applications.* Springer Publishing Company, Incorporated, 2013.

[303] Tejaswi Redkar and Tony Guidici. *Windows Azure Platform.* Apress, 2011.

[304] Antony Rowstron, Dushyanth Narayanan, Austin Donnelly, Greg O'Shea, and Andrew Douglas. Nobody Ever Got Fired for Using Hadoop on a cluster. In *Proceedings of the 1st International Workshop on Hot Topics in Cloud Data Processing*, page 2. ACM, 2012.

[305] Sherif Sakr, Faisal Moeen Orakzai, Ibrahim Abdelaziz, and Zuhair Khayyat. *Large-scale Graph Processing using Apache Giraph.* Springer, 2016.

[306] Semih Salihoglu, Jaeho Shin, Vikesh Khanna, Ba Quan Truong, and Jennifer Widom. Graft: A Debugging Tool for Apache Giraph. In *Proceedings of the 2015 ACM SIGMOD International Conference on Management of Data*, page 1403–1408. ACM, 2015.

[307] Juha Salo. Data Center Network Architectures.

[308] Jason Sanders and Edward Kandrot. *CUDA by Example: An Introduction to General-Purpose GPU Programming.* Addison-Wesley Professional, 2010.

[309] Kaz Sato, Cliff Young, and David Patterson. An in-Depth Look at Googles First Tensor Processing Unit (TPU). *Google Cloud Big Data and Machine Learning Blog*, 12, 2017.

[310] Julian Satran and Kalman Meth. Internet Small Computer Systems Interface (iSCSI). 2004.

[311] Gigi Sayfan. *Mastering kubernetes.* Packt Publishing Ltd, 2017.

[312] Mathijs Jeroen Scheepers. Virtualization and Containerization of Application Infrastructure: A Comparison. In *21st Twente Student Conference on IT*, volume 1, page 1–7, 2014.

[313] Jürgen Schmidhuber. Deep Learning in Neural Networks: An Overview. *Neural Networks*, 61:85–117, 2015.

[314] Friedhelm Schmidt. The SCSI Bus and IDE Interface Protocols. *Application and Programming, Addison-Wesley, New York*, 1995.

[315] Nicolas Seyvet and Ignacio Mulas Viela. Applying the Kappa Architecture in the Telco Industry. https://www.oreilly.com/ideas/applying-the-kappa-architecture-in-the-telco-industry (visited: 2019-11-09).

[316] Jawad Ali Shah, Hassaan Haider, Kushsairy Abdul Kadir, and Sheroz Khan. Sparse Signal Reconstruction of Compressively Sampled Signals Using Smoothed 0-Norm. In *Signal and Image Processing Applications (ICSIPA), 2017 IEEE International Conference on*, page 61–65. IEEE, 2017.

[317] Jawwad Shamsi, Muhammad Ali Khojaye, and Mohammad Ali Qasmi. Data-intensive Cloud Computing: Requirements, Expectations, Challenges, and Solutions. *Journal of Grid Computing*, 11(2):281–310, 2013.

[318] Jawwad A Shamsi, Sufian Hameed, Waleed Rahman, Farooq Zuberi, Kaiser Altaf, and Ammar Amjad. Clicksafe: Providing Security Against Clickjacking Attacks. In *2014 IEEE 15th International Symposium on High-Assurance Systems Engineering*, page 206–210. IEEE, 2014.

[319] Jawwad A Shamsi and Muhammad Khojaye. Understanding Privacy Violations in Big Data Systems. *IT Professional*.

[320] Jawwad A Shamsi, Sherali Zeadally, and Zafar Nasir. Interventions in Cyberspace: Status and Trends. *IT Professional*, 18(1):18–25, 2016.

[321] Jawwad A Shamsi, Sherali Zeadally, Fareha Sheikh, and Angelyn Flowers. Attribution in Cyberspace: Techniques and Legal Implications. *Security and Communication Networks*, 9(15):2886–2900, 2016.

[322] Toby Sharp. Implementing Decision Trees and Forests on a GPU. In *European Conference on Computer Vision*, page 595–608. Springer, 2008.

[323] Alexander Shpiner, Eitan Zahavi, Omar Dahley, Aviv Barnea, Rotem Damsker, Gennady Yekelis, Michael Zus, Eitan Kuta, and Dean Baram. Roce Rocks without PFC: Detailed Evaluation. In *Proceedings of the Workshop on Kernel-Bypass Networks*, page 25–30. ACM, 2017.

[324] Konstantin Shvachko, Hairong Kuang, Sanjay Radia, and Robert Chansler. The Hadoop Distributed File System. In *Mass Storage Systems and Technologies (MSST), 2010 IEEE 26th Symposium on*, page 1–10. IEEE, 2010.

[325] Konstantin V Shvachko. HDFS Scalability: The Limits to Growth. *; login: The Magazine of USENIX & SAGE*, 35(2):6–16, 2010.

[326] Kamran Siddique, Zahid Akhtar, Edward J Yoon, Young-Sik Jeong, Dipankar Dasgupta, and Yangwoo Kim. Apache Hama: An Emerging Bulk Synchronous Parallel Computing Framework for Big Data Applications. *IEEE Access*, 4:8879–8887, 2016.

[327] Tooba Siddiqui and Jawwad Ahmed Shamsi. Generating Abstractive Summaries Using Sequence to Sequence Attention Model. In *2018 International Conference on Frontiers of Information Technology (FIT)*, page 212–217. IEEE, 2018.

[328] Nanki Sidhu, Edzer Pebesma, and Gilberto Câmara. Using google earth engine to detect land cover change: Singapore as a use case. *European Journal of Remote Sensing*, 51(1):486–500, 2018.

[329] Dilpreet Singgh and Chandan K Reddy. A Survey on Platforms for Big Data Analytics. *Journal of Big Data*, 1(8):1–20, 2014.

[330] Aameek Singh, Madhukar Korupolu, and Dushmanta Mohapatra. Server-Storage Virtualization: Integration and Load Balancing in Data Centers. In *Proceedings of the 2008 ACM/IEEE Conference on Supercomputing*, page 53. IEEE Press, 2008.

[331] Uthayasankar Sivarajah, Muhammad Mustafa Kamal, Zahir Irani, and Vishanth Weerakkody. Critical Analysis of Big Data Challenges and Analytical Methods. *Journal of Business Research*, 70:263–286, 2017.

[332] Swaminathan Sivasubramanian. Amazon DynamoDB: A Seamlessly Scalable Non-Relational Database Service. In *Proceedings of the 2012 ACM SIGMOD International Conference on Management of Data*, page 729–730. ACM, 2012.

[333] Joseph D Sloan. *High Performance Linux Clusters with OSCAR, Rocks, OpenMosix, and MPI*. O'reilly, 2009.

[334] Aleksander Slominski, Vinod Muthusamy, and Rania Khalaf. Building a Multi-tenant Cloud Service from Legacy Code with Docker Containers. In *2015 IEEE International Conference on Cloud Engineering (IC2E)*, page 394–396. IEEE, 2015.

[335] Daniel J Solove and Danielle Keats Citron. Risk and Anxiety: A Theory of Data-Breach Harms. *Texas Law Review*, 96:737, 2017.

[336] Stephen Soltesz, Herbert Ptzl, Marc E Fiuczynski, Andy Bavier, and Larry Peterson. Container-based Operating System Virtualization: A Scalable, High-Performance Alternative to Hypervisors. In *ACM SIGOPS Operating Systems Review*, volume 41, page 275–287. ACM, 2007.

[337] Jordi Soria-Comas and Josep Domingo-Ferrert. Differential Privacy Via T-closeness in Data Publishing. In *Privacy, Security and Trust (PST), 2013 Eleventh Annual International Conference on*, page 27–35. IEEE, 2013.

[338] Kristopher A Standish, Sam Amiri, Misbah Mubarak, Louisa J Bellis, Takanori Fujiwara, and John L Rayner. Advances in Supercomputing. *Advances in Supercomputing*, page 157, 2020.

[339] Nick Steele, Stan Hawkins, Joe Maranville, and Andrew Bradnan. Single Sign-on for Access to a Central Data Repository, March 27 2018. US Patent 9,928,508.

[340] Stergios Stergiou. Scaling Pagerank to 100 Billion Pages. In *Proceedings of The Web Conference 2020*, page 2761–2767, 2020.

[341] Thomas Lawrence Sterling. *Beowulf Cluster Computing with Linux*. MIT press, 2002.

[342] Michael Stonebraker, Daniel Abadi, David J DeWitt, Sam Madden, Erik Paulson, Andrew Pavlo, and Alexander Rasin. MapReduce and Parallel DBMSs: Friends or Foes? *Communications of the ACM*, 53(1):64–71, 2010.

[343] Michael Stonebraker and Ariel Weisberg. The VoltDB Main Memory DBMS. *IEEE Data Engineering Bulletin*, 36(2):21–27, 2013.

[344] Nikko Strom. Scalable Distributed DNN Training Using Commodity GPU Cloud Computing. In *Sixteenth Annual Conference of the International Speech Communication Association*, 2015.

[345] Jeff A Stuart, Cheng-Kai Chen, Kwan-Liu Ma, and John D Owens. Multi-GPU Volume Rendering using MapReduce. In *Proceedings of the 19th ACM International Symposium on High Performance Distributed Computing*, page 841–848. ACM, 2010.

[346] Jeff A Stuart and John D Owens. Multi-GPU MapReduce on GPU Clusters. In *Parallel & Distributed Processing Symposium (IPDPS), 2011 IEEE International*, page 1068–1079. IEEE, 2011.

[347] Michelle Suh, Sae Hyong Park, Byungjoon Lee, and Sunhee Yang. Building Firewall over the Software-Defined Network Controller. In *16th International Conference on Advanced Communication Technology*, page 744–748. IEEE, 2014.

[348] Alexey Svyatkovskiy, Kosuke Imai, Mary Kroeger, and Yuki Shiraito. Large-scale text processing pipeline with apache spark. In *2016 IEEE International Conference on Big Data (Big Data)*, pages 3928–3935. IEEE, 2016.

[349] Colin Tankard. Big Data Security. *Network Security*, 2012(7):5–8, 2012.

[350] Linnet Taylor and Ralph Schroeder. Is Bigger Better? the Emergence of Big Data as a Tool for International Development Policy. *GeoJournal*, 80(4):503–518, 2015.

[351] Claudio Tesoriero. *Getting Started with OrientDB*. Packt Publishing Ltd, 2013.

[352] D.J. Patil Thomas H. Davenport. Data Scientist: The Sexiest Job of the 21st Century.

[353] Ashish Thusoo, Zheng Shao, Suresh Anthony, Dhruba Borthakur, Namit Jain, Joydeep Sen Sarma, Raghotham Murthy, and Hao Liu. Data Warehousing and Analytics Infrastructure at Facebook. In *Proceedings of the 2010 ACM SIGMOD International Conference on Management of Data*, page 1013–1020. ACM, 2010.

[354] Muhammad Tirmazi, Adam Barker, Nan Deng, Md Ehtesam Haque, Zhijing Gene Qin, Steven Hand, Mor Harchol-Balter, and John Wilkes. Borg: the Next Generation. In *EuroSys'20*, Heraklion, Crete, 2020.

[355] Uchi Ugobame Uchibeke, Kevin A Schneider, Sara Hosseinzadeh Kassani, and Ralph Deters. Blockchain Access Control Ecosystem for Big Data Security. In *2018 IEEE International Conference on Internet of Things (iThings) and IEEE Green Computing and Communications (GreenCom) and IEEE Cyber, Physical and Social Computing (CPSCom) and IEEE Smart Data (SmartData)*, page 1373–1378. IEEE, 2018.

[356] Sarah Underwood. Blockchain Beyond Bitcoin, 2016.

[357] Olivier Huynh Van and Jeff Gray. Systems and Methods for Determining Endpoint Configurations for Endpoints of a Virtual Private Network (VPN) and Deploying the Configurations to the Endpoints, April 19 2016. US Patent 9,319,300.

[358] Abhishek Verma, Luis Pedrosa, Madhukar Korupolu, David Oppenheimer, Eric Tune, and John Wilkes. Large-scale cluster management at google with borg. In *Proceedings of the Tenth European Conference on Computer Systems*, pages 1–17, 2015.

[359] Akshat Verma, Puneet Ahuja, and Anindya Neogi. pMapper: Power and Migration Cost Aware Application Placement in Virtualized Systems. In *Proceedings of the 9th ACM/IFIP/USENIX International Conference on Middleware*, page 243–264. Springer-Verlag New York, Inc., 2008.

[360] LLC VoltDB. VoltDB Technical Overview, Whitepaper, 2010.

[361] Denny Vrandecic. Architecture for a Multilingual Wikipedia. Technical report, Google, 2020.

[362] Aleksa Vukotic, Nicki Watt, Tareq Abedrabbo, Dominic Fox, and Jonas Partner. *Neo4j in Action*. Manning Publications Co., 2014.

[363] Sameer Wadkar and Madhu Siddalingaiah. Apache Ambari. In *Pro Apache Hadoop*, page 399–401. Springer, 2014.

[364] Guohui Wang, David G Andersen, Michael Kaminsky, Konstantina Papagiannaki, TS Eugene Ng, Michael Kozuch, and Michael Ryan. C-Through: Part-time Optics in Data Centers. In *Proceedings of the ACM SIGCOMM 2010 conference*, page 327–338, 2010.

[365] Guohui Wang, TS Eugene Ng, and Anees Shaikh. Programming Your Network at Run-Time for Big Data Applications. In *Proceedings of the First Workshop on Hot Topics in Software Defined Networks*, page 103–108, 2012.

[366] Rory Ward and Betsy Beyer. BeyondCorp: A New Approach to Enterprise Security. 2014.

[367] Eric W. Weisstein. "convolution." from MathWorld – A Wolfram Web Resource. http://mathworld.wolfram.com/Convolution.html".

[368] W Hwu Wen-mei. *Programming Massively Parallel Processors*. Morgan Kaufmann, 2010.

[369] Xindong Wu, Xingquan Zhu, Gong-Qing Wu, and Wei Ding. Data Mining With Big Data. *Knowledge and Data Engineering, IEEE Transactions on*, 26(1):97–107, 2014.

[370] Miguel G Xavier, Israel C De Oliveira, Fabio D Rossi, Robson D Dos Passos, Kassiano J Matteussi, and Cesar AF De Rose. A Performance Isolation Analysis of Disk-Intensive Workloads on Container-Based Clouds. In *Parallel, Distributed and Network-Based Processing (PDP), 2015 23rd Euromicro International Conference on*, page 253–260. IEEE, 2015.

[371] Miguel Gomes Xavier, Marcelo Veiga Neves, and Cesar Augusto Fonticielha De Rose. A Performance Comparison of Container-based Virtualization Systems for MapReduce Clusters. In *Parallel, Distributed and Network-Based Processing (PDP), 2014 22nd Euromicro International Conference on*, page 299–306. IEEE, 2014.

[372] Han Xiao, Kashif Rasul, and Roland Vollgraf. Fashion-MNIST: A Novel Image Dataset for Benchmarking Machine Learning Algorithms. *arXiv preprint arXiv:1708.07747*, 2017.

[373] Wayne Xiong, Jasha Droppo, Xuedong Huang, Frank Seide, Mike Seltzer, Andreas Stolcke, Dong Yu, and Geoffrey Zweig. The Microsoft 2016 Conversational Speech Recognition System. In *Acoustics, Speech and Signal Processing (ICASSP), 2017 IEEE International Conference on*, page 5255–5259. IEEE, 2017.

[374] Qiang Xu, Xin Wang, Jianxin Li, Qingpeng Zhang, and Lele Chai. Distributed Subgraph Matching on Big Knowledge Graphs Using Pregel. *IEEE Access*, 7:116453–116464, 2019.

[375] Xiaolong Xu, Qingxiang Liu, Yun Luo, Kai Peng, Xuyun Zhang, Shunmei Meng, and Lianyong Qi. A Computation Offloading Method Over Big Data for IoT-Enabled Cloud-Edge Computing. *Future Generation Computer Systems*, 95:522–533, 2019.

[376] Corinna Cortes Christopher J.C. Yann LeCun, Courant Institute. The MNIST Database of Handwritten Digits.

[377] Fan Yao, Jingxin Wu, Guru Venkataramani, and Suresh Subramaniam. A Comparative Analysis of Data Center Network Architectures. In *2014 IEEE International Conference on Communications (ICC)*, page 3106–3111. IEEE, 2014.

[378] Xiaomeng Yi, Fangming Liu, Jiangchuan Liu, and Hai Jin. Building a Network Highway for Big Data: Architecture and Challenges. *IEEE Network*, 28(4):5–13, 2014.

[379] Shui Yu, Meng Liu, Wanchun Dou, Xiting Liu, and Sanming Zhou. Networking for Big Data: A Survey. *IEEE Communications Surveys & Tutorials*, 19(1):531–549, 2016.

[380] Yuan Yuan, Meisam Fathi Salmi, Yin Huai, Kaibo Wang, Rubao Lee, and Xiaodong Zhang. Spark-GPU: An Accelerated in-Memory Data Processing Engine on Clusters. In *Big Data (Big Data), 2016 IEEE International Conference on*, page 273–283. IEEE, 2016.

[381] Saima Zafar, Abeer Bashir, and Shafique Ahmad Chaudhry. On Implementation of DCTCP on Three-Tier and Fat-Tree Data Center Network Topologies. *SpringerPlus*, 5(1):766, 2016.

[382] Matei Zaharia, Mosharaf Chowdhury, Michael J Franklin, Scott Shenker, and Ion Stoica. Spark: Cluster Computing with Working Sets. *HotCloud*, 10(10-10):95, 2010.

[383] Matei Zaharia, Reynold S Xin, Patrick Wendell, Tathagata Das, Michael Armbrust, Ankur Dave, Xiangrui Meng, Josh Rosen, Shivaram Venkataraman, Michael J Franklin, et al. Apache Spark: A Unified Engine for Big Data Processing. *Communications of the ACM*, 59(11):56–65, 2016.

[384] Alexander Zahariev. Google App Engine. *Helsinki University of Technology*, 2009.

[385] Zuzana Zatrochova. *Analysis and Testing of Distributed NoSQL Datastore Riak*. PhD thesis, Masarykova univerzita, Fakulta informatiky, 2015.

[386] Dongpo Zhang. Big Data Security and Privacy Protection. In *8th International Conference on Management and Computer Science (ICMCS 2018)*. Atlantis Press, 2018.

[387] Hao Zhang, Gang Chen, Beng Chin Ooi, Kian-Lee Tan, and Meihui Zhang. In-Memory Big Data Management and Processing: A survey. *IEEE Transactions on Knowledge and Data Engineering*, 27(7):1920–1948, 2015.

[388] Xiang Zhang and Yann LeCun. Text Understanding from Scratch. *arXiv preprint arXiv:1502.01710*, 2015.

[389] Ying Zhang, Mohammad Pezeshki, Philemon Brakel, Saizheng Zhang, Cesar Laurent Yoshua Bengio, and Aaron Courville. Towards End-to-End Speech Recognition with Deep Convolutional Neural Networks. *arXiv preprint arXiv:1701.02720*, 2017.

[390] Yu Zhang, William Chan, and Navdeep Jaitly. Very Deep Convolutional Networks for End-to-End Speech Recognition. In *Acoustics, Speech and Signal Processing (ICASSP), 2017 IEEE International Conference on*, page 4845–4849. IEEE, 2017.

Index

For Product Safety Concerns and Information please contact our
EU representative GPSR@taylorandfrancis.com Taylor & Francis
Verlag GmbH, Kaufingerstraße 24, 80331 München, Germany